Children, Place and Identity

This is the first sociological text to focus on how children identify with nation and locality. The authors take a broad social scientific approach to their topic, eschewing the disciplinary partisan tendencies of many childhood researchers. The book is rooted in original qualitative research the authors conducted with a diverse sample of children (aged 8–11) across Wales, but these data are also located in the context of existing international research on place identity.

Children, Place and Identity looks at how children see different levels of space and place: global, national, local and domestic. The book engages with important social and political questions such as whether cultural distinctiveness can be preserved in a context of globalisation, whether we are destined to passively receive dominant representations of the nation or can creatively construct our own versions; and whether national identities are necessarily exclusive. Most importantly, the book focuses on what local and national identities mean to children in an era of cultural and economic globalisation. Throughout the book we hear from the children themselves via rich data from interviews and focus groups that illustrate the book's themes.

Including material on racialisation, language, politics, class and gender, *Children, Place and Identity* will be a valuable resource to students and researchers of childhood studies and the sociology of childhood.

Jonathan Scourfield is a former teacher and probation officer, now senior lecturer in Cardiff School of Social Sciences. Most of his research has focused on gender and aspects of childhood and child welfare. He is joint editor of *Contemporary Wales*.

Bella Dicks is a senior lecturer in Cardiff School of Social Sciences, with research interests in cultural sociology, and a particular focus on placed identities; culture-led regeneration and heritage; and qualitative digital methodology.

Mark Drakeford is a professor of Social Policy and Applied Social Studies at Cardiff University, and Cabinet health and social policy adviser to the Welsh Assembly Government.

Andrew Davies is currently a senior consultant with Wavehill Consulting, having previously worked as a research fellow for the University of Wales in both Cardiff and Aberystwyth. He has written a doctorate on representations of Wales in literature of the romantic period.

Children, Place and Identity

Nation and locality in middle childhood

Jonathan Scourfield, Bella Dicks,
Mark Drakeford and Andrew Davies

LONDON AND NEW YORK

First published 2006
by Routledge
2 Park Square, Milton Park, Abingdon, Oxon OX14 4RN

Simultaneously published in the USA and Canada
by Routledge
270 Madison Ave, New York, NY 10016

Routledge is an imprint of the Taylor & Francis Group, an informa business

© 2006 Jonathan Scourfield, Bella Dicks, Mark Drakeford and Andrew Davies

Typeset in Sabon by
RefineCatch Limited, Bungay, Suffolk
Printed and bound in Great Britain by
The Cromwell Press, Trowbridge, Wiltshire

British Library Cataloguing in Publication Data
A catalogue record for this book is available from the British Library

Library of Congress Cataloging in Publication Data
A catalog record for this book has been requested

ISBN10: 0–415–35126–X (hbk)
ISBN10: 0–415–35127–8 (pbk)
ISBN10: 0–203–69683–2 (ebk)

ISBN13: 978–0–415–35126–3 (hbk)
ISBN13: 978–0–415–35127–0 (pbk)
ISBN13: 978–0–203–69683–5 (ebk)

Contents

Acknowledgements

We are very grateful to the children who agreed to take part in the research that we refer to in the book and to the staff in the primary schools that helped to facilitate the study. The research was dependent on the funding of the Social Science Committee of the University of Wales Board of Celtic Studies. Máire Messenger-Davies and Catherine Maclean gave valuable help on research design. Sally Holland was also a member of the research team, so contributed to both design and analysis. We would like to acknowledge the helpful commentaries and suggestions on parts of the manuscript from Cardiff colleagues Emma Renold and Gabrielle Ivinson. Thanks to Gwen Burd for her work on transcribing the data.

We should acknowledge some material in the book that has already appeared in journals. In Chapter 6 in particular we draw on a paper from *Ethnicities*, Volume 5, Issue 1 (2005), 'Children's accounts of Wales as racialized and inclusive', material from which is reprinted by permission of Sage Publications Ltd, copyright (© SAGE Publications, 2005). A small amount of material in several of the chapters previously appeared in *Contemporary Wales*, Volume 16 (2004) as 'Wales and Welshness in middle childhood' and is reprinted here with permission from University of Wales Press.

1 Childhoods, places and nations

It has long been recognised that a person's identification with nation begins to take root in childhood. Childhood experience is commonly taken to be the bedrock upon which self-identity is built, and national consciousness is regarded by many as a key foundation of a modern person's identity. Childhood is conventionally seen as a time of 'structured becoming', a time defined as preparatory to the values and preoccupations of the adult world which take root within a child self that is still malleable and 'different' (Jenks 2005: 11). National feeling, too, is often seen as something barely conscious that seeps into one's core being as one grows and develops. Ernst Gellner, arguably the most influential theorist of nationalism as fundamental to the *modern* conception of self, asserts that 'the culture in which one has been *taught* to communicate becomes the core of one's identity' (1983: 61; italics in original). Such a view defines childhood as the primal ground in which national cultures take root. In turn, this reflects the idea that national feeling is not natural or instinctive in children but is consciously cultivated in them (by adults), hence, the assumption that a nation's schools are places where dominant discourses of national identity and history are promulgated. As has been pointed out by historians, some of the consequences of the emergence of a national system of education were the increasing separation between the child self and the adult self and the birth of the idea of child *development* (Aries 1962; see Walkerdine 1984). And, as Gellner argues of Britain, among the major functions of the emerging school system of the late nineteenth century was that of instilling national consciousness into children. The idea of a *national* curriculum presupposes, indeed, that children living in the same geopolitical entity should be educated into a similar pool of knowledge-content.

All of this suggests that a consideration of children should be central to the study of national feeling, place-belonging and, indeed, collective identifications of all kinds. Yet we do not know a great deal about how school-age children actually do relate to the idea of nation. The largest body of work on children's identification with national groups is conducted within a cognitive-developmental paradigm (see the reviews in Aboud and Amato 2001 and Barrett 2005). We return to consider this and other approaches to child development in Chapters 2 and 3. A few other studies exist from other social-science traditions, which shed more light on the social context of national identification in children, and these are discussed further in subsequent chapters. However, this is a topic that remains relatively undeveloped by sociologists and other social scientists. Most theorisations of nationalism and place-identification do not take children seriously. Most theorisations of childhood have neglected the spatial dimensions of children's identity (though see James et al. 1998, Holloway and Valentine 2000a). In the rest of this current chapter, we present a discussion that tries to bring together debates about children and identity with debates about places and nations. In doing so, we necessarily outline a field comprising multiple pieces of the jigsaw that is the subject of this book. In bringing the various literatures together, we try to map out the key debates that have characterised these fields and show how they can be brought into dialogue with each other.

In recognition of the growing acceptance that children's own views and voices must be taken seriously, the book will draw on original research with children in a qualitative case study conducted by the authors. This research explored children's attachment to places and cultures through school-based interviews, focus groups and participant observation with children in what has been called 'middle childhood' (Borland et al. 1998), that is, eight to eleven years of age. The children came from a variety of locations across Wales – a stateless nation within the United Kingdom – and a sample of schools was chosen to cover a range of social class backgrounds, regional location, ethnicity, rural–urban environment and language use. Whilst there are obviously some interesting discussions of 'Welshness' that arise from the data, the themes that run through the book are of more general significance. They touch on dimensions of children's lives – such as their categorisations and images of both known and distant others – that underpin more general processes of collective identification. Before introducing the empirical material, we introduce our topic in this first chapter by looking at theories of nation and place identification in relation to children and childhood.

National belonging, childhood and modernity

The question of national sentiment has become a particularly fraught one in recent decades. Classic modernist discourse – from Marxism to liberalism – suggested that national consciousness would wither away as capitalist modernity progressed towards a more cosmopolitan and internationalist sensibility. Nationalism was seen as being out of synch with advanced capitalist and, indeed, communist forms of organisation. Yet there were always dissenting voices. For example, the Austrian political thinker Otto Bauer, who argued in the early twentieth century that a sense of 'national character' was one of the most successful ways of promoting common interests amongst diverse ethnic groups and was perfectly compatible with advanced socialism (see Bauer 1996). Recent decades have seen, if anything, a reassertion of attachment to both localities and nations, although not in the direction that Bauer intended. In the face of post-1980s political realities – including the fall of the Soviet Union, political instability in the Middle East, increasing migration and intensifying globalisation, there has been a notable rise in nationalist and proto-nationalist movements throughout the world (Hall 1993). As Anderson (1996) notes, there has also been a flood of writing about nationalism over the past three or four decades. Much of this has taken issue with the idea that nationalism is out of synch with high modernity. Gellner's (1983) ground-breaking analysis shows how Western modernity was founded upon the promulgation of national sentiment. Through the inculcation of the populations of Europe into state-administered systems of mass education in the late nineteenth century, their allegiance to each nation-state and its industrial-technical requirements was secured, he argues. The overarching administrative system of the modern nation-state successfully incorporated citizens into feelings of nationalist sentiment such that they would lay down their lives for patriotic causes. How is this done? For Gellner, as for others (for example, Anderson 1991, Hobsbawm and Ranger 1983), the modern nationalist ransacks past 'folk' or oral cultures and selects out or simply invents 'traditions' to offer people as (actually spurious) evidence of the nation's unique and long-lived identity. Gellner sees nationalism functionally – its rise in the nineteenth century was essential for the modern transformation of society from agrarian to industrial-capitalist modes of organisation.

Smith (1979, 1996, 1999) takes issue with Gellner's thesis. He agrees that modern populations hold strong attachments to nation and will continue to do so. But he does not believe that such strength of feeling could be manufactured in a top-down way by nationalist discourse propagated in the state education system. Rather, he argues that the nation-level sentiment that emerged in nineteenth-century nationalist movements was not based on state-arranged manipulation but on its connections with real and pre-existing ethnic traditions, customs, ties and symbols. Therefore, for Smith, the nationalist is not the inventor of national feeling so much as the inheritor of earlier forms of ethnic and collective identification. For him, the 'pre-existing cultural materials' that Gellner sees as nationalism's plunder are not simply a collection of disaggregated cultural resources. Instead, they comprise 'names, memories, territories, cultures, identities' that resonate with 'national traditions and experiences that often draw on long histories of ethnic memories, myths, symbols and values' (Smith 1999: 55). For Smith, these cultural resources are passed on from adult to child 'at their mother's knee' (1999: 52); for Gellner, rather, they are taught top-down through the 'anonymous impersonal society' of the national education system (1983: 57). Calhoun (1997) offers a compromise between these two approaches by arguing that although nationalism is essential to the modernisation process of nations, its power lies also in its appeal to an ethnic group's long-standing association with a particular territory.

In fact, what both Smith's and Gellner's accounts have in common is a recognition that people's attachment to nation first takes root in childhood. In this regard, it is surprising that neither writer elects to interrogate further just how childhood and nationalism are intertwined. In fact, these writers' debate has implications for understanding how national feeling arises (or does not arise) in childhood. Are children socialised into top-down, constructed sense of national identity through formal schooling and media discourse, backed up by parents and other adults well versed in national iconography? Or are children cultivated, rather, into a sense of particular ethnic or cultural affiliations through more informal kinds of routinised custom, which may or may not then map onto the more formal idea of nation? Although we cannot provide a definitive answer to this question, we try in this book to map the *range* of identifications children hold with various levels of collective and ethnic grouping. We are interested in exploring to what extent children do manifest an awareness of belonging to a collective identity, what such identities may be, and how they relate to various kinds of identifiable geographical space. By looking at the interaction of a range of levels of identification, we can examine how they may or may not relate to more 'official' or received ideas of national identity.

Globalisation, children and place-identity

The extent to which children feel they belong to particular collective identities, especially those that are locally or ethnically rooted, is becoming a pressing question in times of highly globalised mass media, technology and markets. Certainly, in literature on adults and nationalism, writers such as Anderson (1996: 9) feel that there is now a large question mark looming over the hyphen yoking state and nation. He lists the reasons for this as mass labour migrations (leading to 'portable nationality, read under the sign of "identity" '), the obsolescence of national conscript armies, the increase in globe-wide security concerns such as nuclear weapons and environmental degradation that states cannot resolve, and global flows of finance capital and decentralised systems of production enabled by advanced communication technology (see also Appadurai 1990). Many of these can be said to impinge considerably on children as they are highly active participants in the world of consumer culture. As the flows of mediated global communication in which children are caught up intensify, it might be thought that they would lose all possibility of developing that sense of local or ethnic attachment that Smith, for example, outlines. Their exposure to global advertising campaigns and promotional media and products might well inculcate a kind of 'McDisney' attitude that would supplant more locally based kinds of identification.

Some writers on globalisation and digital media have argued forcefully that attachment to place and stable collective identities is indeed weakening in the face of digital ICTs and the pre-eminence (in the West, if not elsewhere) of computer networks. It has been argued, for example, that 'places are no longer the clear supports of our identity' (Morley and Robins 1995: 87). Meyrowitz (1985), welcoming this trend, proposes that in the face of new communicational technologies, our 'possession' of a sense of place – both spatial and social – dissolves into the more free-floating condition of accessing diverse kinds of informational and cultural space. Many other writers have noted the 'dis-placement' effects of globalising processes (Appadurai 1990, Featherstone 1995, Giddens 1991, Thompson 1995). This is not a new argument. In many ways, it is a version of the 'loss of community' thesis that has pervaded sociology, human geography and anthropology since their inception (cf. Auguste Comte and Ferdinand Tonnies). Tilly, writing in the 1970s, observed that although local ties remained important, extra-local ties were on the increase everywhere. This tended to dilute their salience for individuals such that local solidarities and collective actions were on the wane (Tilly 1973). This does raise the question of how far children call on what Agnew (1989) labels 'relations of absence' (extra-local ties) or 'relations of presence' (local ties) in defining who they are. How far do children attach their identities to actual places and how far do they see themselves belonging to more dispersed groupings based, perhaps, around global marketing and products? And if the latter, does this necessarily cancel out the former?

Robertson (1995) rejects the global/local dualism altogether, arguing that increased global circulation of information does not standardise culture but universalises a language of the local and the particular. So, a sense of locality is understood as an *aspect of* globalisation, not antithetical to it. He notes the rise in recent decades of multiculturalist or cultural-pluralist discourse, which, as Hannerz (1990) argues, rests on the idea that different cultures can be distinguished from each other and must be valued on their own terms. This suggests that place and culture are still seen as strongly linked. Even though cultures are often represented nowadays as being detached from geographical space (for example, as in phrases such as 'gay culture' or 'enterprise culture'), nevertheless people's identification of places with cultures arguably remains strong (Gupta and Ferguson 1992). Contemporary tourist discourse, for example, entrenches the idea that each geographical place owns a definable piece of the global 'cultural mosaic' (Kahn 1995; see also Dicks 2003). In relation to children, the question arises as to how far they identify with such associations between places and cultures. This necessarily concerns how far children are cognisant of a cultural language of place, and we return to this question below (and take it up again in relation to our own research in Chapters 3, 4 and 5).

In relation to children and new media rather than place as such, Buckingham (2004) notes the polarised positions that frequently appear in debates about the 'effects' of globalised technologies on children. Some see children gaining access to a creative and empowering space via ICTs; others are anxious about, for example, the ways in which they may restrict or limit independent thinking or their perceived dilution of the adult–child boundary. Postman announced 'the disappearance of childhood' in 1983, arguing that as children are exposed to more and more detailed views of adult life via the television screen, rather than being shielded from the adult world as in the past, they are exposed to adult values and become less separated from the adult world. For him, this represents a loss – of the *difference* of childhood. Yet arguments such as this cannot easily be verified by actual research, as Buckingham observes: 'we still know very little about how children perceive, interpret and use these new media' (2004: 118). We shall return to the question of children's relation to media and globality in Chapter 4.

Identification and child development

In order to address the question of how a collective sense of belonging such as national feeling arises and how children and adults come to possess it, we need to consider, first, what we mean by *identification*. At base, identifying with nation means expressing the sense of a positive link between the self and others who dwell in the same territorial space. Identification thus turns on the question of the self and its relations of similarity/difference to others. For Freud, it was 'the earliest expression of an emotional tie with another person' (1921, quoted in Hall 1996: 3). As Hall puts it, identity involves, 'a recognition of some common origin or shared characteristic with another person or group, or with an ideal. And with the natural closure of solidarity and allegiance established on this foundation' (1996: 2).

What he means by 'natural closure' is the sense that identification is not, by definition, a conscious process characterised by questioning or reasoning; rather, it manifests itself as the obvious, natural or inevitable affinities that lie at the very foundations of the self. This quality of closure is the target of Gellner's theorisation of nationalism in that he seeks to expose and deconstruct the ways in which national feeling is actually far from being the most obvious and natural kind of identification that it claims to be (Gellner 1983). A different but also influential critique of closure has insisted on the discursive construction of the self and, hence, of identification – that is, its production in social and cultural discourse rather than within the unified Cartesian subject of Western metaphysics (see Bhabha 1990, Billig 1995, Hall 1996.). We shall return to the discursive construction of identification below.

Another strand of identification theory that argues forcefully against an essentialist conception of the self is, of course, psychoanalytic theory. This body of theory, though notoriously diverse, broadly agrees that the self is not a stable unitary core that stretches forth from birth to death. As Hall says, there is no 'bit of the self which remains always-already "the same", identical to itself across time' (1996: 3). Instead, in psychoanalytic theory, the self is always split, due to the Oedipus complex. Interestingly, psychoanalysis sees stages as being essential to child development, but – unlike developmentalism, below – these are seen as taking form in the unconscious mind, rather than in terms of rational cognition. In psychoanalysis, child development is seen as emotional, complex and subjective, with no simple causality between past and present. The past is not progressively left behind as the child matures, but continually impinges on the present (Urwin 1986). In mainstream developmental psychology, on the other hand, development is seen as rational and social rather than primarily emotional or psycho-sexual. Two main approaches in this tradition – the cognitive and the social learning approach – can be singled out. Modelling is a key term in social learning theory, which proposes that children learn how to behave from powerful models around them such as parents and teachers. These processes of reinforcement and imitation force the child to conform to adult expect-ations. As Jenks (2005) notes, such an approach is not out of synch with previously dominant sociological approaches of the structural-functionalist school, such as Parsons', in which children's socialisation is seen as neces-sary for the achievement of social order. Awareness of adults' behaviour expectations leads children to form appropriate ideas of the social world.

In the social-learning approach, ideas are simply reflections of behaviour. Conversely, cognitive psychologists such as Piaget (2001, first published 1962) argue that ideas (for example, of gender or collective identity, appear-ing at different stages in a child's attainment of cognitive 'skills') lead them to modify their behaviour. Piaget acknowledges the influence of affective responses in shaping the developmental process, but for him the structuring of cognition as rational maturation is the key to understanding how children develop. The developing mind is seen as analytically distinct from the 'out-side world' of social processes and relationships. Kohlberg, working in the Piagetian tradition, studied the development of children's reasoning in terms of progressive stages in cognitive ability. He concluded that children passed through six major stages as they moved into adulthood and beyond, in which the nature of their moral reasoning moved from simple assertions of right and wrong to 'conventional' and, eventually, 'post-conventional mor-ality' (see Crain 2003). This suggests that the child develops towards an eventual (adult) state of independent thinking, in which the influence of cultural norms and conventions is superseded. In relation to national feeling, this might suggest that children would move through a stage of conventional identification with the nation, in which they would see loyalty towards one's country as unquestionably right. In later stages, the emergent morally 'advanced' adult would be able to distinguish between situations in which national identification was the right or wrong response by applying such so-called wider and universal values as liberty and justice.

The stage-focused theories of cognitive-developmental psychologists have been subjected to considerable criticism from within the discipline of devel-opmental psychology as well as outside. Since the 1970s, the focus has turned away from the cognitive abilities of individuals towards an increasing appreciation of the social contexts of children's language use and behaviour.

For example, Dunn (1993) has shown how children's sense of who they are emerges less through a process of socialisation by adults as through interactions with their peers and, particularly, their siblings. Hence, rather than imitating their parents, as in social-learning theory, children adopt styles of behaviour that allow them to navigate the social settings of childhood. This is a theme to which we return in later chapters. Outside of psychology, the so-called 'new sociology of childhood' has taken traditional developmental psychology thoroughly to task for treating children as 'human becomings' rather than 'human beings' (James and Prout 1990, James et al. 1998). In these more recent sociological writings, the whole premise of developmentalism is attacked for defining children *a priori* as lacking or deficient in the qualities or abilities that characterise adult rationality. We discuss this debate in greater detail in the two chapters that follow. In Chapter 2, we outline the strengths and weaknesses of different approaches to understanding children, while in Chapter 3, we seek to challenge the disciplinary partisan approach of sociologists who reject developmental perspectives outright.

From within the discipline of psychology, 'critical psychology' has also contributed a radical critique of developmentalism. This takes on board Foucauldian and post-structuralist theories of the child not as an individual rational being but as a subject-in-culture (see Henriques et al. 1984) Working in this tradition, Walkerdine (2004) tries to reach beyond the polarised positions of developmentalism versus psychoanalysis to argue instead for an approach that does not see development as located inside the child but in the 'cultures of practice' in which he or she lives. It is necessary in her approach to consider (a) the particular nodal point that the intersection of often contradictory discourses (for example, of gender, childhood, sexuality, class) offers different children in particular settings, such as the classroom; (b) the power relations of these discourses (in that certain discourses and subject positions are relatively hegemonic and others more marginalised); and (c) that there are complex emotional investments and attachments that children possess in relation to these contradictory positions which makes it very difficult for many children to feel at ease in them. From this perspective, children's relationships to dominant discourses of national identity emerge as unstable (just as adults' are) in that they invite subject identifications, often from a contradictory position. Indeed, subjects' class or ethnic differences may well collide with them. If, for example, one is brought up experiencing what Sennett and Cobb (1972) call 'the hidden injuries of class' or the sense of difference and negativity that minority-ethnic status can bring vis-à-vis the 'majority' culture, the idea of seeing oneself as 'belonging to' the nation (and the nation as belonging to oneself) may be quite an emotionally uneasy subject position to take up. Children should not, in this view, be seen as insulated from psycho-cultural paradoxes such as these. Though these are debates that must remain unresolved in this book, we keep returning to them in the belief that future research with children needs to take seriously the complexity of the question of identification. It should also respond to Walkerdine's proposal that we need to explore what it might mean to integrate the psychological and socio-cultural dimensions of understanding childhood.

Representations of nation and place

Debates in the psychology of childhood turn, we have hopefully made clear, on the question of how the relationship between the individual and culture should be viewed. Culture is clearly central to any discussion of children and broader collective identifications such as place or nation. We have already alluded to the idea that nations are graspable to individuals primarily through the publicly circulating languages, practices and images that constitute discourses. This brings us to consider the various *representations* of nation that are in circulation and the extent to which children do or do not relate to them. Is 'the nation' for children a set of identifiable cultural attributes held to characterise a geographical territory? Or is it something less tangible? Public discourse, as well as the settings of institutional organisation (such as schools or sporting practices) are replete with expressions of national feeling that rely on an assortment of cultural markers. These typically include nation-defining images, symbols, narratives, legends, sporting activities, famous personalities, proclamations of shared values or social solidarity, and so forth. Wales, for instance, is conventionally associated with – to pluck a few well-rehearsed items from the air – the Welsh language, choral song, chapels, rugby, oratory, countryside, mountains, rural villages, tradition, community, sheep, coal-mining, druids, leeks and daffodils. Such cultural markers, though in many cases clichéd, contradictory and seemingly trivial, are important in the sense that they help define the identity of a nation in the public eye. Hence, it is clear that nations are not just territorial entities. Feeling part of a nation or region, as Evans (1999: 2) notes, 'is bound up with the ways those nations and regions are made tangible through repeated and recognizable symbolic forms, narratives and communicative styles'. A number of writers have drawn attention to the power of symbolic resources in instilling a sense of national identity both in individuals and in institutional practices (Anderson 1991, Bhabha 1990, Hobsbawm and Ranger 1983, etc.). Gellner's (1983) analysis invests these symbolic resources and narratives with considerable power to instil in citizens a sense of national identification. And in devolved but non-state political communities such as Wales, the generation of collective images and narratives has long been a primary means of publicly asserting, as well as denying, the coherence of the nation-in-waiting (Gruffudd 1995).

The cultural approach to the nation is closely related to debates on place-identification. Indeed, some writers have connected ideologies of the nation directly to ideologies of place. For example, writers on place have debated the extent to which inhabitants of various spaces (from locality to nation to region and beyond) are utilising a pre-given language of cultural categorisation in order to define their sense of place-belonging, and how this relates to the actual contexts of their own daily lives, social ties and interpersonal relationships. To some extent, this reflects the structure–agency distinction that underpins the argument between Gellner and Smith. How far is a sense of place-belonging inculcated through top-down images and how much of it is a product of the self's own enmeshment in local cultural groupings? It is a debate that is also often conducted in terms of the micro–macro distinction in sociology. Some writers downplay the power of wider cultural ideologies and categorisations in favour of analysing the influence of actors' locations in situated social networks and relationships. In this perspective, discussed further below, places such as nations become meaningful to their inhabitants largely through their own daily social experience of them rather than through representational systems. Increasingly, however, it has been recognised that both dimensions are important (Pred 1983). As geographers Agnew and Duncan argue, 'local social worlds (*locale*) cannot be completely understood apart from the macro-order of *location* (i.e. socio-economic and market factors influencing place) and the territorial "*sense of place*" ' (1989: 2; our italics). Hence, place-identities are best seen as constructed both through people's own social and biographical experience during the life course *and* through wider cultural representations circulating through the media and other sites of representation. Pred (1983) argues that people are not free to produce their own sense of place autonomously, but neither is a sense of place simply injected into them through dominant discourses. Pred is drawing here on Raymond Williams's recognition of the interplay between representational or ideological resources and the 'ordinary behaviour' of everyday lives. That is, inhabitants' sense of place is formed both through their daily experience of the *spaces* in which they live and interact, and also through symbolic representations of *place*. The latter involve the ways in which spaces become imbued over time with particular cultural associations and how they themselves come to act as symbols of particular kinds of values or lifestyles (Lefebvre 1991).

Let's consider, first, the culture/ideology approach to place-identification. A large amount of literature has explored how cultural associations attached to places help to 'produce' them as identifiable entities (Harvey 1993). Shields' (1991) concept of 'social spatialisation' emphasises that these discourses of place do not have merely symbolic effects; rather, they become directive, affecting planning decisions and policies as well as shaping local institutions' modus operandi. It is inevitable that they should also go *some* way to shaping the cultural horizons, attitudes and expectations of inhabitants. This suggests some degree of correlation between cultural identity and geographical space, as we noted above in discussing the global/local debate. In such a perspective, nations, like localities, are to be seen as geo-cultural entities, occupying defined physical space that 'contains' cultural content. The idea that every particular geographical territory can lay claim to a distinct cultural identity or heritage has been central to many nationalist, regionalist and indigenous ethnic movements. However, it is one from which many writers on nationalism have wanted to distance themselves. For example, nationalisms based on 'ethnic' appeals (such as the promotion of cultural values or ways of life) are often distinguished from those based on 'civic' appeals (such as the promotion of citizens' political participation or collective activism) (see McCrone 1998). The ethnic or cultural type of allegiance is often seen as reactionary, since appeals to cultural place-identity always seem to depend on establishing a dialectic of sameness/otherness that excludes those values or peoples deemed 'not like us' (Harvey 1989, Massey 1995). We shall return to the 'instability' of cultural representations below.

If cultural representations are powerful ways of according places with 'reputations' and 'identities', then we can see that there are important analogies between place-identification and nation-identification. Nations have an abstract quality: they cannot be grasped directly by their inhabitants and must instead be made meaningful to them through constantly circulating symbols and images (Anderson 1991, Billig 1995). This is an analysis that has also been applied to other scales of place – including regions, cities, towns and even small localities. All places – big and small – have an abstract quality in that their territorial boundaries can only be grasped from a bird's-eye view. Whilst on the ground, as it were, their inhabitants must develop an *imaginary* of place that allows them to map cultural identity onto geographical space. That is, Englishness or Welshness or Pakistaniness come to be seen as coterminous with physical boundaries, just as the sense of being a 'Cardiffian' or a 'Londoner' implies identifying with both a cultural and a spatial entity. There is also another sense in which national identities are related to more local forms of place-identity. To take the example of Wales, where we carried out the research that we introduce in the next chapter, rural villages in certain parts of Wales have become powerfully associated in public discourse with 'authentic' Welsh identity (Morgan 1983). Schools and organisations in the rural north and west of Wales are more likely to participate extensively in Welsh-language ceremonies and traditions (such as *eisteddfodau*, musical and literary festivals) that are well established in local communities than those in urban-industrial localities in south-east Wales that have developed their identities on the periphery of this particular version of national culture. (Although it should be noted that schools in the south-east whose main language is Welsh – these are a minority but are growing in number – will also be very familiar with eisteddfodau). Hence, certain local place-identities may play quite a central role in shoring up *national* identity – just as national identity may shore up local place-identity. Whilst the 'place' of the nation might be thought of as being hostile to that of locality, in that, for nationalism to take hold, people have to lose hold of their local identifications and begin relating to a wider and more abstract collectivity (practically the entire population of which they will never know or meet), nevertheless, it has been forcefully argued that local-level identifications are crucial to the development of nationalist sentiment (Smith 1996). Indeed, it appears that nation-level associations are themselves reproduced through key local sites that seem quintessentially to embody (or, indeed, negate) that nation's identity. Hence, we talk of the 'heart' of England, or the 'heart' of Wales. That is not to say, of course, that these national-local resonances go uncontested (Bagguley et al. 1990, Massey and Jess 1995). Indeed, there has been a long-standing and almost caricatured split between the rural and urban imaginations of Wales (Day 2002). Nevertheless, contestation does not dilute the potency of symbolic place-myths and associations; indeed, it may strengthen them.

However, while there are undoubtedly many resonances between local-place and nation-as-place, they are not the same thing. Our view is that both need to be seen relationally. That is, nations cannot be understood in isolation from other scales of place-identity. In fact, we should consider a *range* of spatially defined cultural groupings to which people say they 'belong', such as towns, villages, regions, localities or even supra-national entities such as Europe. This is in addition to culturally defined sub-national groupings, such as ethnicities, which have a more complex relationship to territory. We need to consider how the *scale* of place – specifically, its local, regional, national and supra-national levels – may affect the degree to which collective cultural representations are salient to people. They are unlikely to impinge on the horizons of the self all to the same degree. Place on a national scale is likely to be apprehended by both adults and children rather differently than place on a local scale. For instance, whilst inhabitants of a small locality such as a village may not traverse it daily, they can gain a fairly concrete sense of its contours simply through repeatedly moving around it. Bigger places will necessarily assume more abstract forms. Much also, however, depends on how mobile one is. Age is clearly a factor here: children's sense of physical location may be quite restricted – perhaps to a handful of familiar and sanctioned locations around home, shops and school. This is a key theme in Chapter 5, where we discuss the scales of local and domestic identities. It may only be at the relatively small spatial scale of the neighbourhood that children (and, indeed, many adults) can gain a concrete sense of its physical contours. Boundaries *within* the locale may thus be quite readily recognised, even if, as in many children's case, they reach only as far as the very limited space that is designated safe or within-bounds.

Grasping a sense of the nation as place, on the contrary, involves more abstract *representations* of boundary such as maps, logos, metaphors, museum displays, etc. (as Anderson [1991] famously documents in the case of nation-building in south-east Asia). It follows that, especially in early and middle childhood where exposure to and understanding of such representations may not be great, awareness of the nation as possessing a bounded physicality may be quite restricted. Having a nationality may feel more like an abstract and perhaps rather vague identity in comparison with one's daily emplacement in bounded locales. Our data go some way to confirming this hypothesis. Thus, the extent to which representations of place produce a correspondingly clear sense of place-identity in children's or, indeed, adults' minds is open to question. It is necessary to keep in mind a number of different dimensions or levels of spatial-identification that children might have. It follows that national identity cannot be studied in isolation from place-identity, since one's conception of national belonging is always intimately bound up with how one perceives, and how others perceive, the place in which one lives. As Cohen observes, 'local experience mediates national identity' (1982: 13). This is why it is important that locality and nation be theorised relationally: the meaning of each is recast in the light of each other and also in the light of other levels of collective identification that people may have, including globality. That is why in this book we return repeatedly to different levels of children's identification with space, place and collective identities.

The instability of cultural representations

So far, we have been concentrating on how nations and other places are constructed through cultural representations. Representations, however, are not the only way of approaching the question of nation and place-identification. Indeed, the problem with place-defining representations is that they often appear to be far from clear-cut. For example, it is necessary to keep in mind that the kinds of cultural marker attributed to a nation by outsiders are not necessarily the same as those adopted by insiders. And not all insiders and outsiders may subscribe to the same markers as each other. In actual fact, it is often extraordinarily difficult to find agreement on what exactly are the cultural values and symbols that do make up either a nation's or a place's cultural identity. Post-colonial theory suggests there can never be 'closure' in any cultural narrative of the nation, for national identity is too fraught with difference. In this perspective, the cultural appeals and values promoted in the name of the nation can never enjoy a stable or established hegemony as in Gellner's or Anderson's analyses. On the contrary, in this view, any attempt to outline a coherent block of cultural content as the defining identity of a nation will always fall apart. For Bhabha (1990), the very attempt at national representation itself gives rise to instability and ambivalence, because of the impossibility of reconciling appeals to cultural sameness (the 'pedagogical') with the empirical actualities of people's lived allegiances (the 'performative'). His point is that no pedagogical narrative of the nation can gain supremacy because its claims to credibility or authenticity depend on it resonating actively with its addressees – 'the people' – who are both its objects and its subjects. But as soon as they are invited to identify with one narrative, a space opens up instead for them to express others – through appeals to cultural difference, various minority claims and experiences of exile. Hence, the narrative can never establish its terms. For Bhabha, the anxieties of national representation are not, therefore, centred on the 'outside' boundary or the problem of 'other' people in other nations, but on the problem of the 'inside' – the 'otherness of the people-as-one' (1990: 301). In other words, the elaboration of national cultural characteristics involves a constant process of struggle over the question of cultural difference, in which national discourse is continually both denying it and summoning it up. Bhabha's argument is that national discourse, for this reason, is never stable and can never establish dominance. National discourse in this perspective constantly undermines itself for it is always negotiating how to accommodate, come to terms with or repress cultural difference.

In Gellner's theory, by contrast, nationalist discourse – though frequently contested – speaks with a clear and powerful voice. This begs the question as to whether people really have in mind a clear field of cultural characteristics (whether defined or contested) when they think about their nation? Or, indeed, when they think about any place, including even their home town. To conclude that they do would suggest people possess a facility in, recognition and use of place-defining linguistic categories and a vocabulary of cultural comparison with which to articulate them. It is probable that whilst some people will operate with clear place-defining categories of this kind, others will not. But we could say with some certainty that it is a capacity unlikely to be widely found in middle childhood. One suspects that if young children were to produce this kind of elaborated cultural language of place, they would need to have been specifically schooled in it. As we discuss in Chapters 4 and 5, the children we studied employed very little in the way of explicit cultural place-markers in their general talk about where they lived or, indeed, other nations or places. However, they did express quite a strong awareness of spatial, social and cultural *boundaries*. Just because children or adults may not use overt place-defining or nation-defining language does not necessarily mean that they have little or no sense of national or place belonging.

Indeed, the idea that people identify with place through definitive cultural characteristics is not necessarily the best way of understanding nation- or place-identification, particularly where children are concerned. Micro-sociologists studying place, for example, have explored the ways in which people identify with the routine settings they move through and act in: the *locales* that form the contexts of their interactions (see Agnew and Duncan 1989 for a discussion). This approach to place emphasises the situated nature of social interaction and explores how people picture the nature and scope of the various collective spaces they inhabit: what kind of socio-spatial boundaries do people operate with and how do they perceive them? In Chapter 3, we consider how children's readiness to identify with particular national, local or ethnic collectives can be seen as a kind of performance: children will display and claim different degrees of attachment, and indeed, even different attachments altogether, depending on the social context in which they find themselves. The situation of the classroom peer group, for example, constitutes a particular arena for children's *negotiation* of their identities according to the gendered, racialised and classed dimensions of their interrelationships with their peers. Studies in the socio-cultural tradition have shown that children will communicate quite differently depending on the interpersonal context and the various ways in which they feel called upon to respond to communicational situations (Wells 1987). This makes it difficult, of course, to generalise about children's 'stages' of development or 'competencies'. We turn now, accordingly, to a discussion of the social dimensions of place-identification: the lived interactions and experiences through which individuals engage with the spaces in which they move.

Spatialised social interaction and children

Personal and social experience, many writers have argued, remain essential components, even the foundation, of people's sense of who they are and where they belong (Relph 1976, Williams 1961). And this experience is necessarily located in particular physical surroundings; it is always already *implaced* (Casey 1993: 104). Our daily embodied experience of our home locality as well as of 'away' or 'abroad' inevitably shapes how we relate to constructs such as the city, town or nation. In this sense, a sense of place is a *social* construct, arising out of our interactions with others around us. Some time ago, Bott (1957) demonstrated how people's experience of community is defined by their particular location within social networks (of friends, family, work colleagues and acquaintances) rather than in objectively identifiable places-with-cultures. More recently it has been argued (for example by Albrow 1997) that space rather than place is the most useful way of characterising (grown-up) people's identifications with where they live. In this perspective, different groups' horizons and networks constitute different social spaces, overlapping within, but not defined by, the geographical area they share. Inhabitants may reside in the same physical place but may have quite different experiences of it, for their salient points of self-identification are provided by their location within specific social, family and friendship contexts. The extent to which people have connections with 'elsewhere', are mobile outside the locality, have knowledge of and a sense of attachment to other places and identities, both at home and away, are clearly some of the key determinants in forging their sense of where they 'belong' and to which wider collective – if any – they relate. It might be thought, in particular, that a strong sense of identification with one's own locality or region, and perhaps also with one's own nation, would more likely be found in individuals whose social networks are relatively constrained and unvaried.

We suggest that exploring the nature of these social networks is particularly important when trying to understand children's sense of place. It seems common sense to assume that children, due to their restricted mobility and limited social networks, are necessarily more local in their outlook than adults. Yet analysis of the well-rehearsed distinction between 'locals' and 'cosmopolitans' suggests that adults themselves vary considerably in their consciousness of and openness to other cultures (Hannerz 1990, Merton 1957). In Hannerz's discussion, the cosmopolitan is not necessarily the person who travels, but the person who is 'willing to engage with the Other' and 'open towards divergent cultural experiences' – as opposed to the person who seeks to assimilate what is foreign into fundamentally local meaning-structures (1990: 239). It is also the person who is competent in the language of comparative cultural meanings. Therefore, someone may travel continuously, but still remain 'local' in outlook and orientation, whereas the cosmopolitan disposition can be practised equally well at home or away. There is clearly some stigma attached to the idea of localism (Tomlinson 1999). Bauman's (1996) thesis is that current conditions of 'postmodern identity', in which the freedom to choose, acquire and discard are among society's most valued assets, only reward mobility; those who stay confined to their home locales are disparaged and become the objects of state surveillance, suspicion and social control. Localism is conventionally and ideologically associated with backwardness, tradition, parochialism, narrowness, ignorance, simplicity, and so forth, while cosmopolitanism suggests a spirit of openness, intellectual curiosity and adventure (hence, according to Tomlinson, the feeling on the part of many in the developing world that this is simply another ethnocentric Western dualism). Given the tendency to see children as 'earlier', antecedent versions of adult social relations (Urwin 1984), it might be assumed that children, inhabiting more locally constrained horizons, are situated at a developmentally prior stage to the more 'advanced', 'modern' and 'mature' disposition of the adult/ cosmopolitan. Thus, it might be thought that children would identify most strongly with the immediate locality they occupy, even to the extent of being tribal (note the moral panic over teenage gangs and their sense of 'turf'), and that they would identify much more vaguely with more abstract kinds of collective identity such as the nation, Europe, or, indeed, the globe.

It is certainly the case that children's daily experiences, for obvious reasons, are more limited to the immediate locality than many adults'. Their social networks are more circumscribed than those of adults, simply because they lack the means of independent mobility and are located within quite limited spheres of social interaction: those of the family, school, clubs perhaps, and immediate neighbourhood. In addition, children are not likely to have the same familiarity as adults with the vocabularies and images of nation mentioned above. So, whilst children will be routinely exposed to global media images that may be quite diverse, they are likely to be embedded in localised social networks that may be quite limited, predictable and unvarying. In middle childhood, children's experiences are still largely family based (Borland et al. 1998), and this has important implications for how they experience the idea of 'home' and 'away'. Our own research, too, underlines the idea that children's social networks are necessarily restricted and that they have quite vague and generalised notions of wider constructs such as the nation, Europe and the world. We explore this theme further in Chapter 4. But we also suggest that children do operate some quite surprisingly clear spatial demarcations, such as those between 'here' and 'there' and between 'us' and 'them' (centring particularly on the consciousness of *boundary*, as we discuss further below).

It is important, we suggest, not to fall into drawing too easy an opposition between children and adults' experiences. It might be self-evidently true that children have less opportunity to establish wide-ranging or diverse fields of social interaction than adults, but it is also the case that children's own experiences vary quite considerably. Class belonging, for example, is a key source of variation. Drawing on a qualitative study of children living in or near a run-down East London housing estate, Reay (2000) shows how black *and* white working-class compared with middle-class children hold quite divergent attitudes to place. Whilst one of the middle-class boys she studied reported his confident and adventurous journeyings around the London tube lines, a working-class girl, living in a high-rise flat, only ventured regularly as far as the nearby Fentham Road with her auntie. Reay's data show how the working-class children's 'urban landscapes' were much more constricted than their middle-class counterparts. They were also more fearful and anxious about the neighbourhood in which they lived. She concludes, 'horizons are configured very differently if you are working-class . . . [working-class children's] relationship to the wider world, geographically, socially and psychologically, is characterised by boundaries rather than accessible horizons' (2000: 155). In her study, working-class children were more often kept inside by their parents and only allowed out under close supervision. The working-class girls, in particular, both black and white, were especially constrained in their mobility. This finding on social class is different from an earlier study by Newson and Newson (1976). On the basis of their research with parents, the Newsons describe working-class children being more likely to play out in the street than middle-class children. As with Reay's research, boys were described as covering more ground than girls and, in addition, were more likely to be seen by parents as 'outdoor children' and girls as 'indoor children' (see also Hart 1979). Our own work also underlines some differences amongst children when it comes to their identifications with place and nation, and class (as well as gender and ethnicity) certainly emerges as a key source of variation. Chapters 3, 4 and 5 take up these themes in greater detail.

Chapters 4 and 5 discuss findings from our own study data that suggest children's sense of place tends to be more social and relational than it is cultural or representational. Children tend to see the question of space and collective identity in relation to groups of people who are significant to them (whether known or unknown), and their own relationships with them. They frame the topic of their home locality in relation to divisions they know about between *people* – particularly the 'nice' and the 'nasty' people – and the question of national identity becomes one about which language they speak and which language others speak (see Chapters 4 and 7). Questions about living elsewhere are transformed into thoughts about the people they would miss. Hence, the various scales of collective place-identification are understood by children in terms of the self and its relationship to significant others. In some ways, this chimes with Piaget's observation (1965) that young children see the world principally in terms of their own perspective, rather than imagining how others might see it. This also accords with the Freudian view that early childhood is dominated by egocentric thinking (Piaget was heavily influenced by Freud's writings on psychoanalysis, even if the branch of psychology he developed, cognitive psychology, came to be seen as incompatible with the Freudian tradition).

The structure of the book

We follow this chapter's introductory conceptual overview with a chapter devoted to methodological debates: Chapter 2 will summarise some of the key debates about how we gain access to the perspectives of children and how we can research such an intangible phenomenon as identity. There is also in Chapter 2 a description of the empirical research in which the book is rooted and an introduction to its Welsh context. Chapters 3 to 5 are then concerned with fairly general aspects of place identity. Chapter 3 introduces the empirical material with reference to the *process* of children's identification with national and ethnic collectivities, focusing on development, agency and (gendered) social interaction. Chapters 4 and 5 are quite central to the book's concerns. They form an analytic pairing and give an overview of the extent and character of children's identifications with different spatial domains: global and national (Chapter 4) and local and domestic (Chapter 5). The conclusions of both these chapters are discussed together at the end of Chapter 5.

Chapters 6 and 7 then deal with more specific aspects of place identity. Chapter 6, 'Insiders and outsiders', deals with inclusivity and exclusivity. There is discussion of the nation as racialised and how children of majority and minority ethnicity negotiate this. There is also discussion of the relationship between Welshness and Englishness. Chapter 7, 'Ways of speaking', discusses the significance of language and accent to the children and the implications of this for their identification with place. The book then concludes with a fairly brief chapter that brings together the various threads of the book and offers some conclusions of general relevance to the social science of children and place, as well as some discussion of particular questions thrown up by Wales and issues of what it means to be Welsh.

2 Researching children, place and identity

This chapter will discuss theoretical and methodological approaches to researching children's identification with place and nation. Surprisingly, this issue has been relatively little discussed in the national identity literature or, indeed, in the literature on place. The general topic of childhood and children has, however, long been established in academic work, most centrally in sociology and psychology though often in quite polarised and monodisciplinary terms. Each has generated distinctive and indeed multiple approaches to understanding childhood, not all of which sit easily together. There is a general tension between the sociological and psychological 'stance'; more particularly, there are different strands of theoretical commitment within each discipline. Certain traditions in psychology are more attuned to the sociological enterprise, for example, than others. In order to discuss the methodology of researching children, such differences and tensions need to be thought through, not least because the methods proposed – frequently polarising along the qualitative/quantitative axis – are often seen as incompatible with each other. We begin, then, with a discussion of the key theoretical approaches to studying children. We then move on to introduce our own research with children in middle childhood in Wales, and thence to focus in on methodological strategy and technique. We also introduce the national context of the study with a brief introduction to some aspects of the sociology of Wales.

Theorising childhood

Childhood is an area of academic study particularly marked by division and competing paradigms – perhaps not least because the way in which society views and judges children is a particularly emotionally charged arena. The previous chapter briefly summarised some of the major theoretical approaches to understanding children's identity (namely, social learning theory, cognitive developmental psychology, psychoanalysis and critical psychology). These differences are important in so far as they imply quite different ontologies and epistemologies of the child and, hence, quite different methodologies for research on childhood. This chapter will primarily be concerned with research methodologies, but it is first necessary to consider in a little more depth the paradigms upon which these different methodological traditions are built. So we begin with a discussion of theories of childhood.

If we consider the theories of national and place identifications discussed in the last chapter, it is clear that neither place nor nation can be treated as givens. Instead, they have to be seen as socially and culturally constructed, whether through powerful cultural representations (entrenched in school curricula and elsewhere) that shape how we relate to collectivities such as the nation, or through the equally significant social interactions through which we experience both our immediate concrete and more distant abstract collective belonging(s). Understanding the *social* dimension of children's lives, then, whether conceived as interactions or discourses (or both), is key to understanding their identifications with nation and place. This suggests we will need to explore the sociology of childhood if we are to make sense of our topic. And, yet, it is not enough, for we also need to understand how the child's sense of *self* – the 'I' – is implicated in these social constructions – how the child comes to identify himself or herself within them. Here we are talking about concepts associated with 'internalisation'. This is the transformation – however unevenly or problematically – of external influences into internal activities or states. This urges a psychological approach. Yet the place of the social in the dominant psychological approaches to childhood is greatly contested. And in sociological approaches, by contrast, the notion of the self remains underdeveloped. Hence neither will suffice alone.

Our position in this book is that we need to integrate psychological and sociological approaches in order to understand children's identifications with spatial collectivities such as place and nation. Jenkins (1996) recognises the necessarily psycho-social character of identity and conceptualises this as the 'internal–external dialectic of identification'. Theoretical integration is not something that is easily achieved, however, and we would certainly not make the claim that our small study, discussed in the chapters to come, manages to do so. Indeed, this book does not in any sense set out to construct a new 'psycho-social' theory of childhood and place, something that our arguments here can be construed as calling for. It is rather that our investigations into the topic and reading of the literature convince us that a more nuanced and flexible approach is needed if we are really to understand children's subjective worlds. Our starting point is to consider how 'the child' is defined in both psychology and sociology. Hence, we need to ask, 'To what extent can the more established psychological approaches, namely socialisation theory and classically constituted developmental psychology, help us in understanding children's relationship to place and nation?' 'Can more recent so-called critical psychological approaches contribute more?' 'And what, by contrast, does the much-vaunted "new sociology of childhood" help us to understand about children's collective identifications?' In what follows, we take each question in turn in an attempt to understand the contributions and limitations of existing theory and to suggest what an adequate approach to childhood might need to address. In the second half of the chapter we turn to a discussion of methodological strategy and technique.

Psychological theories of childhood

Let us start with the developmental paradigm, which is undoubtedly the most influential and well-established model of childhood today (Harden et al. 2000, James et al. 1998). It informs much of professional child-rearing practice, pedagogy and schooling in many parts of the world, and informs key socio-legal assumptions about areas such as the age of criminal responsibility and debates about child testimony and reliability. In the developmental approach, there has been some attention paid to studying children's sense of national identity (for example, Barrett 1996, Barrett et al. 2003, Jahoda 1964, Piaget and Weil 1951; see also the next chapter). It would be wrong to say that the social context of children's lives is ignored in developmental psychology or that children are seen as passive. On the contrary, it was a central tenet of Piaget and his followers that it is through active engagement with the social world that children's cognitive abilities develop. Yet the social and emotional realms are seen as influences on the developmental process, never constituitive of it (Urwin 1984). Hence, this social world is seen as separate from the child's mind, something that can be 'controlled' for through breaking it down into quantifiable variables (Hogan 2005). This approach to developmental psychology consequently lacks a commitment to and method for understanding the complex psycho-social relations within which children are located (social here should be understood broadly, encompassing a complex of societally derived influences on children's lives, including: social interaction, institutions and ideologies; culture, history and discourse; governmental regulation, politics and the law; as well as economics, spatial relations and geography). To represent these social factors as variables – an approach that necessarily reduces them to (small) numbers – inevitably ignores the complex interrelations amongst them and the equally complex processes through which they may shape the developing child's sense of self.

This blind spot is related to the fact that developmentalists who focus on cognition tend to be effectively uninterested in the child's own worldview or phenemonology. This is because a strict focus on cognition, narrowly defined, rules out taking seriously the subjective dimensions of childhood that in other traditions are seen as constitutive of children's 'identity'. As the psychologist Flavell noted in an overview of cognitive-developmental research, 'when knowledge and abilities are subtracted from the totality of what could legitimately be called "cognitive", an important remainder is surely the person's subjective experience: how self and world seem and feel to that person, given that knowledge and those abilities' (1992: 1003, quoted in Hogan 2005: 23). In other words, a focus on knowledge and abilities alone tells us little about what it means to be a child, even if it could make sense to separate these out at all. As Urwin (1986) notes in her critique of the developmentalist paradigm, social interactions are seen as either speeding up or slowing down cognitive processes, but not as part of the structuring of cognition itself. In relation to nation and place, developmentalism does seem convincing in so far as children would need to be *able* to grasp cognitively abstract constructs such as the nation before they could be said fully to identify with them. Yet this ability can only develop in relation to children's social location as a whole throughout their childhood. Hence, cognition must at some level be a social process. It is in children's own worlds and perspectives that we need to look to discover the actuality of their identifications.

Contrary to this, attempts to see the world through children's own eyes are excluded by much developmental psychology, since it tends to treat children as unreliable informants. This is precisely because it sees them as always 'not yet capable' of competencies defined against a grown-up standard (Hogan 2005). Only adults, it is held, can reliably observe, understand and tell us about children's minds. In addition, this body of work traditionally assumes that 'the child' is a universal or standard phenomenon, with variations from the norm seen as deviations. There is a historical tendency to present the findings of studies conducted exclusively in western Europe and North America as though they applied universally. Much literature now testifies to the fact that childhood is both defined and experienced quite differently in different places as well as across different historical eras. Global cultural variation is recognised by psychologists who follow a sociocultural approach to human development (for example, Cole 1999, Rogoff 1990). There is very little that is universal in relation to the assumptions about children and their development enshrined, for example, in national legal systems. Hence, the age of criminal responsibility, reflecting beliefs about when childhood begins and ends, varies considerably from culture to culture and from generation to generation; it is currently fifteen in Norway, eight in Scotland and ten in England and Wales (Stainton Rogers 2003). In England and Wales it was age seven before 1932, age eight until 1963 and only in 1998 was it raised to ten (Gittens 1998). For Piaget, Kohlberg and their followers, such diversity could only be understood as a set of variables helping to explain the cognitive stages at which children arrive.

Kohlberg's highest stage of moral reasoning – a personally constructed sense of justice – involves the individual applying their *own* conscience, leaving behind the 'stage' in which reasoning follows societal rules and laws (Kohlberg 1969). This suggests religiously or extended-family–organised societies such as many in the non-Western world operate from within a lower stage of moral maturity. Such thinking has justifiably been described as ethnocentric (see Said 1994). Similarly, the classic cognitive-developmental approach accords little if any importance to the powerful ways in which socially constructed gender relations differently shape girls' and boys' ways of thinking. Carol Gilligan (1982) has advanced a theory of gendered development that challenges the universalist assumptions in Piaget's and Kohlberg's work (introduced in the previous chapter). She argues that the care ethic, frequently held up as a defining attribute of femininity, is devalued in Kohlberg's work since it is seen as a stage to be surpassed on a longer journey towards the attainment of a sense of justice. She rejects Kohlberg's idea that morality is about dilemmas that have *a* rational solution; instead, she proposes seeing contextual relativism, notably more of a feminine trait, as an alternative indicator of moral maturity (Gilligan 1987). In sum, the classic cognitive developmental paradigm sees the individual child as a rational 'brain' on a linear path of development whose endpoint is defined in terms of reason, not culture. The desire for objectivity ultimately leaves the actuality of children's experiences opaque (Greene and Hill 2005).

Nevertheless, it is important not to overstate the homogeneity of developmental approaches and, crucially, not to take cognitive-developmental research as representative of all psychological approaches to children that retain a theory of development. Dunn's work (1993, 2005), for example, stresses the need to understand children's development as produced within the actual networks of social relationships in which they live. Hence, she advocates observing children in the real-life settings of their homes and play/school-places, paying close attention to the complex of interpersonal relationships (such as between friends and siblings) in which they exercise their cognitive, affective and social powers. She notes that data from studies using this 'naturalistic' method show children displaying capabilities that are often far in advance of the abilities evidenced in controlled settings through standardised tests. In particular, she argues that studying children's naturally occurring talk yields rich insights into their developing powers of understanding (Dunn 2005). Hence, there appears to be some support for Hogan's contention that developmental psychology is beginning to take children's subjective experiences more seriously and is more willing than before to take account of the historical and social fields in which they are located. Although Hogan concedes that 'it is fair to say that such ideas have not, historically, dominated the field', nevertheless, she claims, 'their influence on contemporary research and theorising is considerable and is increasing' (Hogan 2005: 29).

Hogan has in mind here approaches influenced by Lev Vygotsky, the Russian psychologist writing in the 1920s whose ideas about children's social worlds were rediscovered by a new generation of psychologists working in the 1980s. These are developmental approaches that start with the social world and work back to the child. Their starting point is that children are born into a world already deeply structured and culturally encoded, which they encounter through continually interacting with it and gradually coming to be a fully participant member of it (see Wertsch 1981). In this kind of approach, national identity would not be seen as existing 'out there' in cultural representations or schooling and finding its way into children's minds by some unexplained means (as Gellner's analysis, lacking a theory of psychology or the self, implies). Instead, it would be seen as the product of a gradually unfolding series of interactions between the child and a cultural world in which national distinctions are already presented as inevitable and natural. Whilst still working with a theory of the developing child, this approach would choose to use qualitative methods in natural rather than artificial settings. Work in the socio-cultural or 'situative' tradition has focused in particular on how children learn, always as members of social groups (Brown et al. 1989, Lave 1990, 1991, Lave and Wenger 1991). School classrooms, for example, are seen as arenas wherein children's interactions are powerfully shaped by the social world yet are also negotiated on an individual level.

By contrast, classic socialisation theory treats environments more simplistically as the settings wherein culturally appropriate norms, values and behaviour patterns are learned by children from adults. Socialisation in many psychological approaches has come to mean 'internalisation' (Christensen and Prout 2005). This involves understanding how the social and cultural worlds in which children live come to reproduce themselves in children's minds. For example, gender differences are learnt from adults' gender-stereotyping behaviour (Archer and Lloyd 2002). Hence, parents hold strong expectations about how boys and girls should look and behave; children then learn to conform to these. Conditioning and imitation are the processes through which this learning operates. This tends to see the relationship between the child and the environment as rather mechanistic and unproblematic. Similar criticisms have been made of theories of socialisation from the discipline of sociology. For Jenks (a leading proponent of the 'new sociology of childhood', see below), socialisation theories sees children as merely reactive, tending to 'condemn' them 'to be an absent presence, a nominal cipher without an active dimension' (Jenks 1992: 13). These approaches to understanding children fail to interrogate *how* these learnt values get instilled and lose sight of how the child reacts *actively* to the social situation he or she encounters. The Piagetian developmental approach, by contrast, does at least have the considerable merit of prioritising both of these, although it lacks a means of accounting for the potency of the socio-cultural realm.

Theorising just how children do actively construct meanings within a social context that is nevertheless powerful and constraining has been quite a challenge for the psychology of childhood. Critical psychology is one approach that does explicitly seek to reconcile analysis of subjectivity with analysis of children's 'social worlds' (Richards and Light 1986). Such approaches seek to explicate the ways in which dominant discourses of childhood that define children in certain ways (such as inherently innocent or, conversely, savage) have powerful effects in institutionalising these expectations into the legal system, education system, and so forth (Epstein

1993, Walkerdine 1984). In relation to nations, the prevalent discourse of children's innate innocence coupled with nationalist discourse (inculcated through schooling and elsewhere) would be seen as combining to construct nationhood as an 'object' eliciting patriotic expression in school classrooms. Although coming from a different theoretical perspective, this analysis supports Gellner's argument (1983) that nationalist sentiment is largely constructed rather than inhering (as in Smith's analysis) in lived ways of life. In this approach, children's talk would be analysed as a multiple and potentially contradictory amalgamation of 'texts' showing traces of the various positions and perspectives that make up cultural discourses of place and nation. As Walkerdine puts it, the social is not a smooth coherent force but 'a set of identities or positions, produced within the discursive relations of different practices which do not necessarily fit together smoothly' (1986: 65). Hence, children do not have a unified identity that is theirs; rather, they give voice to contradictions and multiple perspectives that are not inside their minds but in culture (Alldred and Burman 2005). This offers a fruitful line of inquiry for thinking about collective representations as multiple discourses about place, ethnicity, nationality and belonging. These may not add up; they may rather contradict each other (for example, the idea of the nation as a reassuring 'we' identity versus the idea of its multiculturalism and plurality). Hence, we should not expect children (or indeed adults) to produce coherent accounts of what it means. This approach does not see children growing into coherent reason; instead, their talk is understood as similar to adults' and crossed through with contradictory positions.

Discourse theory does not, however, succeed so well in explaining how children may recognise themselves within these discourses. How do children relate 'self' to 'nation' in the sense of coming to invest in it emotionally? This body of work struggles to find ways of understanding children's subjective agency in the face of these powerful discourses. It frequently appears instead that individuals vanish into a concept of the available subject-positions offered by competing discourses. A similar disappearing act, though differently theorised, underlies the conception of children in the social learning approach just discussed. Children are seen as empty vessels who (paradoxically) nevertheless can learn; this begs the question of what constitutes the pre-social self that is able to assimilate the externally derived stimuli. In other words, the child is taken as always-already rational, thus positing a 'cogito' that pre-exists socialisation. In discursive approaches, by contrast, the child is seen as entering consciousness only through entry into language and thus into discourse. The child-self comes to be seen as produced by and in culture, and individual agency disappears altogether. To avoid this kind of reductionism, Walkerdine and others turned to psychoanalytic theory in order to explore how the contradictory subject positions that define, for example, girls' socially expected roles mean that they often experience being split or torn between competing identities (Henriques et al. 1984). Walkerdine insists on the affective and non-rational dimensions of these processes, recognising that children are actively investing emotionally in subject positions, not simply being defined by them.

Sociological approaches to childhood

Whilst social and critical psychology are, de facto, concerned with theorising the relationship between self/mind and context/world, the sociology of childhood has found it less problematic than psychology, for obvious reasons, to focus on the child as an entirely social actor. Early sociological work on children assumed a model of socialisation that was not dissimilar to the social learning theory discussed above. The most influential figure here was Talcott Parsons. His analysis of the 'personality system', the 'social system' and the 'cultural system' posits the individual as being under the control of a hierarchy of nested systems that are structured according to the 'functional imperatives' of societies – namely, pattern maintenance, integration, goal attainment and adaptation (Parsons 2002, first published 1961). In pattern maintenance, for example, the social system is geared to maintaining the stability of 'patterns of institutionalised culture'; this involves the *internalisation of values* concordant with the belief system in the structure of an individual's personality. Central to this are the 'mechanisms of socialisation' – the processes through which 'the values of society are internalised in his [*sic*] personality' (2002: 369–70). Parsonian sociology thus makes frequent use of psychological concepts, although there is no explicit psychological theorisation of the self or consciousness. The proposition is that children are socialised into key values that are essential for the stability of society. Parsons observes that such processes are not straightforward and may involve strains and tensions in the individual's motivational commitment. However, the tendency in 'stable' societies is towards conformity. The implication for a theory of children's national identifications would be that any society needs its members to be socialised into a recognition of its distinctive identity and to feel loyalty towards this (a Parsonian 'value' translated into the 'norm' of national feeling); hence, the social system conditions the personality system such that national feeling becomes a highly desirable norm that individuals 'identify' with. The personality system is handled in the main by the family, which embodies the key environment for the successful socialisation and emotional support of the child. Once formed, the personality that emerges in childhood is stable and unchangeable.

Parsonian structural-functionalist sociology is now considered outdated, but it is arguable that the concept of socialisation retains considerable influence in relation to theories of childhood. This is perhaps because, in common with developmental psychological approaches, the child is seen as fundamentally different to adults, requiring powerful conditioning processes to make him or her conform to adult norms. As Jenks (2005) notes, this belief in children's fundamental otherness has been remarkably persistent and widespread in Western culture, dominating educational policy and pedagogical practice in the UK for decades. Recent sociological approaches to children take issue with the idea that children's differences at different ages are natural and argue instead that these differences are always social (James et al. 1998). The so-called 'new sociology of childhood' (of which Jenks is a prime founder) suggests that they are competent and active participants in all kinds of social scenarios – such as making social distinctions, expressing or withholding judgements about others, drawing and redrawing boundaries between here/there or self/other, initiating talk or behaviour designed to exclude or include others, and so forth. Such a perspective examines how children's thoughts about where they 'belong' and who they 'are' are part of the much more generalised patterns of social interaction produced in the key settings (especially of school) in which they find themselves. This approach argues that 'the immaturity of children is a biological fact but the ways in which that immaturity is understood and made meaningful is a fact of culture' (James and Prout 1990: 7). A new wave of largely qualitative sociological studies of children in the 1980s and 1990s began to analyse childhoods as fluid and shifting 'worlds' and children as competent social actors, worthy of study on their own terms (Connolly 1998, Corsaro 1997, Qvortrup et al. 1994, Thorne 1993). These researchers adopted to varying degrees a social-constructionist paradigm, understanding children as active social beings and childhood as constructed through culture, society and history (Christensen and Prout 2005).

This work has served to reinvigorate the field of childhood studies and to develop a plethora of mainly qualitative research techniques with which to investigate the meanings that children make. However, in its outright rejection of developmental perspectives, it exhibits a certain degree of hyperbole and a tendency to cast all developmental research as unassailably wrong-headed. In the next chapter, we focus on the limitations of a refusal to countenance children as developing beings.

Qualitative methods for researching children

We have so far arrived at a position that, whilst not ruling out quantitative or standardised methods, favours largely qualitative approaches to researching children *given the demands of our topic*. This is because since we are concerned with their subjective experiences and feelings, investigating as we are their national or place identifications, we need methods that can elicit the meanings children themselves generate rather than meanings constructed within researchers' instruments. This does not mean that quantity is ignored; qualitative approaches often make use of concepts of frequency. For example, inevitably when we talk in the chapters that follow about significant markers of identity we mean those that cropped up most often in fieldwork. Nevertheless, our focus is on the *interpretation* of meanings that, as far as possible, have been allowed to emerge through interaction with children and have not been imposed through standardised coding or ratings systems. Furthermore, strategies for eliciting these meanings have to be flexible and, in our view, plural. In researching this particular type of collective identification, we are dealing with a very slippery and quite abstract phenomenon. We cannot, it is plain, observe children in the act of identifying with either place or nation. This is something that emerges not so much in observable behaviour as in and through verbal expression. Hence, we need techniques that encourage children to talk. And these are difficult to construct in relation to children in middle childhood who – developmentalist controversies aside – do not necessarily find lengthy periods of verbal self-expression either easy or engaging. In addition, the topic of identity itself presents problems for it is a subject matter constructed by professionals, not one that is used by children (or indeed many adults) themselves. In other words, it is an '-etic' rather than an '-emic' category. Anthias expresses the implications of this well in relation to adults:

> Researchers in the field often know that they cannot find useful or interesting answers by asking direct questions about identity. Asking someone a direct question about their identity often produces a blank stare, a puzzled silence or a glib and formulaic response. This is not only because research subjects have not understood the question, but also because they cannot easily provide answers. [...] there are ways round the problem of asking about identity in this upfront fashion, and experienced researchers are often able to tease out answers that refer to identity. Moreover, researchers in the field know from experience that it is best to allow subjects to talk about themselves, their lives and their experiences, and their 'identity' will emerge from this narration.
>
> (Anthias 2002: 492)

There is also an argument that identities are too complex and contingent for it to make any sense to ask direct questions of research participants about how strongly they identify themselves with particular groups. In other words, we need methods that will allow children's expressions of national identification to emerge in the course of interactions that do not appear overly artificial or awkward. This may well involve a combination of more direct and more indirect kinds of questioning. What we need to establish, above all, are methods that allow children's own meanings to emerge.

In earlier methods of qualitatively researching children, their own perspectives were often seen as impossible to research. King (1978: 8), for example, considered it virtually impossible to 'understand the subjective meanings of very small children' and developed techniques in the classroom for avoiding eye contact with them, to the extent that he elected to take refuge in the Wendy house. More recently, a cluster of ethnographic studies has focused directly on the subjective worlds of children themselves; yet it is necessary to acknowledge that this is not as easy as it may look. The new sociology of childhood stresses the need to try and understand children as active social actors in their own right rather than interpreting their behaviour as indicators of which developmental stage or level of learning they have arrived at. But this does not mean that one can somehow close one's adult eyes when doing research with children and see the world through the child's eyes instead. Thorne describes how the sheer size differential in adult–child interactions as well as differences of status and power mean it is impossible to 'pass' as one of them: 'My greater size; my access to special relations with the principal, teachers and aides; my sheer status as an adult in an institution that draws sharp generational divisions and marks them with differences in power and authority, posed complicated obstacles to learning from kids' (Thorne 1993:16).

Pollard (1987: 103) similarly observes, 'one cannot be a real "participant" or expect to be treated as a "member", but one can be participatory by interaction'.

One of the major difficulties raised in the literature on researching children concerns their tendency, being commonly subject to adult direction, to be easily influenced by their perception of the researcher's agenda. Interviews with children, in particular, can place heavy demands on children to conform to the social expectations of the adult. Hence 'children may give answers that are detemined more by their desire to please than by their desire to be truthful' (Greene and Hill 2005: 9). Studies have shown that children will endeavour to answer even nonsensical questions, and that they will often say 'no' when they do not understand (Waterman et al. 2001, cited in Greene and Hill 2005: 9). Children can, of course, lie, and they can also be adept at evading and mocking adult authority (Corsaro 1997). On the other hand, adult–child interactions can hardly be said to be routinely characterised by lies and deceit; children may in fact be more likely to make things up to each other than to adults. Interviews do give the opportunity for children to articulate their experiences and opinions directly to an adult about a focused topic and can yield rich data (Harden et al. 2000). This strength is also a weakness, however, since the interview requires of the child quite a high degree of linguistic competence and confidence in self-expression; where these are lacking, it may easily deteriorate into a 'teacherly' interrogation. As an alternative, the use of focus groups rather than one-to-one interviews can provide a less threatening context for children to express themselves in. They have the added advantage of constructing a setting (albeit still an artificial one) in which children are engaged in social interaction with their peers. If children's friendship and peer groups are recognised as crucial arenas in which they develop and negotiate their identities, the use of group-level discussions may well be considered essential. Yet the obvious danger with child focus groups is that if the requirement on the part of the researcher to be non-directive is adhered to, they can fall apart into chaos. If it is not, they can end up being rigidly controlled and their original purpose forfeited.

For this reason, talking methods such as interviews and focus groups are often supplemented or even replaced by more creative methods that do not demand the child's giving lengthy verbal accounts. Various kinds of play and games, together with verbal prompting techniques, creative tasks and a whole array of visual aids have all been recommended as engaging children more effectively in research interactions (James et al. 1998). Their use is becoming increasingly common, and we adopted one or two of these methods ourselves in our own research design (see below). However, it should be acknowledged that not all activities deemed 'fun' or 'accessible' by adults will be seen as such by all children; furthermore, the decision to use creative tasks to the exclusion of talking falls back on assumptions of children's innate otherness (Harden et al. 2000). Such techniques may favour more creative children and inhibit those with different skills (Backett and Alexander 1991). In addition, they can present the non-specialist researcher with perplexing material to analyse, particularly when it comes to drawings. Some very interesting work has been done by image-trained specialists analysing children's drawings, which illuminate the cultural meanings and self–other relations embedded within them (for example, Van Leeuwen 2000). The text-trained researcher, by contrast, may find herself with rather fewer insights to draw on. Nevertheless, creative methods can be very useful if used to elicit conversation and verbal talk, as we found in our own project.

For these kinds of reasons, it is often advocated that more lengthy periods of interaction are required between researcher and children and, hence, that participant-observation methods be adopted that allow children to get used to the researcher's presence. The strategies available to the researcher wanting to observe children vary along 'an observational continuum' (Graue and Walsh 1998: 100) from more interactive to more passive. Renold (2002, 2005) conducted a lengthy period of observation of children in the classroom. She found that her stance in relation to the children (how much she 'participated' in as opposed to simply observed their social worlds) was not entirely under her own control as the children positioned her in a number of different social roles in relation to themselves. This required being flexible and open to a constant process of renegotiation of what she could and could not do in her interactions with them. At different times, she engaged in various kinds of participant observation, including 'watching', 'listening', 'sharing', 'learning' and 'collaborating'. In more passive 'watching' modes, she was seen by the children as a spy, a journalist or a supervisor/teacher; in more active 'sharing' modes (where she freely answered their questions and exchanged information) she became a 'friend' or 'big sister'. It is clear that such roles can only be built up after a long period of mutual acquaintance, which means that fieldwork with children is often a lengthy and time-consuming business. Renold describes very well the tricky process of constantly needing to reassure children that you will not breach confidentiality and that you will not 'tell on them'. Such questions are not only about obtaining the best research data; they are also ones that involve being clear about one's ethical stance in relation to the power differentials of adult–child relations.

Ethics

Researching with children is particularly vulnerable to ethical problems. First, there is the question of avoiding harm. There is the blatant fact that some adults can and do abuse children's powerlessness in order to further their own desires, whether sexual, authoritarian, for physical domination, or whatever (Scourfield and Coffey 2006). All researchers have to ensure they do not expose children to risk of harm. Second, however, there are more subtle influences that also have to do with inequalities of power, but which will be there to trouble even the best-intentioned and principled researcher. These involve how we represent children's views and how we can avoid the temptation to 'speak for' the child in a way that reinforces the idea of children as an 'other', fundamentally outside of the dominant norms of adult society (James et al. 1998). That kind of thinking leads children to be denied a voice of their own. Attempts to 'give voice' to children's perspectives should not be denigrated, of course, but they are still open to the charge of translating children's experiences and concerns into adult agendas. Hence, the researcher–researched relationship gets entangled with the adult–child hierarchy (Alldred and Burman 2005). In many ways, there are few, if any, solutions to this dilemma. The unavoidable power imbalances put into play when adults research children have led some researchers to advocate according children a more active role in the research process. For example, Kellett et al. (2004) have conducted a research project that involved ten-year-old children as fieldworkers. It is clear, however, that such an approach will not be feasible or appropriate in all projects.

Central to the ethics of research with children are the issues surrounding informed consent. Cohen and Manion (1994: 350) propose four issues to be aware of in applying procedures for informed consent: competence, voluntarism, full information and comprehension. Clearly, young children are not as able to meet these terms as adults. They are usually located in settings such as family and school in which they are subject to adult authority and have low status so that they may not feel free to refuse a request to participate in research. They are also unlikely to be able to understand the implications of the research project and its topic, and for this reason the information given to them, being of necessity adapted to their level of comprehension, cannot be as full as it would be for adults. Hence, for many reasons, children will not be able to choose as freely as adults whether to consent to participate in a study (Morrow and Richards 1996). In managed, directed and timed interactions such as focus groups and interviews, the researcher can be more assertive in ensuring that the children are explicitly given the opportunity not to participate and instead to give their 'informed dissent' (Morrow and Richards 1996: 95). In participant observational situations, however, especially when the participants are interacting freely with others (as in playground settings) it is much more difficult to seek and obtain consent. Renold found that her eleven-year-old schoolchildren were often ready to tell her in no uncertain terms when they were not willing to let her listen into a conversation. Doing participant observation with younger children who have not yet developed these skills and who may understand virtually nothing about the issue of protecting privacy can be more ethically contentious. Every project, ultimately, has to look to its own research design to ensure ethical risks are minimised; however, to an extent there will always be a balance to strike in recognising the particular vulnerabilities of children and according them sufficient autonomy such that good data are generated.

Our own project: methods adopted

Our own project sought to explore the ways in which children talk about the nation and the places in which they live. We selected six primary schools to take part in the research, chosen to represent a purposive sample of the diversity of life in Wales. These were selected on the basis of information about the socio-economic, ethnic, geographical and linguistic character of their various locations obtained from a variety of sources. The Welsh schools' census provided us with some information on the socio-economic make-up of each school (through free-school-meal quotas) and the Welsh Index of Multiple Deprivation was also consulted, which provides a ward-by-ward breakdown of social and economic deprivation in Wales. Linguistic indicators were obtained from two principal sources, first (and more crudely), the schools census, which gives a breakdown of the percentage of pupils taught through the medium of Welsh. Second, the 1991 census results were consulted, which provide more detailed information about the linguistic character of communities in Wales on a ward-by-ward basis. We chose three English-medium schools and three Welsh-medium schools: a sample which overrepresents the Welsh-medium sector, since only 20.3 per cent of primary school pupils in Wales had at least part of their curriculum delivered through the medium of Welsh at the time (National Assembly for Wales 2001). This decision was based in part on the centrality of the language to debates about Welshness past and present. It offered us the opportunity to explore diverse, marginalised and contested identities.

We spoke to a total of 105 children over three months in late 2001, conducting a total of eighteen focus groups and fifty-four in-depth interviews. The children were drawn from the eight to eleven age bracket from a range of social classes, ability ranges, ethnicities, nationalities and linguistic identities. We used solely qualitative research methods, namely, focus groups (of six children, three groups in each school) and semi-structured interviews (nine in each school). Where children were bilingual Welsh–English, they had a choice to participate in either language. In order to engage the children, we used some visual prompts such as a map, a video clip and postcards, and varied the style of discussion by using, for example, a sentence-completion exercise and sorting of cards. For the card-sorting exercise, we asked children, in focus groups, to choose identity label cards that described them. This was a similar exercise to that used in the British Psychological Society's (BPS) millennial project on children's views of Britishness (Barrett 2002), but with qualitative rather than quantitative aims in mind. The batches of cards included the labels 'Welsh person', 'English person', 'British person', 'European', 'from [named local town or area, e.g., Cardiff]', 'black', 'white', 'Asian', 'boy', 'girl', 'religion [several]' and 'you choose'. This last card was blank, and children could add any other identity label they wanted. We wanted to know what children thought about nationally dominant collective identifications with place. We calculated that we could not list all potential ethnic/national categories and keep the children engaged, so we had to add this blank card for minority identities. We gave examples of how it could be used and the children were enthusiastic in adding extra identities on this card. We described their choice as a 'secret vote' in so far as their classmates did not need to know what they had chosen if they wanted to keep it to themselves. We did, however, then invite any comments they wanted to make about each of the cards both in focus groups and interviews, and most children were happy to discuss their choices both with the interviewer and in front of their peers in the focus group. We also kept our own notes of their choices. The exercise proceeded in three stages:

1   Children decided which of the cards to keep (that described them) and which to reject (that did not describe them).
2   They were asked to choose one card only from this batch that was the most important to them.
3   They were given back the whole set, asked to write on a card another thing that was very important to them, such as a person, pet, sports team or interest, and then choose between the entire set which was the most important.

It was the children's discussion of this exercise that interested us more than quasi-quantification of the responses. The focus groups, as well as acting as a social context where the production of identity could be studied, also functioned as a platform from which to draw a sample of children with something interesting to say about themselves and their identity choices to take part in individual interviews.

It is important to record that we do not see our research project as attempting to reveal the one authentic voice of these children, as there can only be a 'multiplicity of authentic voices' (Connolly 1997: 163). Van Ausdale and Feagin (2002) have observed that the presence of a 'sanctioning adult' will inevitably affect what research projects reveal (in this case about racialisation). They write that 'when it comes to much research on race, the right answer the children are expected to give is that "we are all the same inside" '(2002: 14). This message does indeed emerge in our data, as will be shown at various points in the book. We were also struck, however, by the extent to which unwitting racialisation of Welshness emerged, and that some children were willing to conduct a conversation about national belonging that seemed naïve to any discourse of political correctness about ethnicity.

Any researchers studying anything other than a topic that is strictly about schooling should of course have reservations about school-based research on children's views. It was inevitable that the school context affected what the children said and how they said it. As Strange et al. (2003) note in a recent paper on the effects of school context on the research process, questions of timetabling, time constraints and absenteeism all impinge on the quality of the data, as do classroom norms. These norms include the positioning of adults in the teacher role, gendered peer-group interaction (see Chapter 3) and, of course, children's expectations of acceptable discourse within the school. The effect of school ethos and curriculum on national and ethnic identity is an interesting and important issue in itself. The question of informed consent in schools also needs to be questioned, as already noted (David et al. 2001). However, we considered discussions in schools to be a familiar enough arena for the children as to be a relatively unpressurised opportunity for them to air their views, and the influence of the school on the discussion was one of the issues we were keen to explore.

As we noted above, qualitative research does not preclude using numbers, but it uses them quite strategically to describe the parameters of the sample assembled rather than for purposes of standardisation or generalisation. In fact, data can be both quantified *and* interpreted; they do not have to be seen as exclusively qualitative or quantitative (Bryman 1988). Quantifying data is often seen as useful in particular for describing and mapping a field; qualifying it for purposes of 'drilling down' into the meanings generated. Hence, in our own study we quantify our data in noting which markers of identity were mentioned most often by the children and in commenting on how the frequency of identity markers varied between the six schools.

Children and national identity in Wales

Our main focus in this study was the attempt to explore the intersections of place and nation in children's lives with reference to their particular sociocultural positioning – such as gender, ethnicity and, importantly, whether they were attending Welsh- or English-medium schools. At this point, it is necessary to consider in a little more detail the particularities of Wales and Welshness as these provide important parameters to the study. National identities in different countries and cultures cannot be straightforwardly compared as if they are local manifestations of the same social processes. Jenkins (1997) questions, for example, whether nationalism in Northern Ireland and Wales can even be regarded as the same phenomenon.

Wales is a stateless nation within the UK – albeit one with some devolved powers – with a population of just under 3 million (out of nearly 60 million in the whole UK). It is a relatively poor country in comparison with England and Scotland, with household income being some 10 per cent below the British average (Day 2002). Wales is often thought to be marginal within dominant notions of Britishness. Hechter (1975) characterised its relationship with the British state as one of internal colonialism, although this was a highly controversial claim at the time and most commentators remain unconvinced (see the reviews of these debates in Day 2002 and Williams 2005). Around 20 per cent of the population of Wales speak the Welsh language. This language gives Wales an obvious claim to culturally distinctiveness, but its significance to Welsh identity is highly contested. As would be expected in the context of the global dominance of the English language, the Welsh language has struggled to be other than a private low-status language (May 2001). The past few decades have witnessed some recovery of its status, with a Language Act that has improved bilingual provision in the public sector and in official documentation. Most importantly, there has been an increase in Welsh-medium education. However, there is still considerable concern about the erosion of Welsh as a community language and the language of the home (see Jenkins and Williams 2000).

Our research sample was designed to take account of the different emphases that different groups and areas within Wales place on the importance of the language and the independence of Welsh identity. Hence, our sample broadly reflects voting results during the 1997 Welsh devolution referendum; three being in areas that voted 'yes' to devolution and three in areas that voted 'no'. Wales has often been spoken about in terms of a three-way split between its more Welsh, less Welsh and most Anglicised regions (Balsom 1985, Roberts 1995). We note that Balsom's 'three Wales model' has been questioned by many commentators (such as Day 2002, Williams 2005). Williams sees the model as a 'museum piece' (2005: 14). Notwithstanding valid criticisms of this model as essentialising regional identities, it is worth noting that the schools in our sample were evenly spread between what Balsom terms 'Y Fro Gymraeg' (Welsh-speaking heartland), 'Welsh Wales' and 'British Wales'. The schools are described in Table 2.1. Culturally appropriate pseudonyms are used for all children, schools and specific locations. Where we mention more general geography that cannot identify specific schools, such as counties (for example, Gwynedd, Powys) and the capital city of Cardiff, we are referring to actual locations.

Our sample was, of course, not intended to be wholly representative of life in Wales: rather it was settled upon in order to take account of regional differences within Wales whilst simultaneously offering us the opportunity to explore diverse, marginalised and contested identities. It is worth noting that there is regional difference across Wales in terms of the politics of 'race'. Only one of the schools, Highfields in Cardiff, is ethnically diverse to any extent, reflecting the population of Wales both numerically overall and also

Table 2.1 The research sites

Highfields School: an English-medium inner-city Cardiff school with a multi-ethnic intake. The free-school-meals quota was close to the Welsh average. Cardiff is the Welsh capital, a city of around 300,000 people.

Petersfield School: English-medium and serving a socially deprived council estate in the eastern valleys of south Wales, which is a generally deprived post-industrial region. The estate is in the town of Llanhywel. More than half of the children in this school receive free school meals.

Llwynirfon School: English-medium, in a bilingual area of Powys in rural mid-Wales where between 20 and 35 per cent of the population are able to speak Welsh (1991 census). This school has a very low proportion of children who receive free school meals.

Ysgol y Waun: Welsh-medium and not deprived (in terms of children receiving free school meals) in a largely anglophone area of north-east Wales and not too far from the border with England. The school is located in a small town, Ffynnon Las and its catchment area includes both urban and rural areas.

Ysgol y Porth: Welsh-medium in an area of rural Gwynedd (north-west Wales) where over 80 per cent of the local population speak Welsh. This school has a low proportion of children receiving free school meals. The small town where the school is based is called Bryn Tawel.

Ysgol Maesgarw: based in a village in a deprived area of the western valleys of south Wales (a generally deprived post-industrial region) where large numbers and a significant proportion of the population are able to speak Welsh. The proportion of children on free school meals was well above the Welsh average.

---

in terms of regional concentration of minorities. This was a school that parents seemed to choose because of its cultural diversity. Bahira moved to the school when she started wearing an Islamic head scarf (*hijab*) as she would have been the only one to do so in her previous school. Joe's mother (Joe is white) chose the school because she thought it was 'not a racist school'. In terms of language politics, the 'problem' of English incomers diluting the Welsh language is especially highlighted by language campaigners in the area surrounding the Gwynedd school, Ysgol y Porth.

Children in Welsh-medium schools study everything except English through the medium of Welsh. The children in English-medium schools have to study Welsh as a National Curriculum foundation subject and in the context of discussions about the nation in interviews and focus groups they very often referred to learning Welsh in school. Although our opportunities for participant observation were very limited, informal time spent with children around the school in and between lessons and in the playground revealed some interesting patterns of language. What we observed in this regard generally supports the findings of other research carried out on the Welsh language in schools in Wales. In English-medium schools, Welsh was learned as one of several school subjects, and none of these children was heard naturally speaking Welsh outside of these lessons. Children in Welsh-medium school all used Welsh in classrooms. All of them spoke Welsh fluently enough to be clearly understood, but for those children who were learning Welsh as a second language, degrees of fluency varied considerably. There seemed to be a considerable variety of school ethos with regard to language use. So, in Ysgol y Waun (north-east Wales, very little first-language Welsh-speaking in the local area), the children spoke English in the playground but seemed to feel rather guilty about this; many persisted in speaking Welsh in interviews even though it was clear that they would have been more fluent in English. Ysgol y Porth (north-west Wales) seemed generally relaxed in its bilingualism. This is one of the parts of Wales where the Welsh language is strongest and both languages could be heard in the playground. In Ysgol Maesgarw, despite the school being in a part of Wales traditionally thought of as naturally bilingual and with relatively high levels of Welsh-speaking ability – the western valleys of south Wales – the children tended to speak English in research interviews and seemed happier to admit that Welsh was a language they only really spoke in school. Our impressions of this school seemed to confirm the general pessimism that has been expressed about the Welsh language in this part of Wales, a pessimism that was confirmed by the 2001 census. Only one of the schools featured language use other than English and Welsh – Highfields in Cardiff, the most ethnically diverse of the schools. In interviews and focus groups in this school, languages mentioned included Arabic, Somali, Pushtu, Bengali and Urdu.

Issues such as the extent to which children identify with the national language, or, conversely, de-emphasise its importance to their sense of identity are fundamental to the arguments pursued in later chapters. Children, as Chapter 1 discussed, are seen as crucially important to any attempt at nation-building. Stephens (1997a) has observed that constructions of children can be pivotal in the structuring of modern nation-states. There is some conscious nation-building going on in Wales at present, as the country has recently gained further measures of self-government in the form of a national assembly that was established in 1999. There is also the context of the forming of Cymuned, a lobby group campaigning for the preservation of Welsh-speaking communities. As Day (2002) notes, this controversial development has seen accusations of exclusivity and even racism being made on both sides of the debate. As we note below, the promotion of 'Welsh-speaking communities' involves a consideration of migration patterns and cultural belonging that have implications for ethnic diversity, whatever position is taken in the debate (Williams 2003).

Aside from these more controversial elements of the Welsh national-cultural scene, one obvious way in which politicians can attempt to influence children's views of the nation is the school history curriculum (see Phillips 1998). Any nationalist vision will require the co-option of children. In Wales, Welsh-medium education is increasing, in an attempt to make a more fully bilingual nation, and this is having a certain effect, as can be seen in the rise in numbers of Welsh-speaking children between the 1981 and 2001 censuses. There are youth organisations that operate within nationalist discourses, for example, the British nationalism of the guiding and scouting movements and the cultural Welsh nationalism of Urdd Gobaith Cymru (the Welsh youth league). Stephens (1997a) notes that the work on children and the nation in her special edition of the journal *Childhood* explores how certain constructions of childhood have been shaped by, have legitimated or have challenged particular constructions of the nation, but adds that few of the articles in that special edition present empirical material on how children understand their identities in relation to nationalist visions. Our book is an attempt to do this in relation to Wales.

One of the key dimensions we explore is the multiple intersections (in Wales, as in any nation) between race, ethnicity and national identity. The 2001 census shows the ethnic origin of the Welsh population to be 97.9 per cent white. Cardiff has 8.4 per cent minority-ethnic population and much of Wales, with the exception of cities on the south Wales coast, is around 98–9 per cent white. Wales is in one respect more cosmopolitan in terms of people's origins than most of Britain, however, because of the large number of people born in England who live there (Giggs and Pattie 1992). In terms of the politics of identity and belonging, the Welsh language tends to predominate public debate. Charlotte Williams (1999a) notes that in some ways 'race' is less of an issue in Wales than England precisely because Welsh identity is so contested. There is less of a sense that there is something clear and well-defined under threat than in some other parts of the UK. There is some continuity between the history of minority-ethnic people in Wales and the more general history of black Britons (Fryer 1984). There are also some important differences. In comparison with much of the UK, some of the black settlement in Wales is particularly long-standing. This is especially true of Cardiff, but also of smaller numbers of black families with a long history spread across Wales. Many of these are dual heritage families. There is also a long history of racism, overlooked in some romanticised visions of Wales and despite the relatively long history of minority ethnic people in Wales, there is a powerful legacy of 'Welshness' being seen to equate to whiteness (Williams 1995).

Whilst most readers of this book outside of Wales are realistically going to be more interested in the more general social-scientific implications of the data and discussion, we would robustly defend the value of research on Wales for its own sake, and not only as a case study for exploring wider social scientific questions. Wyn Jones (2004) has observed that there is a relative dearth of social-scientific research being conducted in Welsh universities that is specifically and intentionally about Wales. We hope this book will make a contribution to the research evidence about Wales as well as contributing to more general debates about children and place identity. We should also explain to readers who are primarily interested in Wales that we have, of course, been obliged to limit the Wales-specific discussion for the sake of those readers with a more general interest in childhood studies.

Conclusion

We have attempted in this chapter to sketch out some debates concerning the study of children. We have drawn out some of the tensions between conceptions of children and identities in traditional psychological research on cognitive development, socio-cultural approaches to child development, critical psychology, traditional sociological work on socialisation and the (now not so) 'new' sociology of childhood. We have commented on the implications of these different paradigms for researching children. The study that the book is based on is qualitative and is most influenced by the new sociology of childhood, but we also maintain the need for a psycho-social approach to understanding children's identities, and the following chapter will go on to explain more about this, with reference to some of our own empirical material. The research project was conducted in Wales in late 2001, so we have to bear in mind we are exploring a particular series of regional contexts within a particular stateless nation with its unique history. Whilst Wales is interesting in its own right, we spend much of the book trying to draw out insights of general social-scientific interest. We begin this in the next chapter by considering the process of national and ethnic identification in children.

3 The process of children's national and ethnic identification

In this chapter, we explore the topic of children's identifications with significant collective others – those they see as different from themselves, and those they see as the same. All of this involves the need to understand and interpret the quite complex processes of self–other categorisation that children employ. These can be seen as part of the building blocks out of which children construct their sense of nation, collective belonging and ethnic identification. Richard Jenkins (1997) argues that the boundary between 'ethnicism' and 'nationalism' is indeterminate. He defines an ethnic group broadly as based on 'the *belief* shared by its members that, however distantly, they are of common descent' (Jenkins 1997: 9–10, italics in original), and this definition can encompass national identity. We agree that the assertion of national identity is very close to the assertion of ethnicity in its demarcation of boundaries between peoples and that the assertion of both national and ethnic identity involves the symbolic construction of community (Cohen 1985). The whole of this book is, therefore, centrally concerned with ethnicity as thus broadly defined. Nevertheless, there are differences between national and ethnic identity – such as the idea that nations are bounded geographical spaces, whilst ethnicities have a more ambiguous relationship to space and place. McCrone (2002) has noted that in Britain there is a tendency for 'national' identities to be connected with constitutional issues and territorial politics, whereas it is often assumed that 'ethnic' identities refer to 'race' and these are typically discussed in the context of multiculturalism. Our approach differs markedly from this. We start from the assumption that children are variously enmeshed in a range of collective identifications operating at different levels, including ones that that blur the boundary between ethnicity and nationality by turning rather on questions of 'Where do I belong?' and 'Who do I relate to?'. However, we use the terms 'ethnic' and 'national' separately in this chapter's title since some of the research data we refer to here, such as the assertion of an Islamic identity, are in fact concerned with ethnicities that are not tied to the nation.

Unlike ethnicity, nationalism and national identity are explicit projects of the state (Jenkins 1997). Despite this unavoidable political dimension to the topic, we must acknowledge that this chapter is more about children's culture than it is about political science, since it is grounded in discussion of the meanings children themselves use in talking of their senses of collective belonging. We are primarily concerned in the chapter with *how* children talk about themselves in relation to the nation and other collective identifications. Of course, it is not possible to disentangle the cultural and the political within any discussion of imagined communities, nor within the ongoing internal–external dialectic of identification (Jenkins 1996, 1997). We do not attempt any disentangling in this chapter. Political and cultural discourses of the nation obviously form the context to what children say about the nation, as discussed in Chapter 1, but our emphasis in much of the current chapter is on what children *do* with the idea of nation (Bechhofer et al. 1999; Thompson 2001). In what follows, children's national identifications, being the prime focus of our study, receive more attention than the topic of ethnicity, though our discussion remains sensitive to the extent to which both are inevitably intertwined.

As noted in Chapter 1, there is relatively little published social-scientific research on children's relation to the nation in comparison with the existing body of work on adults. There has been some work on representations of the nation for and through children and on how childhoods are constructed via top-down nationalist projects (see some of the papers in the collection edited by Stephens 1997b, Meek 2001 on children's literature and Exell 2006 on Wales). There has been anthropological work on children and culture, but not so much on children's sense of spatial boundaries. Holloway and Valentine (2000a) have argued as social geographers that the new social studies of childhood need to encompass a more sophisticated consideration of social space. Space is discussed in some recent writings (such as James et al. 1998), but to focus on the nation is a somewhat newer angle within the sociology of childhood. There are a few sociologically oriented studies of children's identification with the nation, such as Carrington and Short's (1995, 1996) work on England and Scotland, Howard and Gill's (2001) research on Australia, Hengst's (1997) research on England, Turkey and Germany and Segrott's (2006) on Wales. Not surprisingly, however, given its historical dominance of the academic study of children, the discipline where perhaps most research activity can be found on children's views of the nation is that of developmental psychology. Despite coming from more sociological backgrounds ourselves, the work of child-development researchers was hard to avoid when we embarked on our research, since the British Psychological Society's developmental section chose the topic of children's views of Britishness for its millennial project (see Barrett 2002). To a limited extent, we engage in this chapter with the work of developmental psychologists on children and the nation.

We have chosen to foreground here a discussion of social processes that reveal both tensions and common ground between sociology and psychology. Following the overview of different disciplinary approaches to understanding children in the previous chapter, one of the main aims of this chapter is to challenge sociologists' and psychologists' lack of recognition of each other's work on identity. We reflect on three social processes that we argue are important to understanding national and ethnic identities in children: child development, agency and social interaction (with particular emphasis on the gendered dimension of interaction). Our overall argument is that none of these three social processes should be the exclusive preserve of either sociologists or psychologists and that an adequate explanation of social identities in children needs to draw on aspects of both disciplines.

The development of children's thinking about nations and ethnic groups

As noted in Chapter 1, identity has of course been a major topic for psychological study for some time. The concept of identity is inevitably a social psychological one and those studying it will place more emphasis on psychological or sociological aspects, depending on the traditions within which they are working. There is also a substantial body of work on psychoanalytic perspectives on identity. It is certainly not our aim in this book to provide a comprehensive review of all psychological work on identity. What follows is a fairly brief appeal for an open, balanced and inclusive social-scientific approach to the study of children's national and ethnic identities, using the primary example of the development of children's thinking. The argument in this section of the chapter refers to some evidence from our own research, but inevitably a qualitative sociological study of identities cannot match the terms of inquiry of psychological research questions designed for quantitative investigation and much of the argument therefore refers to other people's research and theorising.

As noted above, an important strand of research on children's views of nationality comes from developmental psychology. It was the topic for the millennium project of the BPS's developmental section, which involved BPS members across Britain in research using standardised measures available on the society's web site. This is an important body of work, and some of the existing sociological work on children's national identities (for example, the collection edited by Stephens 1997b) does not consider it at all, probably because of the general lack of communication between disciplines. Dominant in psychological work on this topic have been developmentalists, though concepts from social psychology such as social-identity theory and self-categorisation theory have also been brought to bear (Barrett 2005, Rutland 1999). We go on to discuss below the development of children's thinking. Cognitive development is of course only one specific aspect of psychological development, but it is both relevant to the construction of collective identities and also interesting to engage with because it is relatively controversial.

We cannot attempt to review satisfactorily the large body of literature on children's thinking about national groups, so we simply mention here a few of the key insights. Barrett (2002, 2005) provides useful summaries of the key messages from this body of research. The largest body of work has been conducted within a cognitive-developmental paradigm. There is a general consensus amongst researchers who work within this paradigm that the importance children attribute to national identity increases between five/six and eleven/twelve years of age. There are substantial data from this body of work on the significance of geographical knowledge and national symbols and children's views about people from other nations. Research on inter-group bias, which is very relevant to children's views of the nation, shows the general picture from cognitive-developmental research to be one of an inverted-U relation between age and prejudice: children become more preju-diced in the earliest years of primary school and this then fades by the end of middle childhood (Aboud and Amato 2001). Some other research findings have, however, questioned this relationship between age and prejudice or group identity (Barrett 2005, Rutland 1999). Barrett cites contrary evi-dence: 'national in-group favouritism at the age of 6 is not universal [. . .] some children do not exhibit changes in national attitudes between 6 and 10 years of age [. . .] and attitudes to enemy out-groups sometimes become more (rather than less) negative between 6 and 10 years of age' (Barrett 2005: 276).

As we noted in the previous chapter, the imposition of age-bound devel-opmental stages on children has been questioned in recent years by critical voices from within the psychology discipline (see also Burman 1994, Stainton Rogers and Stainton Rogers 1992). It has also been criticised by sociologists of childhood for universalising childhood (not appreciating cultural diver-sity), for downplaying the significance of social influences and for seeing children as 'becoming' not 'being', therefore not worthy of study in their own right, and effectively denying them all agency (James and Prout 1990, James et al. 1998, Jenks 2005). It seems that developmental*ism*, namely a narrow approach to understanding children that only considers supposedly biologically driven changes over time and does not accord sufficient weight to either socio-cultural context or children's agency is indeed inadequate for understanding children. A good example of its limitations can be seen in work on the development of racism. Van Ausdale and Feagin (2002) observe that young children have traditionally been seen as originally innocent in terms of racism through their lack of cognitive grasp of group categorisation. Much developmentalist research on the topic has focused on adult-defined mental activities rather than the social context of peer interaction when sanctioning adults are not present. Van Ausdale and Feagin themselves found children as young as three showing racially discriminatory behaviour and learning this from social interaction.

An almost outright rejection of developmental psychology has, however, become a given in sociological writings on childhood. We believe such an automatic rejection of developmental approaches to children may need some rethinking, at least in relation to the specific issue of national and ethnic identities. We argue this on the grounds that developmental psychology is more open to consideration of social processes than caricatures of it allow, and also that it is perfectly possible to accept that stages of development are indeed implicated in shaping identities, whilst recognising the complex social nature of the interactional settings and situations of children's experiential worlds. We have noted already that not all researchers of child development are so narrow as to only regard cognitive development as relevant. Things have moved on since the important contribution to understanding children's national identities from Piaget and Weil (1951). There has been debate about Piaget's cognitive stages in relation to national identity since the 1960s (see Jahoda 1964), and in more recent research there is debate about just about everything else to do with the development of national identity. Martyn Barrett, one of the most prolific psychologists researching this topic gives the following verdict, in a chapter that reviews the psychological evidence on children and the nation:

> There are four main theoretical frameworks that have been applied to children's development in this domain: cognitive-developmental theory (CDT), social identity theory (SIT), self-categorisation theory (SCT), and social identity development theory (SIDT). None of these theories is able to explain satisfactorily the empirical findings reviewed in this chapter.
>
> (Barrett, 2005: 275)

He goes on to conclude that a more complex theoretical framework is required, which encompasses 'media, educational, familial, experiential, cognitive, and motivational factors' (2005: 280). In this, he is underlining the necessarily multifaceted nature of children's identifications with nation, and appears to be calling at least implicitly for a more interdisciplinary approach. It is widely accepted by psychologists that children do not passively learn their views of in-groups and out-groups from their parents and peers but 'play a more active role in the biases they develop' (Aboud and Amato 2001: 65). Piaget himself saw children as actively engaging with their physical and social environments, but more prominent in some recent research on child development has been an emphasis on the active creation of developmental experiences contingent on particular settings (see the summary in Borland et al. 1998). The criticism that developmental psychology does not respect cultural diversity may be historically valid, but is difficult to sustain as a blanket judgement in 2006, in the light of work that clearly does encompass culturally specific development (see, for example, Cole 1999, Greenfield and Cocking 1994, Rogoff 1990). Cole (1999: 74) asserts that 'cultural mediation of development is a universal process expressed in historically specific circumstances'.

Cognitive development is of course only one aspect of children that child-development researchers study, but to take that as an example, need it necessarily be anti-sociological to accept that ways of thinking change as children grow up? We do not have to take the view that cognitive abilities develop independently of social influences. It is possible to follow Vygotsky's ideas (see Chapter 2) about the necessarily social and cultural nature of child development and still be interested in what children typically think about national ethnic collectivities at different ages in different social contexts. It is not controversial to observe that a term such as 'British' will very likely mean little or nothing to a toddler who cannot yet talk, because of limits to that toddler's cognitive abilities. We have to acknowledge that this is in part due to biological limitations. The extent to which, and the ways in which, individual children conceive of social difference are clearly important factors in shaping how they picture social groups and their own relationship to them. These are likely to be determined, in our view, through the complex intertwining of cognitive ability and social experience that needs to be seen as both structured and agentic. Clearly, the issue of prejudice cannot be reduced to cognitive ability alone; neither, however, can it be realistically explained in the case of young children without some reference to children's developing capacity to think through complex cultural boundaries such as 'insiders' and 'outsiders'. The question at stake is a matter of emphasis, essential though that emphasis may be: that is, whether this capacity is essentially innate and only *influenced* by social processes (conceived of as separate to cognition) or whether it is the product of complex interrelations between psychological processes and social constructions/interactions. We find the latter approach more convincing, though admittedly difficult to theorise adequately given the largely discipline-bound climate of the present time.

Of course, it is also the case that developmentalism is not just an academic approach, but is widely embedded in today's social institutions. James et al. (1998) argue that we might expect children to perform differently at different ages not on developmental grounds, but because society is structured on the basis of developmental assumptions, through the school curriculum and its learning stages, through the age of criminal responsibility, lawful sex and marriage, and so on. Whatever our theoretical assumption about age and stage, it is surely enlightening to consider (and indeed measure, albeit with methodological and theoretical caveats) how identities develop over time. We need evidence, for example, in order to go beyond unsupported assertions that identity is more important (or more contested) now than in the past. We need to find out empirically the extent to which people do typically identify with collectivities in different social contexts at different stages of life (however you might understand these stages). For example, the conclusion from psychological research that amongst a sample of English children, at the age of five/six children's gender, age and local identities were typically more important to them than their national identity, but national identity then increased in importance through middle childhood, typically overtaking age and local identity by eleven/twelve (Barrett et al. 2003) is genuinely interesting to anyone trying to understand children's relationship to place (even though these quantitatively derived findings may not be considered sufficient on their own). It seems deliberately contrary to refuse to accept the idea that children's awareness of the world changes in some respects as they spend more time in it.

The points we have briefly raised so far could be seen as theoretical justifications enough for a more dialogical approach between sociologists and psychologists researching child development. Theoretical justifications should not, moreover, need to be on either sociologists' or psychologists' own terms, as this is against the spirit of interdisciplinarity that we are advocating. However, to consider the theoretical case from sociology for a developmental approach we can turn to the work of Nick Lee (1998). Lee is unusual in questioning the theorising of children as 'beings' and not 'becomings' that most recent writing on the sociology of childhood has come to adopt. He issues a challenge to what he sees as the 'sociological prejudice' of favouring 'the mature and self-possessed over the immature and dependent' (Lee 1998: 460), arguing that society should be understood as incomplete, provisional and developing for both adults and children. Whilst Lee himself is not arguing for an acceptance of child-development research, we would like to make this link. It seems to us that to reject out of hand the idea of development, that is, of incremental change as children grow older, is to propose studying children as though they were no different than adults. This view appears to characterise the theoretical assumptions of the 'new sociology of childhood' (whilst being contradicted by its recommendations for child-friendly methodologies). We would also follow Lee in applying an 'immature sociology' to the development of national identity in people of all ages. Whilst it may be the case that many children do not understand the difference between, for example, Welsh and British national institutions, neither, it should be said, do many adults (especially since the National Assembly for Wales is still relatively new). 'Development' need not, therefore, be only the province of child psychology. Using the insights of Lee and James et al. it should be permissable to take a sociological interest in ages and stages even if one understands these as primarily socially – or psycho-socially – located.

There are indications within our dataset of some of the developmental limitations on children's identifications with national and ethnic collectivities. For example, not all children in middle childhood understand geopolitical boundaries. A certain grasp of these boundaries is required if children are to make any sense of available national identities and of rituals such as national days of celebration. There are many boundaries and complexities to contend with: Wales is within Britain but has its own separate national identity as well as two languages which bear the same names as two nationalities. Britain is also part of Europe. There are villages, towns, counties, regions, countries and continents – all of which require a grasp of geographical and political concepts. Examples of confusion follow: 'Is

Cardiff just one big country?' (Satnaam from Highfields School); 'What's the difference between English and Welsh, and British and European?' (Clark from Petersfield School);

Nicola:	What's European mean?
Andrew (researcher):	From Europe.
Julia:	What's Europe though?
Andrew:	Europe is a continent, isn't it?
Julia:	Are we in Europe?

(Year 4 focus group, Highfields School)

There was also some cultural and linguistic confusion; so, for example, Kathryn thought Italians speak English and Australians speak Irish. As we explain in later chapters, there was very frequent ellision between being Welsh and speaking Welsh, being English and speaking English. Whilst we could not, given our research design, *measure* any association between strength of identity and geographical knowledge, it is worth noting that some other research has found a connection. Barrett and Whennell (1998), for example, in a study of 101 English children aged five to eleven, found geographical knowledge to be correlated with feelings of Englishness and Britishness: the more factual geographical knowledge they had, the more British or English they felt.

We have made a very brief defence of the psychological concept of development in research with children in relation to national and ethnic identities, because although not psychologists ourselves, we found the findings generated by this body of work worthy of consideration and capable of shedding light on some of our own research findings. We go on to discuss some crucial aspects of identity that quantitative child-development research does not, however, capture. We intend this chapter to be as much of a challenge to partisan developmentalists as it is a defence of child-development research to sociologists who reject it. Our position is that we ideally need both sociological and psychological insights, using both qualitative and quantitative methods of inquiry, to capture as much as possible about the character of national and ethnic identities in children. We also need to advance our understanding of how sociological and psychological processes are interrelated in the reproduction of these identities. Since one key objection of sociologists of childhood to the developmental paradigm is its denial of agency to children, we now go on to consider the question of agency in children's national and ethnic identities, with reference to our own qualitative research.

Human agency in constructing national identity

The reclaiming of agency has been a major concern within recent developments in the sociology of childhood. Agency is not a straightforward term, of course, implying as it does theories of subjectivity and motivation as well as a theory of action. However, we can follow Giddens in proposing that agency involves 'the intervention [of a subject] in a potentially malleable object-world' (Giddens 2002: 233). Agency implies the ability to act, rather than simply be acted upon, and hence the idea that the actor 'could have acted otherwise' (2002: 233). It should be said that in much of the sociology of childhood literature there is a relatively underdeveloped concept of agency, and it is frequently taken as shorthand for other terms, such as resistance to norms or self-determination or simply expressing oneself. A more nuanced picture is needed that addresses the dialectic between structure and agency in the sense that Giddens implies.

Agency was a key theme of the UK Economic and Social Research Council's Children 5–16 programme (see Prout 2001) and has been to the fore in recent state-of-the-art sociological overviews of childhood such as that by James et al. (1998). Similarly, Thompson (2001) has recently argued for 'putting people back into nations' in the study of national identities. In contrast to Billig's (1995) emphasis on discourse, Thompson is interested in 'how individuals *actively* employ their "common stock of knowledge" about nations and national identities' (2001: 21, italics in original) and therefore, in his terms, the 'local' rather than 'banal'. He is interested in the *practical* aspects of the reproduction of nations and national identities, and we share this interest. This is not to deny the important discursive and representational resources that work to anchor narratives of the nation in cultural settings – especially those of schools and television programmes. However, our concern is to investigate how, and to what extent, children actively appropriate this language and how they position themselves in relation to these popular images. The role of agency in children's place identities is an important theme throughout the book. As noted above, it is not necessarily the case that psychologists who study identity development in children are too narrowly focused on biology to consider the role of children's agency. Most child-development researchers would consider agency to be limited by stage of development, however, especially in very young children (see Hobbs 2002). Sociology offers crucial insights, both by insisting on children being seen as social actors and by accepting that agency is limited by their location in social, cultural and political worlds – a very different limitation from the kind focused on by most developmentalists.

It is important to foreground questions of structure and agency when considering how children of diverse heritage negotiate their affiliations to places and cultures. Bahira reveals some of the complexities of her identities: 'Because my nan's grandad is Irish, so I put down Irish. My mum's dad is Polish and I have loads of different stuff in me, so it is confusing'.

There are choices to be made for Bahira. In an earlier focus group she described herself as 'British Muslim'. Another girl in the same school, Shamsa, shifted her choice between two rounds of card-posting from 'Somali Muslim' to 'my country [Britain] and my family'. In her interview she then said that she chose British 'because my auntie and uncle are British'. Wasim declared in a focus group at Highfields that he felt 'half English and half Muslim and half Italian. Full Italian, half Welsh'.

There are examples of children in the Welsh study maintaining some English identity even where they are aware this is not approved of. For the overtly 'English' children we spoke to, who have perhaps moved to Wales within the past few years, there seemed to be less of an issue here. They were generally confident in expressing an English identity, even in a region such as Gwynedd (north-west Wales) where English in-migration is highly controversial because of the perceived dilution in the concentration of Welsh speakers. In the area of Gwynedd we went to, it is perhaps less controversial in some respects to be an English child than in other parts of Wales, as all children have a Welsh-medium education, so become proficient in the language. It is towards parents who do not learn the language that there is perhaps most resentment. The children we spoke to who expressed some nervousness about admitting their Englishness were those who can pass as 'Welsh', having been brought up in Wales and having a local accent, but see themselves as being at least part English because of family origin. Melissa saw herself as partly English. She spoke of having English family members and visiting England, but having learned to keep quiet about it: 'I don't know because like, I had this dream once about that. I told somebody in school and they said, "Oh you shouldn't be here, you should be in England" and since then, I don't tell anybody' (interview with Melissa, Year 6, in Petersfield School).

These examples indicate that children are well aware of having to present themselves in certain ways in relation to the categories of nationality and ethnicity under discussion in the fieldwork setting. For children occupying uneasy relationships with the locally dominant cultural 'standard' – be that whiteness or Welshness, or both – as in minority-ethnic or mixed-ethnicity identities, simple assertions of national or cultural belonging are not available. Hence they hedge around the subject and choose amongst proffered labels carefully. Children's agency, then, has to be understood in relation to their consciousness of being located within a world of cultural constraints (what can and can't be said) – the potency of which they are already fully aware. In constructing national identities for themselves, children exercise their agency in negotiating the culturally loaded and unequal terrain of diverse heritage and in the maintaining of an identity that is at least potentially unacceptable to their peers.

In stating opinions about their national identities, the children we spoke to drew on the resources available to them for describing the nation, and their repertoire of ideas about Wales and Welshness was limited (see the next chapter for a detailed consideration of this). This raises the question of whether children have fewer cultural and linguistic resources to draw on than adults. We might expect that indeed they do, having had less time and opportunity to be exposed to the resources that adults would use as points of reference in discussing nationality. We might also expect children to have fewer resources to draw on than adults if we accept that thinking capacities develop over time. It is also true, of course, that many adults find their resources are limited in discussing national identity. Roberts (1995) found in his research in the eastern valleys of south Wales that people tended to use clichés such as chapel, singing and rugby to describe what being Welsh meant to them. Our children more often made reference to birthplace, language, accent or sport. For many adults, as with children, then, there may be little to draw on in constructing a Welsh identity. Some may have an opinion on the Welsh Assembly, or may be aware of some of the more controversial debates about nationhood that are aired in the Welsh media, but others may not.

The limited cultural resources that the white Welsh children have to draw on circumscribe their agency in relation to national identity. An example of this is sport, probably the most important source for the children of what Michael Billig (1995) calls 'banal nationalism': the daily flagging of the nation in public discourse. The children repeatedly talked about supporting the Welsh rugby team and English Premier League football teams. We made a point of asking them what they thought about this since they live in Wales, and varying degrees of reflexivity can be found in their responses. It seemed to take more of an active decision to support a local football team than to support Manchester United, which was by far the most popular option – even for the children in the most strongly Welsh-oriented locality. To support a local Welsh team was to reject the powerful force of the dominant peer-group culture, in which football's appeal is associated with the most internationally successful and well-known teams. Some children did seem to have thought through the possible conflict. Emma had clearly done so, and was proud of her decision to maintain support both for Welsh nation and English football club.

> Yes it is OK because most of my bedroom is stars and moons but then I have got a massive poster of Manchester United. And I've got a postcard and the [Welsh] national anthem [. . .] Most people support Man United in Wales. I can tell you now that there is more than fifty people in this school that support Manchester United.
>
> (Interview with Emma, Year 4, from Petersfield School)

Emma is not making a different choice in this regard from that of other children, but she has made it her own. She is attempting to individualise the standard group affiliations. This particular child says of herself that she is determined to be different from other children. She declares, for example, that she would like to move to the Petersfield estate (she lives elsewhere) even though the houses are boarded up there and she is aware that it is stigmatised in the local area. She told us that if other girls in her brownie pack said they liked sitting down she would say she liked standing up. But Emma stands out in her determination to be different (up to a point). Hers is, perhaps, evidence not so much of a general self-determination in relation to national identity, but that some children are more reflexive than others about dominant discourses they encounter (and perhaps more at ease in either accepting or resisting them). Explaining this must surely require some psychological as well as socio-cultural insights. We do not provide them here, but want to note that a purely sociological explanation seems inadequate to explain this kind of individual variation.

Most children do not seem to question sporting affiliations, and some told us that they had chosen a team to support on the basis of what everyone else was doing. Sport and local/national support is an example of how children's capacity to define themselves 'against the grain' can be very limited. They are not simply following adult influences here. There is a trend amongst adults in Wales for people to support English Premier League football teams and then Welsh national teams, but this is a particularly well-developed pattern in the culture of children. This suggests that children express strong and relatively conformist allegiances within their peer group, and again shows the extent to which children of this age have already internalised clear concepts of what is culturally appropriate within their own group settings. Again, though, this begs the question of how reflexive most adults are about their national identities. Discourses of national belonging are by their very nature restricting. They are all about marking out boundaries between people and, thus, inevitably reveal the pulling power of cultural conformity. Bauman (2000) remarks, in the context of a discussion on nationalism in 'liquid modernity', that ethnic belonging is not a matter of choice: 'the choice is not between different referents of belonging, but between belonging and rootlessness, home and homelessness, being and nothingness' (2000: 73).

Although Bechhofer et al. (1999) place an emphasis on agency and social interaction in the construction of national identity amongst Scottish elites, they recognise that for many people national identity is constructed from a taken-for-granted common stock of symbols and narratives. Pryke (2001), in taking issue with Bechhofer et al.'s paper, makes more of this point, arguing that 'for most people, most of the time being a national just "is" ' (2001: 198). Where we can most obviously see children exercising agency is where there are more choices available to them. For the minority-ethnic children and children with parents of mixed nationalities, the more general topic of identification with places and cultures was more open. That is not to suggest, of course, that these children were not also marginalised and restricted in their identity choice in many respects (see Chapter 6 on the racialisation of Welshness), or that the relative openness of their collective identities might make choices more difficult and fraught, but identification is potentially a more active process for these children who, by definition, have to work out how to position themselves in relation to dominant discourses that for others are relatively unproblematic because they are taken for granted. Thompson explains the role of agency in national identity thus:

> Individuals may not be conscious of how they are actively involved in giving life to national identities when they categorise, but they do use these categories to explain, position and make sense. They do not there-fore view these categories as their own personal inventions, rather they view them as information that is available for them to use in order to make sense of the actions of others.
>
> (Thompson 2001: 28)

Sociology provides insights into the operation of the structure–agency dialectic in children's negotiation of identity that developmental psychologists might take heed of. We can see both the potential for children to be active in making collective identities their own and also the discursive limitations on that agency – limitations that are by no means evenly distributed given the unequal power relations that underpin them. An arena where the active construction of national identity can be captured vividly is in the children's interactions in focus groups, and it is to the role of social interaction in the 'doing' of identity that we now turn.

The negotiation of identity through social interaction

In this section of the chapter we illustrate the central importance in our research of understanding how identity is negotiated in social interaction. Housley and Fitzgerald (2001: 1.1) have observed that in fact this dimension of national identity, the ways in which it is 'produced, recognised and used within the realms of everyday interaction' is relatively under-explored in sociological research. It should be recognised that our research design, with its limited use of participant observation, did not allow us to observe children's everyday interaction in great depth or detail. However, both interviews and focus groups do allow us to reflect on the 'performance' of identity and to compare performances in these different arenas.

One of the principal contributions of Erving Goffman (sometimes referred to as a social psychologist and sometimes a sociologist) has been his emphasis on the contingency of identity work and the dependence of identity on performance in specific contexts of interaction (Goffman 1990, first published 1959). Similarly, the anthropologist Frederik Barth (1998, first published 1969) sees ethnicities as the perpetual subject and object of negotiation (boundary maintenance), and Barth's insights are highly relevant to any consideration of national identity (Jenkins 1997). Bechhofer et al. (1999) draw on the legacy of Goffman and Barth in describing the interactive process of national-identity construction amongst elite groups in Scotland. On the specific question of how children relate to the nation, Jason Hart's paper (2002) on children and nationalism in a Palestinian refugee camp in Jordan describes a thirteen-year-old boy, Qusay, who espoused Palestinian nationalism to his father but also, when away from home, said that Jordan was 'his country'. In a photographic research exercise, the same boy repeated Islamist rhetoric, and when away from older relatives, teachers and religious leaders he dressed in an American style and admitted to his liking of Michael Jackson, music that his father would not approve of. This boy's national identity was not fixed; rather, he displayed different aspects of himself for different audiences. Our data, likewise, reveal this process of the children's presenting their national/ethnic selves for public consumption in specific social settings.

Our data-generation techniques presented the children with a variety of stages on which to act out their identities, both to themselves and to the researcher. The focus groups involved, perhaps above all, performance in front of peers as well as group performance in front of the facilitator, and the individual interviews involved performance in front of a researcher and, perhaps significantly, a researcher (Andrew Davies) who was Welsh-speaking. The children frequently altered what they said in the different contexts. In Maesgarw school, two Year 6 boys, Rowland and Phillip, espoused views in the focus group about British and Welsh nationality and institutions that were in line with mainstream Welsh nationalist political opinion. In his one-to-one interview, however, Phillip took a less overtly nationalist tone, which might suggest his front-stage performance of nationalism was above all connected with his interaction with Rowland. In focus groups in Highfields School, several children mentioned Christianity as important to them in some way. None of these children subsequently spoke about religion in interviews. Their references to religion in the focus groups can most plausibly be understood in relation to the statements of Muslim faith articulated in the groups by some other children. Significantly, those children who mentioned Islam in the group discussions maintained their stated commitment to religion in their individual interviews – suggesting that their self-identification as Muslim is not perhaps so much a matter of social performance as an identity more deeply rooted in their sense of self. One might speculate that in a largely secular society such as Wales, for many white children religious commitment can be 'put on and shrugged off' without strong implications arising for identity, whilst for the minority Muslim children, faith expression was a much more psychologically and culturally salient issue deeply entangled in questions of 'Who I am'.

Another interesting example of the interaction context of identity work was Zubaida's contribution to the Year 5 focus group in Highfields School. Zubaida said that she identifies with Pakistan and Islam, and her 'external' impression management, at least in the context of a focus group about national identities, was all about marking herself out as different. The researcher, Andrew, had been told by the Head Teacher to avoid our proposed question 'Would you go to war for your country?' because there had been some tension in the school since 11 September, 2001. The fieldwork in this school took place the week beginning 17 September 2001. The Head Teacher's account was that some Muslim children had been repeating anti-Western Islamist rhetoric that they were hearing in the mosque and that this had caused arguments amongst the children. To get children talking about how to represent their local area and culture to outsiders, we asked them to imagine that a soap opera was going to be made in their local area. Zubaida, knowing the controversial nature of this context (she later says 'Sh! We're not supposed to talk about that', when the war in Afghanistan is mentioned), offered Osama Bin Laden as a potential character:

Sabirah: Phil Mitchell.
Andrew: You'd have Phil Mitchell.
Wasim: And I'll have Jackie Chan.
Danny: I'd have a footballer.
Andrew: Jackie Chan.
Danny: I'd have a footballer.
Wasim: Yeah, I'll have David Beckham.
Joe: Listen in to all the latest news and being nosy.
Andrew: Yeah.
Danny: I'd have a footballer.
Andrew: A footballer, yeah?
Danny: Yeah.
Sabirah: And Peggy.
Zubaida (quietly): I'd have Osama Bin Laden.
Wasim: I'd have Michael Owen, yeah, I'd have Michael Owen.

(Year 4 focus group, Highfields School)

This is an interesting exchange. Her intention might primarily have been comic effect. We might speculate that she was fed up of the litany of male heroes from sport and marital arts, and mentioned Bin Laden as a challenge to the boys' excitable macho referencing. This group was indeed character-ised by much gendered positioning among the boys, which was not thrown off course by Zubaida's intervention. She does also see her Islamic faith and her Asian origins as marking her out as different in the focus group, so the Bin Laden mention has to be understood in that context. Is she feeling, perhaps, that there is nowhere else for her to go to select a public icon – equivalent in terms of fame to the 'Western' ones mentioned – that will stand for 'her' identity given the current post-9/11 ideological climate? She attempts to get Wasim on side by telling him he is Asian because he has lived in Pakistan and, although he was born in Wales, Pakistan is his 'home country' in her eyes. Wasim is, however, having none of this, saying 'No, it's not my home country; this is my home country; I was born here'.

Zubaida marks out her difference in the opening exchanges of the focus group, and keeps this strategy up throughout. In the early stages of the group she was contributing with one-liners. Later in the group she expands to succinctly explain her views about the places she has lived in:

> I don't like living in Cardiff. Well, it's okay but I don't like it because my home country is um . . . Pakistan, because I went to live there for six months and I've got eight rabbits and I've got lots of friends there and stuff as well. I thought, um . . . that's why because I have got my aunties, my uncles and stuff. Here I haven't got anybody like that. I've got my cousins and stuff but they are in Birmingham. But I like Pakistan better.
>
> (Zubaida, Year 5 focus group, Highfields School)

Immediately following this, we have another interesting exchange. After Joe's attempt to affirm Zubaida's Muslim identity, Wasim, who Zubaida believes is Asian because he is a Muslim and has roots in Pakistan, describes himself as half-Italian. Joe thinks this is 'cool'.

Joe: I like the Islamic community, they stick together well.
Andrew: Do you agree?
Zubaida: Yeah.
Wasim: I like Italian because half my family are from Italia.
Joe: Huh? You're Italian?
Wasim: Yeah, half of it.
Joe: Cool.

> (Year 5 focus group, Highfields School)

To be Italian in this context is to be stylish, sexy, good at football. Joe's 'Cool' is highly gendered. This is an entirely approved-of nationality in the context of a discussion where the boys have been working hard to preserve their masculine cultural capital in the group by referencing more and more symbols of boys' 'cool' – from Beckham to wrestling. They have also been using feminising put-downs ('Billy Elliott', 'cry baby'). Wasim's mention of his Italian connection might also be one way of distancing himself from Zubaida's attempt to co-opt him into a South Asian identity which, as Connolly (1998) has observed, is often a feminised identity in many contexts in multi-ethnic urban Britain. It is also a vulnerable one given the context of racialised discourses proliferating in the UK following 9/11 (most notably in the tabloid press). Obviously, the effects of racism and local national/ethnic hierarchies have to be taken into consideration. Whatever the motivation, the 'work' of identity is being done here through interaction. The children's discussion is an artificial one in a sense, with them being brought together for a research project, but they will of course also be drawing heavily on their existing knowledge of and feelings for each other as classmates over several years.

The gendered nature of the exchanges we have just mentioned leads us to another angle on interaction and social identity: West and Zimmerman's contention that 'gender itself is constituted through interaction' (1987: 129). Clearly, gender is not only constituted through interaction as there are powerful structural and institutional forces that reproduce unequal gender relations that have to be acknowledged. However, West and Zimmerman's argument helps to sensitise us to the ways in which national identity can be a resource for 'doing gender'. Several authors have noted the intersection of gender and ethnicity in children's interactions (for example, Connolly 1998; Frosh et al. 2001) and the gendered character of discourses of the nation has been described by Yuval-Davies (1997) amongst others. Because 'Cymro' means 'Welsh man or boy', one boy in Maesgarw asked if the 'Cymro' card was the same as the 'boy' card ('Ydy Cymro a bachgen yr un peth?'), showing that the gendering of the language (Welsh nouns, as in many languages, have a gender) has implications for *social* identity. The developmental research we referred to earlier in the chapter does not fully allow for a serious consideration of how different social identities can overlap and intersect in this way. Similarly, for Zubaida, religious and national identities intersect. This is hardly surprising, since there cannot be any neat conceptual distinction between these terms. They are both 'ethnic' in Richard Jenkins's (1997) terms. The fact that none of the black and minority-ethnic children we spoke to used 'Welsh' as an umbrella identity indicates that Welshness is still a heavily racialised identity (see Williams 1995 and Chapter 6 of this book). What Zubaida's identity performance illustrates is the complexity of multiple identities being negotiated in specific social interactions, a complexity that quantitative identity surveys, whether they are conducted by psychologists or sociologists, will struggle to convey (although see and Lopez 2003 and Phillips 2002 for examples of more sophisticated approaches to quantifying plural and complex identities).

The dependence of social identity on social interaction is a well-established insight in terms of identity in general (see, for example, Goffman 1990), but has not been well developed in relation to national identity until recently (see Bechhofer et al. 1999, Hester and Housley 2002). This idea of social identities as contingent on social interaction is not, however, an insight that is exclusive to sociology. Self-categorisation theory from social psychology (Oakes et al. 1994) claims that all human perception is categorical, and that categorisation is sensitive to the realities of social context and intergroup relations: as Rutland (1999: 57) expresses it, 'social categorisation and in-group favouritism are seen as flexible effortful on-line constructions in context'. It could be argued that quantitative psychological research into social categorisation has at its core more in common conceptually with certain qualitative sociological approaches to the performance of identity (see, for example, Housley and Fitzgerald, 2001) than would appear at first glance. Nevertheless, it is important to recognise that the provenance and circulation of these categorisations are primarily cultural and social, rather than being a facility belonging to innate cognitive processes.

Conclusion

The topic of children's national and ethnic identities is fertile ground for exploring both commonality and tensions between sociological and psychological explanations of childhood and of identity. There are some general implications of the above discussion. We need both to identify those aspects of identity that are amenable to standardised measurement as well as to explore through qualitative research the social processes in which they are enmeshed. Though child development is significant, we should not think of children's identities in terms of a linear process. It is not the case that professionals working with children can intervene to stop prejudice 'forming' at a relatively early age as though it is something amenable to 'intervention', or indeed that it does not develop or change later in life. We should consider both the potential for agency in national and ethnic identities and also the structural and discursive limitations on agency. We have to understand these identities in their immediate contexts of highly differentiated social interaction.

In trying to outline a more nuanced approach that takes seriously both the psychological and sociological dimensions of children's subjectivities, we do not suggest that there are no differences in emphasis or indeed epistemologies between intellectual traditions in different academic disciplines. Clearly there are. Disciplinary boundaries are also very difficult to cross because of decades of separate institutional development. Competition between sociology and psychology is to be expected when these two disciplines often attempt to explain similar social phenomena, from apparently different perspectives and, crucially, from within different university departments that have to compete for resources. There are vested interests in disciplinary separation. It is in fact relatively easy to do what we have done in this chapter and simply recognise the validity of other approaches. It is much harder to synthesise them with intellectual credibility, and we are not claiming to have begun such a synthesis in this book. Eclecticism can be criticised for lack of rigour and intellectual coherence: trying to do a lot of things and therefore not doing them well. But this is a challenge to which sociologists and psychologists should be prepared to rise. There is the important practical consideration of where one can publish interdisciplinary research so that it will actually get read, but again that should not be insurmountable. As it is, there are eminent scholars cited in this book whose work does in fact get read across disciplines (for example, Goffman, Billig and Walkerdine). This is especially true of critical psychologists who have attempted to construct cross-disciplinary psycho-social understandings of child development, but is perhaps less evident among the 'new' sociologists of childhood.

This chapter has focused on the *processes* of national and ethnic identification. The following two chapters, while taking as read that stated identities are contingent and have to be understood in the context of social interaction, will attempt to give an overall assessment of the children's identifications with different places and different spatial domains. In doing so, observations will be made about the apparent strength of different identities. We do not claim that these observations are straightforwardly generalisable even within Wales, let alone elsewhere. However, there are interesting ideas to pursue about the significance of place in middle childhood and in order to do so we have to make some assessment of identities as they are articulated by children themselves. This involves recognising that the prevalence of certain meanings needs to be accounted for (something that necessitates a degree of quantification), but also that these meanings are not self-evident nor amenable to standardised analysis. Instead, they have to be *interpreted* by the researcher in relation to both existing theory and his or her understanding of the 'grounded' categorisations arising from the data. Nevertheless, we have also to acknowledge the small scale of our study and the necessarily contingent nature of the conclusions drawn.

4 Global and national dimensions of place identity

In order to understand how children relate to the idea of 'place', we need to appreciate that places can take different forms and be experienced on a number of levels. Massey (1994) has argued that places do not have simple boundaries in the sense of divisions that frame enclosures, nor do they have single, unique 'identities'. Instead, they tend to be full of internal conflicts and differences. She also cautions against making too simple a distinction between terms such as the local and the global. Instead, every place can be seen as the focus of a distinct mixture of wider and more local social relations, with this very mixture producing effects that could not simply be repeated elsewhere. This necessary complexity arises too when the 'subjectivity' of place is considered, since places mean different things to different individuals and social groups. Children will have a variety of particular relationships to place, the complete determinants of which are unlikely to be straightforwardly identifiable. For example, age-related limitations on children's mobility and breadth of cultural knowledge need to be set in the context of particular lives lived in particular localities and kinship networks. For this reason, Holloway and Valentine (2000a) argue that the new social studies of childhood need to develop a more sophisticated understanding of spatiality that takes account of this complexity.

This chapter and the next (which form a thematic and analytic pairing) are structured according to different levels of spatial domain: global, national, local and domestic. It might be thought that the arguments of Massey (and Holloway and Valentine in relation to children) make this subdivision within and between the two chapters somewhat artificial. Indeed, we would wish to challenge any attempt to construct neat bounded categories of global, local, domestic and so on. Nevertheless, we knew we wanted to ask children about the range of place-identifications that they held, and this meant asking them about their representations and experiences of place at a variety of levels – from the locality in which they lived to the nation to which they belonged, and beyond this to the images and knowledge they held about more distant people and places. In this way, we were able to draw a picture of the concentric circles of place-knowledge and place-feeling through which the children expressed their senses of 'where' and 'who' they were (and hence where and who others were). Accordingly, although these various domains are certainly connected, they can also be correctly identified as having different kinds of significance for different children. We support the breaking down of artificial barriers between the categories of 'global' and 'local', and recognise that they are always relational. Yet it is also clear from our data that different levels of space and place are experienced in different ways by the children we spoke to, precisely because of the social location of middle childhood. This chapter tackles the global and national dimensions of the children's place identification. The main summary discussion of these dimensions will take place not in this chapter but at the end of the next one, as by then we will also have presented our findings on the local and domestic dimensions. Given the stated scope of this book and of the Welsh children research, there is unsurprisingly much more space devoted in this chapter to national identities than to the global dimension, but it is the global with which we begin.

The global

In asking children to think about places outside of their own immediate experience, we are inevitably inviting them to think about the relationships between themselves and others, and between where they currently 'are' and what it might be like over 'there'. Specifications of self/other and here/there relations were the principal terms through which the children in our study spoke of place. Given this, we were interested in the degree to which they saw these boundaries as expressing relations of similarity or difference. Did they see Europe, for example, as very different from, or rather similar to, Wales? To what extent could they picture themselves as belonging to Europe? On the whole, our findings suggest that children do not hold very clear or well-defined senses of place-difference at the more abstract levels of nation, Europe or the world, and rather readily see themselves as quite similar to distant others. Certain boundaries – notably the Welsh/English national one – are more salient to the children, as might be expected, but even here they had few cultural markers or resources to hand in describing it. The reasons for this are quite complex and difficult to determine satisfactorily from the limited data available. But we suggest that the children's familiarity with globalised media images and a generalised media discourse of multiculturalism and geographical mobility (real or imagined) played a part in diluting any strong sense of place-delineation between here/there and self/other. In addition, the status of Wales as a largely white and relatively monocultural country (with the exception of particular locales, as in our one ethnically diverse school in Cardiff) may well go some way to explaining these children's relatively undeveloped sense of ethnic or cultural difference. At the same time, and to return momentarily to arguments about developmentalism addressed in Chapter 2, it was also clear to us that the children's age-limited experiences were a factor in preventing them from operating with much in the way of an elaborated language of cultural place-difference, not withstanding its presence on classroom walls (and indeed, in the media) via displays about Wales and other cultures. Children simply lacked the life experience and vocabulary to engage in talk about cultural differences. Even the Welsh dimension in the Welsh-speaking schools was not as clearly elaborated as we might have expected. We noted in Chapter 1 that various writers have asked whether in an era of globalisation children lose a sense of local or ethnic attachment. We raised the question of whether in the early twenty-first century children are more likely to attach their identities to delineated places or to see themselves as belonging to more dispersed groupings based around global marketing and products. We also raised the question of whether these two dimensions of identification need necessarily be mutually exclusive. It is these kinds of issues we consider in the discussion that follows.

There was considerable variation in the children's knowledge about other places and other countries. Geopolitical knowledge may be limited by how much experience they have of travelling to other countries (Rutland 1998, though see also Bourchier et al. 2002 who did not find such an association). National and local dimensions of place identity were a more overt focus of our research than the global dimension, but we did ask the children to describe to us other European countries, using a map as a prompt for discussion of an imaginary journey. What the children told us in discussing this journey echoed the findings of Holloway and Valentine's (2000b) study of Internet conversations between children in Britain and New Zealand. The British children in their study identified with New Zealand as another affluent Western country. When we asked the children in our study to imagine a journey through western Europe, the most common view was that people in these countries are 'just the same'. Where they mentioned differences, they almost always referred to language, although occasional mentions were also made of dress and diet. A few children expressed negative views about Germany (see also Barrett and Short 1992). These negative views were justified with reference to the Second World War, football violence or specific stories from their parents about meeting 'unpleasant' Germans. When discussing their home country in comparison with other parts of the world, there was some awareness of experiencing relative comfort. There were a few comments made about the territory being free from war and about the UK being comfortably off in comparison with many countries.

We asked the children to do a sentence completion exercise with prompts such as 'In ten years' time I would like to be living in——' In response, a small majority saw themselves moving away from their local area in future, often seeing themselves in 'glamorous' leisure spots such as holiday resorts in Europe or the USA. This is perhaps to be expected in a context of globally circulating imagery of glamorous locations. In Jukarainen's (2003) research on the borders of Finland with slightly older children, there was a tendency to favour the idea of moving to large cities in future – Tampere, Turku,

Helsinki, St Petersburg, Moscow, Stockholm. The children were also more likely to want to move to the UK, USA and Germany than across the nearest border. Shopping and entertainment were frequently mentioned, affirming 'the conception of today's youth as significant consumers' (2003: 225).

Whilst demographic trends in fact suggest that most people stay within Britain and indeed within their local area (see, for example, ODPM 2001 for evidence from England), most of these children seemed to readily envisage moving away and moving abroad in the future, at least when they were presented with an explicit question that asked them to consider where they wanted to be in ten years' time (which could be seen as creating a methodological artefact to some extent). This finding may be linked to an idea rooted in Welsh history and popular culture, which instructs its listeners that 'You've got to get out to get on' – that personal progress is not simply aided by mobility, but is a precondition of it. That the children often see their future in countries such as the USA might suggest not so much an awareness of global cultural diversity as an ability to see other places as part of their own social worlds. So when asked about future location, they were perhaps most *familiar* (from television in the main, we might speculate) with Western, developed countries. They could perhaps see continuities between their own selves and the people who lived in these places. In other words, they did not express much awareness of the 'otherness' of other places. On the whole, the fact that the children can see themselves moving away from home may tell us more about the children's familiarity with media images of certain high-status locations than it does about their actual intentions or their imagined future mobility. These places are physically distant but could be seen as being close to the children's own experience in a cultural and communicative sense. In considering the children's imagined future mobility, we should note that our sample included only one school with children of very diverse ethnic backgrounds. We might expect that a group of children with family connections abroad may well have a different sense of connection to other countries and that those with family origins in the global South might prioritise affluent Western countries less than did our largely white sample of Welsh children.

These children live in a world dominated by global flows of capital. Many of the goods they consume are manufactured in developing countries by global corporations and marketed on an international scale. Consumption is very significant in the children's lives and a whole range of consumption opportunities are increasingly marketed at children (Buckingham 2004, Cook 2004). Over time, we can see globalising tendencies in children's media – television, magazines, the Internet – in the sense that material produced by companies from the USA in particular is consumed in many countries. Multichannel television has increased this tendency, with American channels such as Jetix and Nickelodeon doing well in the UK. In fact the television programmes the children in our study spoke of as their favourites were as likely to be British programmes as they were American. Occasionally they mentioned a programme from Australia or Japan, but there was no reference made to any TV programme from Wales or in the Welsh language, despite half the children being fluent in Welsh. We should, of course, note here that the proportion of programmes available in Welsh in comparison with English language programmes is very small indeed. There are plenty of references within the dataset to aspects of childhood consumption that we could see as globalised. For example, English Premier League football is very popular, with boys in particular but also with many of the girls. Premier League games take place within the borders of England, but they are clearly a global concern in so far as they are marketed to all corners of the globe. The contemporary preoccupation with celebrity emerges, as in the following excerpt, where it is reproduced as the automatic option for an identity 'other than Welsh':

Andrew: Okay, so what I want you to do, is to either write down on the 'you choose' card something else, if you want to be something else other than Welsh.
Emma: Like popstars?

(Year 4 focus group, Petersfield School)

This preoccupation needs to be understood in the context of what Buckingham (2004: 115) terms 'a self-referential' global arena of television where 'the guests are pop stars or actors from soaps, the games and the pop videos are ads for other commodities and the prizes are other media artefacts'.

Some of the features of their local areas they chose to highlight were leisure facilities that are not in fact locally distinctive at all. When asked how they would describe their local area to people in Australia if they were to move there, they often mentioned sites of consumption and leisure that in fact exist throughout the UK and to varying extents across the West. Wasim from Highfield School, in the next excerpt, tells us he likes Wales because of the urban leisure facilities that Cardiff has: 'I like Wales because it has got lots of shops, lots of stadiums, it's got lots of football stars, cricket stars. It's got big pitches to play cricket, lots of big parks'.

We return to discuss the significance of the global dimension at the end of the next chapter, where we consider the overall picture of attachments to spaces and places. To summarise very briefly here, there was evidence of the children identifying with other affluent Western countries and seeing people in them in general as 'just the same' as them. When asked to imagine future location, most of the children could see themselves moving away from their home areas and often to glamorous locations abroad with which they were familiar via their media consumption. More generally, globalised consumption featured quite strongly in the children's talk. We return at the end of Chapter 5 to the question of how important the global dimension seemed to be in relation to other spatial domains.

The national

If, as we have suggested so far, children possess some facility in imagining themselves part of a global community, albeit one that is largely ill defined, where does this leave their sense of national distinctiveness? In this section, we consider some of our findings on the topic of national feeling and identification (though it should be noted that this chapter does not exhaust the theme of resources for national identity, which runs throughout the book; there is, for example, more on the theme in Chapters 6 and 7). The dimensions to be considered include both how salient the construct of 'the nation' is in children's sense of where they personally 'belong', as well as how far children utilise a language of cultural distinctions that delineates one nation from another. Hence, we need to consider both the subjective and objective dimensions of national consciousness. There is, for example, a commonly held view that children are potentially capable of holding very strong national allegiances, as in the following quotation:

> My father says he loves his country as much as ever, but he has a different way of fighting now, through his children. From now on he's going to use his children as weapons, he says, because children are stronger than armies, stronger than speeches or articles or any number of letters to the government. One child is worth more than a thousand guns and bombs, he says.
>
> (Hamilton 2003: 117)

These words are from Hugo Hamilton's autobiographical account of his childhood and refer to his father's Irish nationalist project, enacted primarily through his parenting. Obvious examples come to mind of the extremes of nationalist co-option of children: the Hitler Youth, child soldiers in many parts of the world (see Cohn and Goodwin-Gill 1994, Stargardt 2005). On a more mundane and everyday level, as noted in Chapter 1, children are subject to many forms of banal nationalism (Billig 1995) that are much less overt than these obvious examples of aggressive nationalism. They encounter national (and nationalist) discourse in school, at home, around their local communities and via the media they consume. Children are, therefore, immersed in environments where national distinctions are still very much on display. The question then becomes to what extent children recognise and pick up on these cultural referents, and to what extent they see their own identities as defined through such terms.

Resources for national identity

There are several different aspects of the everyday reproduction of national identities. There is the daily flagging of the nation that Billig (1995) describes. In the lives of the children we spoke to, this social process is in fact fairly overt, as they sit in classrooms on a daily basis that have wall displays of Wales, Britain, Europe and the world. In all the schools, Wales was highlighted in such displays. There were significant differences in emphasis between the schools, however (see also Exell 2006). In the Welsh-medium schools there was a particular version of Welsh culture on display, involving the kinds of musical, literary and oral traditions that are performed in *eisteddfodau*. In the one genuinely ethnically mixed school in our sample, one is immediately struck by the word 'welcome' written in at least a dozen languages over the front door, and wall displays reflect the cultural and ethnic diversity of the school.

Another aspect of the everyday reproduction of national identities is the judgements about the nationality of others that we make, mostly unconsciously, on a daily basis, judgements about national *habitus*. Bourdieu's (1986) concept of habitus – applied to national identity by De Cillia et al. (1999) amongst others – refers to socially acquired dispositions that are manifested in outlooks, opinions and embodied phenomena such as deportment, posture, ways of walking, sitting and so on. This is a process that it is difficult to study without extended participant observation. However, the children we spoke to revealed something of these judgements in their negotiation of identities in focus groups and in their commenting on an imaginary journey taken with the aid of a map through Britain and Europe.

The two processes we have just described, banal nationalism and the identification of national habitus are, of course, relatively opaque to the children, as they are to most adults, because these processes work by being taken for granted. Our research design, dominated as it was by semi-structured talk, was geared in the main towards the children's stated opinions about their identities. These drew on the resources available to them. We noted in Chapter 3 that the children seemed to have a limited repertoire of ideas about Wales and Welshness to draw on and that this raises the question of whether this can be explained by their being children rather than adults. Most of this section of the current chapter will be given over to discussion of the most significant markers of nationality in the children's talk. We should note at this point that we are not referring here to what actually *matters* to people – the internal, subjective dimension of identity – as our access to that as researchers can only ever be limited, but rather we are concerned with what the children spoke of as distinguishing Wales and Welshness from other nationalities. Not surprisingly, talk about what a nation means to people often (but not always) refers to what makes it *different*, rather than what it has in common with other places.

We refer in what follows to 'resources for national identity', but there are overlaps with the idea of identity 'markers' introduced by Bechhofer et al. (1999). Identity markers are 'those characteristics which are perceived to carry symbolic importance either as a signal to others of a person's national identity, or which might be mobilised by the individual themselves in support of an identity claim' (Bechhofer et al. 1999: 527–8).

Whilst we would not want to make too much of this conceptual distinction, we prefer the similar but – in our view – slightly broader concept of 'resources' for national identity. These are external points of reference for an aspect of the children's spatially expressed boundaries, that of national groupings. By 'resources' we intend to encompass banal nationalism – that is, the everyday cultural points of reference for distinguishing nationalities. In our view 'markers' is a rather flat term which implies reference points (birthplace, accent, name and so on) that have little cultural depth and that accomplish little more than the marking of a symbolic boundary. We see the term 'resources' as both capturing the potential depth and significance of key national reference points and also as emphasising the potential for individuals to make creative use of these reference points – to exercise agency (the very point Bechhofer et al. are arguing). That said, we also occasionally use the term 'markers' ourselves, in recognition that there is considerable conceptual overlap here. The key resources we discuss here are place of birth, language and sport.

Which resources are important to people will of course vary according to local, national and cultural context. In the case of the (adult) landed and cultural elites in Scotland (Bechhofer et al. 1999), natality, ancestry, place of residence, accent, name and appearance all figured as prominent identity markers. Davies et al. (2006) found from the qualitative element of their research with adults in Swansea (Wales) that the three main resources for Welsh national identity were the Welsh language, sport and opposition to English (and occasionally British) identity. Jenkins (2005) argues that the comparative study of children's national identity resources can help us understand the relative strength and political salience of collective identities. He gives the example, first, of Northern Ireland, where national/ethnic loyalties are highly colour-coded in kerbstones, flags and football shirts (see Connolly and Healy 2004) and different histories are learned in different schools and, second, of Denmark, where nationality is not nearly so conflicted and the everyday presence of the national flag is taken for granted.

In what follows, we start by discussing the content of the main resources used, focusing on the three important resources of birthplace, language and sport. We then go on to discuss the meaning of these resources and the significance the children gave to them.

Place of birth

Place of birth was the dominant marker of nationality for the children. There was a general tendency for them to prioritise country of origin when referring to technical nationality, either referencing their own birthplace or that of their parents. Emma, in the following excerpt, illustrates a typically clear ability to assign national labels unambiguously to family members, largely on the basis of where relatives are 'from': 'My step-father is English, my dad is Welsh, my mum is Welsh, everybody is Welsh. Jenny is half – my sister is half English and half Welsh – because Tim, my mum's boyfriend is from England and my mum is from Wales'.

It is striking that with regard to the Welsh/English national distinction, few children had difficulty in deciding how to assign the categories, and many were confident with delineations such as 'half' or 'partly'. The children were more likely to refer to their family's origin than their own. In middle childhood, children's experiences are still largely family based, and identities are to a large extent constructed through family relationships (Borland et al. 1998). So it was common, for example, for children to speak of being Welsh if their mother and father were Welsh, but perhaps 'half English' if one parent were Welsh and one English. Although there is something to be said here about the social location of middle childhood, we should note that many adults also make reference to parents' birthplaces when allocating nationalities to themselves and others. There was also an awareness from the children of alternative ascriptions of nationality; that your own place of birth, your place of upbringing or even your current location could override parental origin (see also Kiely et al. 2001). Joanna (Petersfield) said 'You would still be Welsh even if you were from like England' and Siôn (Highfields) is certain he is Welsh although his parents are from England because he himself has been born and brought up in Wales. Parental influence seems to be important for Siôn. He told us his father in particular is very pro-Welsh. Siôn said he 'hates' England. Whether the children chose their birthplace or their parents' birthplace was individually negotiated. There was no dominant identity rule in operation, although for the majority of the white Welsh children, the issue to be decided involved negotiating a single national boundary: the Welsh–English one (or occasionally the Welsh–British one). For the minority-ethnic children on the other hand, there were complex choices to be made. Here, no clear pattern emerged, though as we discuss in Chapter 6, these children were reluctant to embrace 'Welsh' as an umbrella identity. A variety of arguments were used for accepting or rejecting national identities.

> My family were born there so I am Pakistani, aren't I? I feel Pakistani as well. Like I am Pakistani myself, I've been there.
> (Muhammad from Highfields School in Year 6 focus group)

> I'm Muslim, I'm a British Muslim, but my Dad's from North Africa. I lived there till I was five, since I was one. But I don't really like it there because it's too hot.
> (Bahira from Highfields School in Year 6 focus group)

> I chose British, because my auntie and uncle are British.
> (Interview with Shamsa Year 6, Highfields School)

It should be also noted that several (white) children said they were 'proud to be Welsh' or 'proud of my country' without being able to say why except for 'I was born here'. Place of birth is a fairly powerful resource for national identity in its own right, and we might speculate that this is especially so when it coincides with parental birthplace, or with some other reinforcing identity marker such as length of residence.

Andrew: Let's go through these then, each of their own, a few of you have mentioned this one, a Welsh person, how important is it to be welsh then to you?

Paula: Really important

Andrew: Why is it important to you, Paula?

Paula: Because you are born in Wales.

(Year 4 focus group, Petersfield School)

Lisa: Dwi 'di dewis Cymro neu Gymraes oherwydd bod fi wedi cael fy ngeni yn Cymru, a dwi wedi byw yna gyd o fy mywyd.

[I've chosen 'Welsh person' because I was born in Wales and I've lived there all my life]

(Year 5 focus group, Ysgol y Waun)

Language and identity

Amongst the most important markers of Welshness the children spoke of were accent and language. In relation to accent, which we do not discuss in detail at this point, we should simply note that having an accent they see as distinctive makes children aware of their difference from others, both within Wales and when mixing with other British children. Many of the children were aware both of being categorised by others and of categorising themselves as different on the basis of accent. Chapter 7 deals with both accent and language in detail. Language is an important issue of place identity in a world where the English language is forever increasing its power and reach and because the issue of language is of particular salience to identity in bilingual contexts. The language dimension is introduced here specifically as a resource for national identity, whereas in Chapter 7, the everyday significance to the children of differences in language and accent are discussed more broadly.

There was very frequent confusion in the way children reported their views of language and identity: being Welsh and speaking Welsh; being English and speaking English. This is to be expected in the context of the generally close relationship found in surveys of national identity between the ability to speak the Welsh language and identification with the label 'Welsh' (Heath 2003) and the historical connection between Welsh nationalist politics and Welsh-speaking communities. Although the collapsing of linguistic categories and nationality is, of course, interesting in itself, we tried to avoid too much confusion by using the labels 'English person' and 'Welsh person' in our card-sorting exercise. The collapsing of categories was much more difficult to avoid in the Welsh-medium schools, where we used the cards 'Cymro/Cymraes' (Welsh boy/girl) and 'Saes/Saesnes' (English boy/girl). These labels, though more often used in contemporary Wales to mean nationality, were traditionally used by Welsh speakers to signify belonging to the Welsh-speaking Welsh people, and some Welsh speakers still use the terms in this way. This collapsing of categories is sometimes avoided by adding a more specific tag – Cymry Cymraeg (Welsh-speaking Welsh people) and Cymry Di-Cymraeg (non-Welsh-speaking Welsh people). These are terms from adult society and were not used at all by the children in this study. Another confusion lies in the term 'Cymraeg' which technically means 'Welsh-speaking' but is commonly used to mean Welsh nationality. There is also the term 'Cymreig', which means 'of Welsh origin', as in 'Y Swyddfa Cymreig' (The Welsh Office), but this tends not to be used in relation to people's national identities and was not used at all by the children in our study. Below are examples of children talking about the Welsh language or the English language when we were expecting a discussion of nationality. This occurred frequently, in every school.

Andrew: Ydych chi'n teimlo bod chi'n Gymraes neu'n Gymro?
Lindsay: Yn siarad?
Andrew: Wel, siarad neu siwt chi'n teimlo – mae fe lan i ti.
Lindsay: Adre dwi'n siarad Saesneg.

[*Andrew*:   Do you feel like you're a Welsh boy or girl?
Lindsay: Speaking?
Andrew: Well, speaking or how you feel – it's up to you.
Lindsay: At home I speak English.]

(Year 4 focus group, Ysgol y Porth)

Andrew: Which do you think is really most important to you of any of them, or are you not sure?
Mark: I'm Welsh really.
Andrew: Are you British first or Welsh first or what would you say you are?
Mark: British really.
Andrew: British first and Welsh second.
Mark: Yeah, because we do Welsh but we speak English.
Andrew: Yeah. Okay and how do you feel about speaking English and being Welsh?
Mark: It is easier than speaking Welsh.

(Interview with Mark, Year 6, Llwynirfon School)

It is interesting that Mark, in this last excerpt, wants to describe himself as British on the basis of language. It is also interesting that he sees Welsh as something we 'do', English as something we 'speak' and British as what we 'are'. Welsh seems to figure here as a school subject rather than a cultural or even a linguistic identity. Mark is unusual in saying that people who speak Welsh are 'probably' more Welsh than he is.

Andrew: What sort of children do you think go to these kinds of schools [Welsh-medium]?
Mark: The people are more Welsh than me.
Andrew: Do you think they feel more Welsh than other people feel?
Mark: Mm. Probably.
Andrew: Do you feel less Welsh than they feel?
Mark: Yeah because I speak more English than Welsh.
(Interview with Mark, Year 6, Llwynirfon School)

Unlike Mark, almost invariably children told us they thought non-Welsh speakers were just as Welsh as Welsh-speakers. Yet the hierarchy of Welshness according to language use that Mark refers to is a version of Welsh identity that is very familiar in contemporary Wales, and one that many non-Welsh speakers vigorously contest. Haf (a first-language Welsh-speaker from Bryntawel) told us she was not sure whether or not non-Welsh-speaking Welsh people are really Welsh or not. This very uncertain comment is the nearest we got to finding a Welsh-speaking child claiming a superior level of national identity on the basis of language. It may well be that Welsh-speaking children were reluctant to make such claims in interview due to a consciousness, however subliminal, of their politically controversial nature.

As other qualitative research on Welsh identities has shown (Davies et al. 2006, Roberts 1995), non-Welsh speakers also often made reference to the Welsh language when speaking of their own Welshness. We could optimistically speculate that this is evidence, as current rhetoric from the National Assembly and the Welsh Language Board proclaims, of the Welsh language being seen as belonging to everyone in Wales. However, when non-Welsh-speaking children referred to the Welsh language in connection with their 'Welshness', it often seemed as though there was an extremely limited repertoire of identity markers (of any kind) available to them. It is possible that in the absence of anything else they could think of, they were making reference to something that did not in fact mean all that much to them. This is one possible interpretation of Aimee's interview below.

Aimee: I just knew that one described me the most.
Andrew: You don't have to tell me which one it was if you don't want to.
Aimee: It was Welsh one.
Andrew: It was the Welsh one, was it?

Aimee: Yeah.
Andrew: Okay. Why did you choose that one?
Aimee: Because I don't know. It was just the one that, um, 'cause mostly
               I like speaking Welsh but we don't speak much of it at home. The
               only thing my dad says is like 'Bore Da' [Good morning] and
               'Nos Da' [Good night] and stuff like that. He don't say much
               Welsh.

(Interview with Aimee, Year 5, Petersfield School)

Of course, the fact that Aimee's father uses these Welsh language greetings in
a town that is totally dominated by the English language and where Welsh
would rarely be heard in public is in itself an indication of family support for
the Welsh language. It could therefore be that the Welsh language is important to Aimee's national identity. Perhaps the Welsh language genuinely is a
badge of difference for children like Aimee, even though she does not know
much of it and would not use it outside of occasional Welsh lessons in
school.

Sport

Sport is an important aspect of banal nationalism for most people, as it is
one of the social domains where national boundaries are most frequently
and overtly marked. Sport was associated with patriotism and national triumph for the children. To generate discussion, we showed them a film clip of
the Welsh national anthem being played at the start of a rugby international.
To quote from just one focus group (Year 5 in Llwynirfon), the comments
that followed this film clip included 'It makes you feel successful', 'It just
makes me feel really proud to live in Wales' and 'It just makes you feel good
inside to be Welsh'. Even in the context of actual sporting failure this clip
was associated with imagined triumph. So Lynn, when asked how she would
show on film what Wales is like, referred to a football match she had
attended that Wales had lost. She associated the nation with triumph over
others in sport.

Andrew: What then if somebody asked you to make like 30, 40 seconds of
               film like that to show people what Wales is like, what would you
               show them, what would you make?
Lynn: I would make them win against Finland. I would just through a
               quick clip.

(Year 4 focus group, Petersfield School)

Comments like this indicate the extent to which televisual and other publicly
mediated demonstrations of national sporting success can be emotionally
salient to children and to their sense of collective belonging and how they
feel about it.

That said, there are not simply blanket national affiliations on offer in sport of course. Some sports are more (locally) national than others, as Gianni explained when he told us that 'Rugby is more Welsh than English and football is more English than Welsh'. It was noted in the previous chapter that nearly all the children said they supported both the Welsh national rugby team and an English Premier League football team – typically, Manchester United (who at the time of our fieldwork had dominated the English Premier League for several years) and that the children seemed happy to claim this dual, Welsh-English affiliation rather than feeling compelled to choose. Indeed, this flexibility means that children can feel included in a range of sporting spectacles and outcomes in their sense of which 'side' or collectivity they relate to. Whilst in Chapter 3 we quoted Emma as asserting her agency in maintaining dual sporting affiliations, other children spoke overtly about following the crowd, or indeed simply choosing the most successful team. In William's case this means supporting England rather than Wales as a national football team:

William: Well my friend said one day when I was reception. And then I went along with everyone and copied them a little bit and then he said, 'Oh so what football team do you support William?' and I said 'What do you?' and he said Liverpool. And then I went round to this house then and we saw a football match playing and then that was it.

Andrew: Okay, great, and who is your favourite player for Liverpool?

William: Michael Owen.

Andrew: Michael Owen. Okay, great, and you said England as well for football?

William: Yeah.

Andrew: Okay, great, and how do you feel being somebody from Wales supporting England at football?

William: Well most of it's (.) well I said I wanted to support them because they have more chance of winning and I don't particularly like a team losing.

(Interview with William, Year 5, Llwynirfon School)

Probably because of the much greater interest in football than any other sport from the boys in particular, and bearing in mind the relatively poor international performance of the Welsh national football team, identification with a Premier League team seemed to be more important than any potential national affiliation. This is illustrated by the following excerpt, in which Mark responds to a question about national teams by perhaps giving away the rivalry that really matters.

Andrew: What about when it comes to football matches in the house? Who supports England and who supports Wales?

Mark:	Well my brother supports Manchester United and I support Liverpool.

(Interview with Mark, Year 6, Llwynirfon School)

Sporting affiliation and identification is in fact one social domain where we can see a distinct difference between middle childhood and adulthood. Several of the children spoke of being baffled by adult emotions in relation to sport, specifically where their fathers get loudly excited. These comments were made by some of the boys as well as some of the girls. In the following excerpt, however, this could be an issue of gender as much as one of age. Paula and Lynn could be distancing themselves from what they might see as the male domain of baying for your team. Boys are perhaps expected to learn this performance of national pride more quickly or easily than girls. Jason joins in the discussion only to imagine himself joining in the glory, reminding us of the gendered dimension of national-identity performance, or the national dimension of 'doing gender', as noted in the previous chapter.

Paula:	Every time Wales does a goal or whatever you call them, he goes like this 'YEAH', until I go 'Shut up Dad'. And then he goes 'No you're supposed to be supporting your country'.
Andrew:	Yeah, okay.
Jason:	If I played for Wales I would do a dummy.
Lynn:	When we went to the match it was Finland against Wales and Wales scored and my dad he got me on his shoulders, lifted me up and we were like on the top thing and I banged my head [*laughter*]. And my dad was like 'Yeeeees!' and he ignored me.

(Year 4 focus group, Petersfield School)

In this excerpt, Paula's main response to the experience she recounts is that she felt 'ignored' by her dad. It seems that children, or perhaps girls in particular, may well feel that adult preoccupation with national sports-team affiliations is quite irrelevant to them and, perhaps, even unwelcome.

The significance of resources for national identity

It is important to consider how the children construct national identity via available resources and what the available resources mean to them. Despite the limited resources they have to draw on, to some extent the children we spoke to can be seen to be active in constructing their national identities, within discursive limits, making selective and creative use of the resources available to them. One example was of the construction of identity in relation to the school curriculum. In Petersfield school (eastern valleys), the children had been learning about the Second World War shortly before Andrew arrived in the school as a researcher. The war then featured in the children's talk about place and identity in a number of ways. In the secret ballot card-sorting exercise we used a 'you choose' card for children to add anything important to them other than a connection with a place or culture. One of the children (Melissa) wrote on this card 'World War Two' and the reason that 'my mother's father was in World War Two'. Melissa was selectively using this particular discourse of the *British* nation since she can see a connection to her own family history – a connection that no doubt her teacher has encouraged her to make. The recent influence on this choice of identity illustrates the very contingent nature of identity and the dependence of identity on performance in specific contexts of interaction. The same child would not necessarily have made the same choice a year or even a month later.

Rowland, in Ysgol Maes Garw School, also drew on twentieth-century history to argue his point about self-determination. Throughout the focus group he made Welsh nationalist arguments, about, for example, the need for the Assembly to have more power than it currently has. Then in the context of a discussion about who should decide on a new road through the local area, he argues that local people, including children, should take the decision, by overtly drawing on nationalist history. He raises the possibility of someone wanting to 'turn Maes Garw into a reservoir'. Here he refers to the history of Tryweryn, a Welsh-speaking area of north Wales where a village was flooded in the 1960s to provide water for (English) Liverpool. This story is a powerful one still in contemporary Welsh nationalism featuring in the political slogan 'Cofiwch Tryweryn' (Remember Tryweryn) – and was the subject of a belated apology by the City Council of Liverpool in November 2005. It may be of course that Rowland is repeating parental arguments. He may have heard one or more of his family members talking about Wales in these terms. Nonetheless, he is choosing to air them in public, and is, hence, active in making creative and selective use of the knowledge he has to display his political and national identity to his peers. It is often unclear as to what extent the children are repeating parental views, and research with the whole family would be needed to explore this. Joe, from Highfields School, said in a focus group that he 'chose Welsh and they (parents) are not anywhere near Welsh'. We might see this as an expression of his claim to individual agency in relation to his national identity, but his declaration that 'I'm the only one in my whole family that's Welsh' could well be a familiar family narrative.

A general claim we would make about our data is that there was little in the way of distinctive cultural content for the category of 'being Welsh'. In this finding our research confirms Carrington and Short's (1995, 1996) studies of English and Scottish children's perceptions of Britishness in middle childhood. They found a large majority of the children citing 'what might be regarded as "surface features" of the national culture' (1995: 226) or defining 'national culture in concrete terms' (1996: 210) such as birthplace, residence, family connections and language. Only around 10 per cent of Carrington and Short's (1995) English sample made reference to 'cultural habits' and the proportion was lower still in Scotland. In our study, apart from the resources mentioned so far – birthplace, language, accent and sport – and two isolated references to ethnic history, which we go on to discuss in Chapter 6 in the context of racialisation, the children had little to go on in describing their Welshness (or indeed, Englishness or other nationalities). This does, of course, beg the question of what *is* distinctive about being Welsh in a culturally globalised world, other than perhaps language and location. Apart from supporting a Welsh national sports team, being born within the country's borders or claiming an affinity with a language that has an almost unique connection to the borders of the Wales, what else is there? This may be an uncomfortable question for those who do not identify with the Welsh language in any way but nonetheless passionately proclaim their Welshness. We do not express any view on the matter ourselves here, but have to note that it is not surprising this question surfaces in popular debates about what it means to be Welsh. Given the increasingly global nature of cultural flows (Appadurai 1990) and the dominance of the English language, constructing a Welshness with a distinctive cultural component is a challenge. It is, of course, open to those living within the borders of Wales (or having their origins there) to define themselves as Welsh in so far as they are not English (see McIntosh et al. 2004 on Scotland). This issue is raised in the next chapter as it relates to the topic of defining insiders and outsiders.

Whilst it is not possible for us to generalise our findings to a wider population, it is worth noting that 'Welsh' was in fact the identity label most frequently selected by the children when we offered them a variety of labels in a 'secret ballot' card-sorting exercise. National identifications were certainly chosen more frequently than local ones in this exercise, although as we explain in the next chapter, there is some tension between this finding and other aspects of our data on the significance of place. Noting the popularity of the 'Welsh' identity label does not of course tell us much about differences between the children in the meaning of this label, and it is to diversity that we now turn.

Variation between children in terms of national identity

Later chapters refer to differences between schools in terms of class, language, accent and 'race'. We make some relatively brief observations here about differences between the children in terms of national identity. The question to be considered is how the markers of national identity differ for children according to the differential power relations (such as social class, gender and regional politics) that are in play in the everyday contexts of children's social worlds.

The first thing to note is that ethnic origin was an important variable influencing how the children within our sample spoke of national identity, and this issue is considered in depth in Chapter 6. Within the limits of our study we are not struck, however, by obvious patterns of difference in national identity according to class or gender. It was not possible to make very reliable comparisons between schools in terms of social class, as although the schools were carefully chosen to reflect a range of class backgrounds (according to data on free school meals), we only spoke to eighteen children in each school and the research design was entirely qualitative, which did not allow for measurement of variation as such. However, we can note here that within the limits of what a qualitative design can tell us, there were not any marked differences according to class or gender in the ways that children talked about national identity or chose identity labels in the card-sorting exercise. This was in contrast to the social class differences apparent in how the children spoke about their local areas, as we explain in the next chapter.

There is one observation we can make from the Welsh study about regional variation in national identity. The children from Bryntawel (Ysgol y Porth), which is in a part of north-west Wales where 80 per cent of inhabitants speak Welsh, expressed a stronger sense of distinctiveness within Britain than did children from the other schools. This implies that, when we consider self-identification, the children from Bryntawel were more aware of their difference from others within the UK than were the other children. The Bryntawel children were quickly able to say which identities their parents would choose, as though national-identity talk was common currency at home. They were aware of speaking a different language from the rest of Britain. Jane worried that if she were to move to Australia she would 'colli'r iaith' (lose the language). They thought that the characters in the Welsh-language soap opera *Pobl y Cwm* (*People of the Valley*) were not that different from local people, but people in *EastEnders*, however, which is set in London, were clearly of a different nationality and language. In the extract that follows, Haf could be referring with 'Saesneg' and 'Cymraeg' either to language, nation or both, as these words have both meanings.

Andrew: Ydi'r bobl yn *EastEnders* yn wahanol i bobl ffindech chi yn Bryntawel 'te?
Llyr: Yndyn.
Andrew: Pam maen nhw'n wahanol 'te? [. . .] Beth sy'n wahanol amdanyn nhw 'te?
Haf: Maen nhw'n Saesneg a 'dan ni'n Cymraeg.

[*Andrew*: Are the people in *EastEnders* different from the people you'd find in Bryntawel then?
Llyr: Yes.
Andrew: Why are they different then? [. . .] What's different about them then?
Haf: They're English and we're Welsh.]

(Year 5 focus group, Ysgol y Porth)

As with adults, discourses of nationhood vary according to region. So debates about nationality are more vivid in Gwynedd (in north-west Wales), for example, than in the eastern valleys. The children in Ysgol y Porth made some reference to the 'Cymuned' debate about language and citizenship that has been especially centred on Welsh-speaking localities such as theirs (see pages 37 and 133). One child, for example, when asked what he most disliked about Wales wrote 'mae gormod o bobl yn siarad Saesneg' (too many people speak English). A few children in this school described the town in which they lived as 'Welsh-speaking'. On entering the town, one could not avoid the Cymuned poster stating 'Ardal Cymraeg yw hon' (this is a Welsh speaking area). Bowie (1993: 169) comments of north-west Wales that 'the whole question of identity is framed very much within the politics of the Welsh language'.

Britishness did not emerge as an important identity for the children in Ysgol y Porth. In Llwynirfon, however, a mid-Wales market town where around 30 per cent of the local population speak Welsh, the children sometimes referred to themselves as British. Welsh identities seemed to emerge slightly more strongly from discussions in Petersfield, which serves a very deprived and non-Welsh-speaking community in the eastern valleys of south Wales, despite the fact that several of the children have family roots in England. There could be an issue of class here. Llwynirfon is a largely middle-class school, and this might plausibly explain the children's greater propensity to utilise the more abstract and official term 'British', whereas the children of Petersfield might, we could speculate, see 'Welsh' as a more appropriate identity label for working-class people, perhaps in contrast to a 'posh' Englishness (see Chapter 6) or Britishness. However, the differences were relatively subtle. Other studies have found much more marked differences in national and ethnic identity according to social class. Differences are particularly marked where class intersects with levels of overt conflict. In Northern Ireland, there is a connection between levels of conflict in communities and social deprivation, although 'the relationship is not a perfect one' (Connolly and Healy 2004: 11) and there are some contrary examples. Connolly and Healy's research shows vividly the differences between children from different class backgrounds in how aware they are of sectarian conflict. In their case study areas of high conflict (which are socially deprived), the majority of three- to four-year-olds were very aware of symbols of their own community. By the age of seven/eight, children in areas of high conflict showed markedly negative views towards the other community, whereas children in the low-conflict middle-class areas from both Protestant and Catholic communities were relatively unaware of violence or divisions except for problems caused by 'bad people'. The children's ability to differentiate 'good' from 'bad' people in divided localities also figured as a class issue in our own study, though in a less highly charged context than Northern Ireland. We return to this issue in the next chaper.

Principles of national identity in childhood

In Chapter 3 we explained that two important aspects of social interaction were implicated in children's 'doing' of national identity: first, that what you claim as your identity depends at least partly on the specific social context (for example, whom you are talking to and where) and, second, that expressions of national identity can be gendered. Of course the children are not particularly conscious of either of these aspects of interaction. There are, however, principles of national identity in childhood that we would see as more consciously articulated. We use the term 'principles of national identity in childhood' as these seem to be overarching beliefs held by most of the children about what is appropriate *for children*.

When we explicitly asked the children about identities, with national identities prominent amongst the options, most were quick to express a strong sense of national identity. They usually spoke of the importance of being Welsh, though some mentioned a dual or multiple nationality, which they often connected to place of birth – either their own or that of their parents – as noted above ('half English, half Welsh', 'quarter Italian, quarter Welsh, half English'). In fact, virtually all the children displayed an unhesitating facility in labelling and quantifying their own national belonging and those of their family members. When the children talked more generally about attachment to places, however, there was not nearly so clear a sense of the strength of national identities. One of our stock questions was about what they would miss if they had to leave their home area and move to Australia. Almost all of them said that they would miss their friends:

> My friends, definitely my friends. They are part of my life really, my friends. I can't live without them, most of the time.
> (Interview with Siôn, Year 6, Highfields School)

Andrew: Beth fyddet ti'n colli am le wyt ti'n byw nawr?
Lisa: Ffrindiau, teulu. Cwn yn barcio yn y nos.

[*Andrew*: What would you miss about where you live now?
Lisa: Friends, family. Dogs barking in the night.]
> (Interview with Lisa, Year 5, Ysgol y Waun)

To an extent, these responses could, of course, be seen as something of an artefact of our particular research design. However, the data suggest that the children show little idea of there being any cultural difference if they were to move to Australia or that they would miss any places. Many of the children said that it was important to them to be Welsh, but there were few references to anything as abstract as Welsh 'culture' or, in fact, any other kind of national culture. The general ideas seemed to be that life would be much the same in another English-speaking country, but that particular people left behind would be missed. It was people, rather than places, that seemed to matter. This suggests, we argue, that although children may feel confident in utilising national identity labels with little hesitation, their actual place-attachments are experienced in intensely local terms – to family and friends. In other words, when we asked them what they would miss if they moved, they answered in terms of *local* people rather than through any reference to the *national* label just uttered. When they spoke of the nation, they were repeating a familiar and well-rehearsed boundary label; when asked to think about content (what they would miss) their answers referred to life as locally lived. This lends weight to our argument about the import-ance of attending to the variety of spatial imaginations expressed by children and how they intertwine with each other. In many ways, it is unsurprising that the national realm is translated into the local, and is likely to be charac-teristic of most adults' worlds too: as Cohen (1982: 13) observes, 'local experience mediates national identity'.

Our exploration of children's national identifications and their relation-ship to other identifications continued with our focus group card-sorting exercise, described on p. 33. In the first stage, we asked them to engage with various collective identities, and in the second stage we asked them all to fill in an extra free-choice card with reference to anything they wanted, but the oral prompts included 'a person you are close to', 'a pet' and 'a hobby'. The children most often wrote the name of a family member for this free-choice card. We then asked them to choose from the entire set – collect-ive and more personal identities – as to which meant most to them. There was a range of responses, as one might expect, but most commonly the children chose the individualised second-round card out of the complete set. This suggests that children will choose a personal family member as important to them over and above a national or collective identity.

Of course we have to be cautious what we conclude from this focus group exercise. Some conferring went on, which further supports the notion of the interactive, contingent character of collective identities. We should also note that in a relatively ethnically homogenous group of children there may be a tendency for national and ethnic identities to be in the background because they are so taken for granted. All but one of the schools in our sample were indeed fairly ethnically homogenous. A relevant example of other research here is Hengst's study (1997), which found that children of Turkish origin in Germany were more likely to give themselves a national/ethnic label than were the white English and German children in his sample. However, despite these sensible notes of caution, we could see the result of our two-stage card-sorting exercise as supporting a conclusion that known and significant others – most often close friends and family members – are more important to children's sense of identity than local/national/ethnic collectivities. We return to this theme in the next chapter.

It is interesting to note that national identity was often seen as something open to change and contingent on one's current location, in contrast with some other aspects of identity, which are fixed. So Jack, for example, saw gender as more of an essence than nationality.

Andrew: So did you have to choose in between those cards, why did you find it difficult to choose between them?

Jack: Because this one is like the country and then 'boy' is like what you really are.

(Interview with Jack from Petersfield School)

This suggests that a nationality for the children is more about where you are (or came from) rather than who you are. It does not on its own constitute the 'you'. Nation and region were at times said to be unimportant according to a universalist ethic that people are 'just the same' in other countries. Nathan's interview is an example of this tendency that surfaced quite often in discussions with the children.

Andrew: Beth mae dod o Gogledd Cymru yn meddwl i ti, yn golygu i ti? [What does coming from north Wales mean to you?]

Nathan: Lot ond dwi ddim yn rili, I don't really care where I'm born. [A lot but I don't really, I don't really care where I'm born.]

Andrew: Yeah? So is it just? Is it important to you or—?

Nathan: Mm. It's just the same. It would be just the same if I was born anywhere else.

(Interview with Nathan, Year 4, Ysgol y Waun)

Probably the most concrete cultural content of 'Welshness' was filled by the children's perceptions of their immediate environment, rather than by any sense of characteristics that distinguished one nation from another. Jenny from Llwynirfon, a rural market town in mid-Wales, told us that Wales has 'loads and loads of hills and landscapes and things like that'. In contrast, Siôn, from inner-city Cardiff, saw Wales as 'tightly packed'. These children's sense of 'Wales' mirrored their sense of their immediate locality. 'Wales' was neither more abstract nor even, perhaps, more remote, but was in some sense coterminous with the local area in which they lived. That is not to say that these particular children did not understand local and national boundaries, as with the examples of geographical confusion in Chapter 3. Our point is, rather, that these children did have a sense of place that was culturally filled, but it was more influenced by their sense of their local environment than by some more distant received idea of the nation. Rather similarly, several of the London-based Welsh-speaking children interviewed by Segrott (2006) associated Wales with rurality. This construction for them was, again, related to their immediate local environment, but in this instance as an obvious contrast with where they lived.

The question remains as to how much of the relative weakness in the children's sense of national identity is explained by their stage of cognitive development – for example their undeveloped facility with more abstract cultural concepts – and how much by the locally confined social context of children's lives at this age. There is also the question of how different adult responses would be. Our research does not allow these questions to be answered, in that we did not set out to research cognition nor to compare children to adults. However, children's attachment to immediate family and friends can most plausibly, we suggest, be understood in terms of their embeddedness in social worlds defined by immediate interpersonal horizons. To put it down to purely cognitive ability and wilfully to ignore these power-ful social factors would, we feel, be blinding oneself to the obvious. In this sense, we would expect adults' experiences to be more varied, but not neces-sarily to be starkly opposed – for most adults, too, will be likely to articulate terms such as 'the national' through experiences that are always local and personal.

Conclusion

An overall discussion of the significance of place in middle childhood will follow at the end of the next chapter. That discussion will consider all four spatial domains: global, national, local and domestic. At this point, we simply summarise the main points raised in this chapter.

We identified the key resources the children used in talking about Welsh-ness as language, birthplace and sport. Most reproduced culturally domin-ant ideas about the meanings of these national markers. Some of the children could be seen to be making creative use of these resources and to be exercis-ing a degree of agency. All of these resources are very likely to be referenced by adults too (as Davies et al. [2006] note with regard to language and sport in Wales) – but we observed that some children do not feel the same kind of passion about sporting loyalties as their fathers. This brings us to principles of national identity in middle childhood. The children did demonstrate a facility with applying and quantifying national labels, and used the Welsh label readily in relation to themselves. Indeed, when Welshness was explicitly on the agenda, they would say it was important to them. However, in more general talk about attachment to places, there was a sense of attachment to known and significant others being of primary importance. In general, we found little filled-out cultural content for the nation in the child-ren's talk. There was little sense of there being cultural differences between Wales and other parts of Britain and the West. We argued earlier that the concept of 'resources' for national identity allowed for national reference points to have thicker/deeper cultural content than the terminology of 'markers' of national identity. Having now considered how the children in the Welsh study employ key resources of nationality, we have to conclude that there seems in fact to be relatively little depth involved for most chil-dren. We return to this question of whether the children have a culturally filled concept of place in the following chapter. The last point to reiterate is that we found relatively little variation between the children in how they related to the nation according to gender or social class. The following chapter will also take up this issue of variation between the children, with particular reference to class and local identity.

5 Local and domestic dimensions of place identity

As explained previously, Chapters 4 and 5 are an analytic pair. This chapter continues the overview of the significance of place, with reference primarily to the Welsh study but also along the way to research from elsewhere. The chapter is structured according to the local and domestic spatial domains, with a distinction being made between the area surrounding home and school (local) and the home itself (domestic). Considerably more attention is given to the local dimension of place identity.

The local

Approaches to the study of children and locality

There are, of course, many different ways of studying children in localities. There are research approaches from several different academic disciplines which focus on different aspects of children's experiences. There has been increasing interest in children in spaces and places from geographers, which can be seen in the recently established journal *Children's Geographies* (see also Holloway and Valentine's edited collection, 2000c). There has been significant work done on children's use of space (see, for example, Factor 2004, Hart 1979) and related work on environmental design and planning for child-friendly places (Chawla 2002). There is a substantial literature on environmental psychology (see for example Bourchier et al. 2002, Chatterjee 2005, Korpela et al. 2002). There is also work on youth in localities. The issues in 'youth' are arguably different from those in middle childhood. As Hall et al. (1999: 506) observe, youth is 'an expansive moment', with young people often laying claim both to extra personal space within the home and to a new freedom to move around and make use of space in their localities. Childress (2004) notes that in the teenage years, young people's spatial claiming or marking of territory can be the site of intergenerational conflict. Children in middle childhood, in contrast, tend to be much more socially and spatially restricted than teenagers, at least in the West.

Children's experience of locality can be highly contested, especially when we consider global social and economic variation. Adult conflicts over space obviously have an impact on children. For example, Poveda and Marcos (2004) describe the ongoing contestation of children's use of space and place by reference to a stone fight involving Gitano (Gypsy) children in Spain. The spatial dimension of ethnic conflict has an important impact on children's lives, as we noted in the previous chapter with reference to Connolly and Healy's research (2004) on Northern Ireland. In the poorest parts of the global South, there are many 'street children', a complex phenomenon as Ennew and Swart-Kruger (2003) point out. Children become displaced and are affected by war or, indeed, are involved as combatants (Boyden 2003, Boyden and de Berry 2004). Boyden (2003) observes that even during times of great adversity such as war, children consciously act upon and influence their environments.

This section of the chapter is primarily about what locality means to the children we studied in terms of their self-identification. In other words, we are interested here in how children's talk about their immediate environments contributes to their sense of who they are. In what follows we deal with several aspects of identification with place: the children's imagery of their locality (both their town and the district in which they live); their emotional attachment to place and their perception of quality of life in their community. We should acknowledge at this point that other chapters in the book also refer to locality. Some of what the children say about locality is also about the nation and is related to national imagery, which was the focus of the previous chapter. Locality 'boundaries' can also be racialised (see Chapter 6) or can refer to language and accent (see Chapter 7).

We had various different strategies for asking the children about locality. We asked them to imagine a soap opera was being made in their home area and to tell us what the soap would need to include if it were to give people an idea of what life was like there. (Obviously, some of these data tells us more about children's perceptions of soap operas than anything else.) We asked them what they would tell a child moving to their area from London about the place and how they would show them around. We asked them what they would miss if they moved from their home area to Australia and also what they would take with them to remind them of home. We asked them to do a sentence-completion exercise on where they would like to be living in ten years' time and why. These techniques taken together provided us with a number of insights about children's relationships to their home environments, and we discuss these in what follows.

A child's eye view of locality

In most of the schools there was an interesting distinction between how the children represented their home town and their immediate locality. When asked what they would show people to tell them about their home area, they either answered with reference to their home town, in which case they assumed a kind of tourist gaze and concentrated on prominent institutions and leisure sites, or else they made reference to the immediate locality in which they lived, in which case they gave child's-eye accounts concentrating primarily on play spaces. The immediate locality was, not surprisingly, more vivid to them, although within the 'tourist gaze' they included reference to children's fun sites which they could also speak about with enthusiasm and in detail.

The child's-eye view of immediate locality highlighted facilities and features that circumscribe their own daily pathways, rather than those that might be identified by a generalising gaze.

Andrew: Why do you think I'd settle there?
Joseph: You can go down the field and get lots of friends up there and there's some shops – Lidl [supermarket] is up there.
Andrew: Is there a lot for children to do around here, or—?
Joseph: Go down the field and play football on the farm and a garage quite close to the two of the shops . . . so kids go there to buy sweets and stuff.
                        (Interview with Joseph, Year 5, Ysgol Maes Garw)

It's half close to the rec [recreation ground]. All you've got to do is go down by Safeways [supermarket] and take the short cut, walk down the grass and there you are.
                        (Interview with Jason, Year 4 focus group in Petersfield School)

These two comments are typical in that the speakers define where they live in terms of the presence and location of areas to play in, including fields and parks. As Rasmussen (2004) notes, it is not necessarily the officially designated 'places for children' that appeal so much as the 'children's places' they make their own. These might be particular corners of official play spaces or tucked-away spaces which adults might not even notice: a 'goal mouth' between two bushes or a patch of earth (or for Joseph and Jason perhaps the 'farm' or the 'short cut').

As we will explain in more detail later in the chapter, the children were very aware of what was safe and what was not. Emma here is alluding to her own experience of getting lost and Lisa is perhaps referencing local childhood folklore about the dangers of the river:

And when you go down the long hill there is loads of turnings and all of that and you get really muddled up and go round corners and come out and (.) don't get lost as it is really big.
                        (Interview with Emma, Year 4, Petersfield School)

Lisa: Paid â fynd i'r afon.
Andrew: Pam 'ny, 'te?
Lisa: Mae'n sinking sand.

[*Lisa*:   Don't go to the river.
Andrew: Why's that then?
Lisa: It's sinking sand.]

(Interview with Lisa, Year 5, Ysgol y Waun)

In relation to their home town, the students mentioned historical sites (such as castles), prominent public institutions ('the Market Hall') shops and sports venues. These tended to be sites thought suitable for visitors. Bahira was explicit about this when mentioning Cardiff's Millenium Stadium 'because it's where most tourists go'. Many of these sites were places the children themselves took pleasure in, often places for consumption. In particular, they mentioned shops and restaurants with targeted provision for children. Gianni said, 'If you was an eight-year-old kid then you'd have to know about Woolies (Woolworth's)'. Siôn recommended a particular supermarket for shopping because of its toy and sports sections. The references to tourist sites give an impression of how the children see the image of their home areas.

As noted above, children's immediate localities were most vivid, no doubt because of their experience of walking and cycling round them, playing in them, rather than travelling past in cars as would probably be the case in their local towns. Shamsa in the following excerpt reveals a conscious hierarchy of place. She starts and then corrects herself, explicitly stating the order of importance of different places: home area first, followed by school and then the city:

Andrew: What do I need to know about this place before I arrive, you know, Blackmoor, Cardiff and the school? What would you tell me?
Shamsa: The school I go to. No. The area I live in and then the school and then the city.

(Interview with Shamsa, Year 6, Highfields School)

Because of the intimacy of their experience in them, places within the immediate locality could in fact be seen as being more significant to the children than most other dimensions of place (such as the national or the global). We noted in the previous chapter that when we asked the children to select cards according to which identity label meant most to them, few selected local identities. Despite this and the primacy of national identities in the first round of card-sorting, we would argue that the overall picture from our data is that locality is more significant to children in their everyday lives than other dimensions of place and space. Later in this chapter we further localise this argument by asserting that the domestic domain seems to be most important of all. The picture is further complicated, however, by our observation that it is people-in-place more than places themselves that seem to be most important to the children. We explain this interpretation of our data in the following section.

Attachment to place

At this point, we move on more directly to the question of attachment to
local places. Our interpretation of our data is that place as a culturally filled
and bounded category does not really feature in these children's social
worlds. In other words, they do not use much in the way of a language
of place-identity. The children generally identify with people rather than
places. Where they do talk about places as important, it is usually because of
the people associated with these places. Places are characterised often in
terms of the nice or nasty people in them. It was noted in Chapter 4 that
when asked about moving from Wales to Australia, it was people rather
than places that the children typically said they would miss. This same
response often arose in relation to locality. Gianni's interview is an example.
When asked about place he talks about people:

Andrew: And what about Bryntawel then – how important is Bryntawel to
         people?
Gianni: Well, it's important to me because if I moved away, I'd be really
         sad because I'd be missing all my friends and stuff. They're really
         nice around here.

                           (Interview with Gianni, Year 4, Ysgol y Porth)

In some instances where children might initially be thought to be talking
about places, in fact their responses seem to be more to do with people. So
William said 'I'd probably miss the neighbourhood that I've got friendly
with'. His mention of being 'friendly' might imply he is referring to the
people rather than the physical environment. Haf, in the following excerpt,
makes a rare statement of attachment to place. She does so on the basis of
her long association with it but also because of family.

Andrew: A beth am Fryntawel 'te? Siwd ardal yw e 'te? [. . .] Pam ydi e'n
         bwysig i ti?
Haf: Oherwydd dwi'n gwybod pa ffordd i fynd. Oherwydd dwi 'di
         bod yma ers gês i eni.
Andrew: O reit, ie.
Haf: A mae 'na rai o teulu fi'n byw yma ac dwi'n licio Bryntawel.

[*Andrew*:   And what about Bryntawel then? What kind of area is it? Why's
         it important to you?
Haf: Because I know which way to go. Because I've been here since I
         was born.
Andrew: Oh right, yeah.
Haf: And there are some of my family living here and I like
         Bryntawel.]

                             (Interview with Haf, Year 5, Ysgol y Porth)

This excerpt shows well the general pattern of responses to place, in that Haf's explanation of her attachment turns on its familiarity to her: the fact that she can orient herself within it and that her family live there. Place to her is where she feels at home.

There were interesting patterns of response according to gender in the sentence-completion exercise: 'In ten years' time I would like to be living in—'. Twice as many boys as girls said they wanted to stay in their home area in future. However, the girls were rather more likely than the boys to mention people as their reasons for their choice of location and in many cases they saw themselves in a future caring role in relation to these people. So, for example, Jasmin wanted her own house so she could have 'my boyfriend all to myself' and Joanne wanted 'a nice house with a lovely family'. Eleri wanted to move to Holland because her uncle lived there. Aimee wanted to stay in the house so that she could 'look after my Mum and Dad'.

The following excerpt shows these children agreeing that their home village is important, but not *that* important. Again it is people and social relations that seem most significant – friends to Dafydd and home, rugby team and school to Rowland. The suggestion is that wherever you lived you would have these ties. The place itself does not have unique qualities.

Andrew: What about Maes Garw then? Is that important to anyone living in this area or Cwmglo?

Dafydd: I want to live in Maes Garw sometimes and I don't want to leave.

Rowland: I didn't put it in the box.

Dafydd: I wouldn't want to leave my friends like.

Rowland: It's important to me but—

Phillip: It's not that important.

Dafydd: No, I know it's not that important.

Phillip: If I lived in Cwmglo it's exactly the same.

Rowland: If I lived in any place it would be exactly the same it's just, I knows Maes Garw, play rugby for it, my home's there, I go to Maes Garw school.

(Year 6 focus group in Ysgol Maes Garw)

In the following excerpt, Nathan cannot conceive of any particular quality of his home area other than particular shops.

Andrew: What would I need to know about the area here?

Nathan: It's just the same as any other area but some areas might not have same kind of things as this and then here might not have as much kind of things as the other area things.

Andrew: What sort of things?

Nathan: They might not have a day and night shop or an Esso shop or

a Kwik Save shop or something. They might have a Tesco one
instead.

(Interview with Nathan, Year 4, Ysgol y Waun)

It should be noted that it can be difficult for children or adults to conceive
of different places as culturally filled-out – as identifiably distinctive, the
expression of which requires facility in a language of comparison. Nathan's
words raise the question of whether a stronger attachment to place depends
to an extent on some knowledge or experience of other (different) places
with which 'home' can be compared. It may be that Nathan's only experience is of comparable but broadly rather similar places, in which case it is
entirely understandable for him to say that what distinguishes his home area
from any other is the different brand of shops, especially when patterns of
retail and consumption mean that certain brands dominate high-street shops
across Britain. Indeed, it is striking in virtually all extracts that children
used the names of local stores and supermarkets as signposts for orienting
themselves around their locality.

We have noted that it is the social and relational dimension of place that
seems most important. The children in our Welsh study tended to define the
locality where they lived by the people they encountered within it. When we
consider the children's assessment of these people, there was a prevalent
distinction made between 'nasty' people, or bullies, and 'nice' people. Scott,
for example, told us some people in his area are 'hoffus ac yn ddoniol'
(amiable and funny) and some are 'drwg a chas' (naughty and nasty). There
were examples from most of the schools of children complaining about
criminals or bullies in their local area and also of people in their locality
being generally nice and friendly. Noise, crime and danger from drunken
adults were more of an urban preoccupation (and we expand on this below),
but many of the children in two of the three more rural schools also had
rather divided images of the local community. This returns us to the salience
of boundaries in children's conceptions of place: as we shall see below, these
nice/nasty divisions were used to map different areas of the localities in
which they lived. The children often characterised particular places as
having concentrations of nicer or nastier people, and we expand on this
theme in the next section of the chapter.

Variation between localities

In this section, we look at our data in terms of the different localities in
which children resided. Here, it should be remembered that we selected our
localities carefully, according to criteria of predominant social class, urban-
ity/rurality and Welsh-/English-speaking. All of these criteria are significant
in that they have implications for the kinds of environments children are
living in. Risk and safety generally preoccupy the children in all the localities. The presence or absence of crime is often referred to. Murders have

iconic importance and were mentioned in three of the schools; violence in general seems to be particularly troubling; rowdy drunken adults often feature in general talk about places and quality of life. There is an acute awareness of bad behaviour from other children (always *others*) – bullying in particular, but also vandalism.

The children's perception of their own locality was, of course, related to their experience and knowledge of elsewhere (as noted above). One question we asked was how a child would find a move from London to this area. Both rural and urban areas of Wales were positively contrasted with London as 'much quieter'. London was generally seen in fairly negative terms as easy to get lost in, having too many cars and too much crime. Similar comparisons were made by children in relation to more local places. This highlights the ways in which children make use of *boundaries* in expressing their sense of place: 'here' tended to be defined in relation to 'there'. In Maes Garw, for example, in the western valleys, the nearby town of Swansea was seen by Rowland as beset with social problems in comparison with his village:

Rowland: Some of them live on the street and some of them beg and some of them are a bit like drugged. Some of them are a bit mental, some of them are on the streets.
Phillip: Some of them are tidy [decent].
Rowland: Most of them are tidy walking along but some of them are psychopaths.

(Year 6 focus group, Ysgol Maes Garw)

Similarly, Mandy said of the same regional comparison that 'schools up here haven't got no bullies and no nasty people or like drugs'. This brings us to the rural–urban dimension of the dataset. As Vanderbeck and Dunkley (2003) note from their US research, the rural–urban divide is important to a process of 'othering' through which children construct their sense of self and this can be a complex process, with children associating themselves with certain narratives and distancing themselves from others.

Four of our schools could be categorised as being more rural than the others. Maes Garw is a village in the mainly rural western valleys. Bryn Tawel (Ysgol y Porth) and Llwynirfon are both small towns in rural areas with sparse populations. Ffynnon Las (Ysgol y Waun) is a small town in a fairly rural area but is not far from the metropolitan area of greater Merseyside (north-west of England). The two schools that could be termed 'urban' are Highfields in inner-city Cardiff and Petersfield which is in a large town in the eastern valleys. Whilst, as noted above, there was a tendency for children in most of the schools to speak of their local community as being divided between the nice and the nasty, there was a fairly marked tendency for children in the more rural schools to describe their locality in more positive terms than did children in the two more urban schools. So, for example, in contrast with the sometimes graphic crime stories of children in the urban schools, the only problem with people in Ffynnon Las that Bryony could cite was to do with traffic etiquette: 'Some are a bit ignorant – they don't let go in the car. When they're like coming your way, there's no point in just going (.) they should let you out, but they don't' (Year 4 focus group, Ysgol y Waun).

Llwynirfon in particular was generally described in fairly idyllic terms. Children repeatedly talked of there being less crime, few cars, more space to play and better mobility for children than in busier places. There was a clear sense of comparison with elsewhere. This suggests that even if the children themselves have little experience of other places, the comparisons they make (positive ones in the case of Llwynirfon) show they clearly do have some knowledge of elsewhere, whether this knowledge is gained from school, media or families. These same issues – crime, play space, cars and the related freedom to roam – surfaced in other rural schools, though with less unwaveringly positive framing than in Llwynirfon. Mobility is beginning to emerge as important in middle childhood, with these children starting to become more independent (Borland et al. 1998, Matthews et al. 2000):

> There's two places I can go by myself – the park and the um (.) shop. My mum might think it's dangerous for me to go and walk down the park in Australia.
>
> (Interview with Nigel, Year 5, Ysgol y Porth)

Jasmin: Because . . . like in London, you are not, you can't go down town or anything so you have to go in the car with your mum. I don't like doing that.

Andrew: Right, you like to walk.

Jasmin: I like to walk, yeah.

David: I like to go on my scooter and stuff.

John: On my bike sometimes, on my roller-blades and skateboard and stuff.

(Year 4 focus group, Llwynirfon School)

Some recent research on rural youth has challenged the idea of a rural idyll (Glendinning et al. 2003, Matthews et al. 2000). However, it is interesting to note that Glendinning et al. found rural life to be a more positive experience for the younger age group they surveyed (eleven- to sixteen-year-olds) than for the older teenagers (fifteen- to eighteen-year-olds). Llwynirfon in particular (though also the other rural areas to a lesser extent) is presented by our research participants as a positive environment for middle childhood, sometimes with a conscious awareness that people at different stages of the life course might have a different view. So, although Molly says her mother cannot get to work because of the town's isolation, Molly herself is positive about its benefits: 'Even though it is small it's got lots of clubs and everything'. There were a couple of comments that perhaps prefigured the disenchantment the studies cited above found from older children who were disappointed at the lack of consumption opportunities: Jenny, for example, said the town was 'quite boring at the weekends'.

Of course, we cannot make sweeping generalisations about rural and urban life from our highly selective sample. As Valentine (1997) notes with reference to parental discourses of rurality, places have multiple meanings and identities. More intensive data collection in these more rural communities would no doubt have revealed tensions that our interviews and focus groups did not uncover. In fact, social class was arguably more strongly associated with concerns about crime than the urbanity of the district. Even in Llwynirfon there were divisions within the town. Jenny spoke in negative terms of an area called 'Maesdu', where 'lots of naughty children live [. . .] like Gary Brookes, who is in our class'. This tendency to divide local people into the nice and the nasty rests upon a clear demarcation between the more affluent and the less affluent areas of the locality and needs to be understood accordingly in terms of social class differences. This strikes us as a significant issue audible in most children's talk on their locality.

Petersfield School has one of the highest proportions in Wales of children living in families on benefits. It is situated on the edge of a very deprived council estate. In Petersfield, above all, we could see that concern about crime had a serious impact on how the children identified with their locality. Their concerns echo what Reay (2000) and Morrow (2001) found in their research with children. As noted in Chapter 1 of this book, Reay's study shows how working-class children's confidence in and freedom to move around and about their local area is considerably more restricted than their middle-class peers. Like Reay, we found that children from the more working-class schools used more local reference points than the children in the other schools. Most often, they told us they liked where they lived but did wish that it was a 'nicer place'. They typically described their home area as generally 'rough', but then distinguished between the respectability of people in particular streets, as in the following excerpts:

David: It is quite a rough place. It is quite poor so you have rough places
            as well so you know not to go there.
Andrew: Yeah?
David: Like Y Fan and Telford Close.
                                    (Interview with David, Year 6, Petersfield School)

> In some of the streets the children are really naughty but in some other
> streets of Petersfield, they are really good and kind, and make friends.
>   (Interview with Joanna, Year 6, Petersfield School)

Of all the schools, this tendency to differentiate between different streets within the local community was most marked in Petersfield. Mention was made in each of the schools in our study of specific problem areas in the locality. These were usually designated by the children as being outside their own home areas, but the exception to this was the Petersfield estate. Here the children were clear about which particular streets on the estate were respectable and which were not. Notions of respectability can be seen as central to working-class identities and to middle-class ascriptions of working-class identity (Skeggs 1997). A process of marking boundaries of respectability – usually connected to concerns about risk and safety – was common to all schools. In Petersfield, however, these boundaries were within the children's own community rather than between their bounded community and unrespectable 'outsiders'. Despite the boundaries being internal to the community, however, the Petersfield children distanced themselves from the 'bad' areas and 'nasty' people. They saw themselves as the respectable and well-behaved ones. Reay notes the same kind of process in her research on a deprived London housing estate. The children in her study constructed 'divisions between themselves and pathological others' as a strategy for 'fighting free of negative emplacement' (2000: 157). The working-class children in our study also clearly distinguished themselves from the 'nasty,' 'naughty' or 'rough' others in their community. As Reay observes, this indicates that these locally entrenched narratives about the rough/respectable places possess considerable power – power to make children feel personally and psychologically vulnerable to being tainted by them and, hence, at pains to distance themselves from them.

Again, this points to the salience of social space in the construction of identity, in that space is always classed (as well as gendered and racialised). Who 'I' am and who I am not are constructs mapped onto those of where I can go and where I cannot. This mirrors research by Southerton (2001) on adults and social class living in an English new town, showing that even amongst groups of people living in the same locality with few conspicuous social differences, marked narratives of the 'other' using the language of class were in evidence (largely expressed through distinctions of taste, money and morals). This enables different classed groups to articulate their sense of who they are by reference to who in the locality they are not. These differences are mapped onto spatial distinctions between clearly labelled local areas with distinctive reputations. Although children's facility with this language is relatively undeveloped in comparison to adults', the same class-loaded discourses are clearly making their presence felt.

We can see here that cultural discourses (in this case, received ideas about the reputations of particular streets in the locality) operate through the particular social networks that individuals traverse in their daily lives (in this case, those that restrict the children's mobility to the local area). Cultural discourses are expereinced and made meaningful through individuals' ordinary lives lived in local physical environments. This echoes Raymond Williams's (1961) arguments about the interdependence of cultural representations and actual human experience. The children's social networks are no doubt suffused with the discourse of respectability and unrespectability, so that children and adults they encounter on the estate are categorised accordingly.

The domestic

To sum up our arguments so far, whilst immediate localities are most vivid to children and are perhaps more meaningful than most other spatial domains in terms of their everyday experience, the children's talk about where they live does not deploy a language of clear cultural place-distinctions. Places themselves as identifiable geo-cultural entities do not figure in children's discourse. In other words, they have little recourse to a language of the objective qualities of place. For them, places are equatable with their own everyday subjective experiences, which necessarily turn on the people they know both directly and by reputation: they are no more and no less than that. Nevertheless, we have also been at pains to point out that this subjective experience is not by any means devoid of the imprint of culture. To the contrary, children are clearly drawing on the culturally given categories of class-based distinctions in their descriptions of the local areas. They know which are the rough places and which are the respectable ones, and they categorise people – including classmates – accordingly. Hence, we can see children utilising a language of class distinctions that is inevitably stigmatising in the sense that it depends on and reproduces relations of social inequality.

This brings us to the question of home and family. Many of the children discussed their attachment to place in relation to other attachments, especially family relationships. Here too, the children were keenly aware of divisions between people (especially marital separations) and of their own often uneasy location in respect of them. Following the second round of card-sorting in the focus groups, the children were invited freely to choose a person or thing that was important to them. Very many of the children chose family members and subsequently spoke about the importance of their families. Morrow's study of children's and young people's perspectives on networks and neighbourhoods (in an ethnically diverse town in the south-east of England), found that 'a number of elements of social life appeared to be sources of a sense of belonging, but home and family were the primary ones' (Morrow 2001: 19). Given the centrality of the family in middle childhood (Borland et al. 1998, Brannen et al. 2000, Smart et al. 2001), for these children their 'place' is above all their family home. As Bahira put it, 'the only important thing is my house'. In one of the focus-group card-sorting exercises, where the idea of a hybrid choice caught on (there was some conferring), the children's choices included 'teulu a'r byd' (family and the world), 'teulu a bwyd' (family and food) and 'teulu a'r ty' (family and house). Another child wrote 'Friday' on their choice card in the second round – 'oherwydd rwy'n mynd gyda dadi' (because I go with Daddy).

We were struck by the children's willingness to speak openly both in focus groups and in interviews about feeling upset by parental separation. A vivid illustration of the intersection of people and place was provided when children with separated parents spoke about a more complicated identification with place because their time was spent with different parents in different locations:

> Rwy'n hoffi byw yn dau ty oherwydd mae Mami gyda boyfriend a nawr mae Dad gyda girlfriend.

> [I like living in two houses because my mum has got a boyfriend and now my dad's got a girlfriend.]
> (Nerys, Year 4 focus group, Ysgol Maesgarw)

> *Andrew*: So what about these then, did anybody find it difficult to choose one?
> *Clive*: Um, it was bit for me because my mum and dad are split up but I still go and see him every weekend and his home town is in Newtown.
> *Andrew*: Right.
> *Clive*: And I was just trying to take him into account as well because they are split up. I miss him.
> (Year 5 focus group, Llwynirfon School)

For these children, the family is not a unitary location, but another divided one. Clive, above, feels the need to consider his father when thinking about place identity. There is more than one place for him to identify with. He has a dual loyalty and dual place-identification. Another child, in the excerpt below, overtly linked her family with her national identity when she told us she did not approve of her father's view of her locality.

> My dad, because we live up there and they lives in Swansea he makes fun of us and says we're up with the sheep, and makes jokes about us. And he says we're, like, sheep speak Welsh and that, but I don't see my other dad much because he always makes fun of us up here.
> (Interview with Mandy, Year 4, Ysgol Maesgarw)

Here, the description of what Mandy's dad thinks of her locality is framed in terms of two divisions: 'us' up here (the people she lives with) versus 'them' in Swansea, as well as Welshness versus non-Welshness. We see here the intersection of domestic, local and national spatial domains. The division in the family is framed through the symbolic division in stereotypical national imagery (being/not being like sheep and speaking/not speaking Welsh), making her recognise that her family 'up here' is being categorised by her absent father as a cultural other. This is one of the few occasions when children mentioned specific stereotypes about national identity. Mandy raises this stereotype in order to reject it. This example highlights the ready availability of national imagery as a language for *adults* to use in characterising their own fractured family relations. It also shows a child assigning her father to an other category, via his use of national (or more accurately regional) stereotypes. For the most part, however, children saw their parents as being the same as them:

Andrew: Okay, what if I asked your parents the same thing? Do you think they'd choose the same card as you?
Jenny: Yeah.
Andrew: Yeah, yours would, would they? Why would they choose that one?
Jenny: Because, um, they're like the same people really.

(Year 6 focus group, Llwynirfon School)

Discussion

As promised, because this and the previous chapter constitute an analytic pair, the following discussion will make reference to both chapters. We consider in what follows both the question of which dimensions of space and place seem to be most significant to the children and also the implications of how the children do or do not identify with place. An important question arises as to how much of our findings are explained by the social (or developmental) location of middle childhood itself, and how much by what we know of adult forms of place-identifications. To what extent can the place of middle childhood help explain how children in middle childhood understand place? We cannot offer a comprehensive answer to this, as our study was small in scope and based in one country. What we can do instead is to present an analysis that tries to do justice to the various dimensions and levels through which children experience the concepts of place we are exploring. Our analysis acknowledges that the social networks in which children are located are frequently circumscribed by age-specific factors, although we do not directly engage with theories of cognitive development.

At various points over this and the previous chapter we have noted that the children do not tend to use categories of place-identification that are culturally elaborated. They seem instead to be utilising a classificatory system based on binary oppositions that divide up people along an axis of risk or threat: the known and the unknown; the nice and the nasty; friends and non-friends. Rather than seeing themselves as rooted in places, they are rooted in networks of people and particularly their families and friends. Local divisions are between nice and nasty people and this categorisation is linked to considerations of safety and risk which are in turn connected to social class divisions and considerations of respectability. National divisions are made primarily according to language and accent (class is sometimes employed here too – see the next chapter on Englishness). When countries are compared on a global level, the dominant discourse is of a world full of people 'just like us'. Some caution is needed in interpreting our data, since we did not explicitly ask the children their views of countries which might be thought to be more obviously culturally distinct from Wales, such as any in the East or the global South. We did, however, ask them about Europe and the main differences perceived here were differences that were rather 'thin' or 'flat' such as language and types of food. The one exception to other countries being 'just like us' was Germany. We suggest that the boundary that is most vivid to the children is the local one between people who are 'nice' and those who are 'nasty'.

Our overall conclusion about the significance of place to the children is that there appear to be few overt place-identifiers in their talk, and we found no evidence of this varying according to class, region or urbanity/ rurality. The children seem to identify with people, as nice/nasty, known/ unknown and so on, rather than identifying with places that have cultural content – which they can represent linguistically through fleshed-out cultural descriptors. Instead, children relate to places primarily through the drawing of boundaries – not ones that they themselves make up, but ones that are clearly derived from pre-given cultural distinctions such as those based on class. We would argue that this stops short of being an elaborated categorisation of place, however. What the children speak of is places having reputations that are constructed within social distinctions made evident through local social networks, so that niceness and nastiness are mapped onto the local environment. To appreciate elaborated categorisations of place we might suggest that you require knowledge of other places that most of these children do not have because of their youth and in some cases because of their localism. Either they have not had the opportunity to compare their locality with others, or at least they have not yet learned a language of cultural comparison. Perhaps, in a sense, the children do not know what they are missing elsewhere in terms of amenities, landscapes, institutional arrangements and so on. The children have more local social networks than adults, because of the localism of middle childhood and their as yet limited facility with the language of geo-cultural comparison.

Such a conclusion conflicts somewhat with studies of children and place by environmental psychologists and geographers who have argued that middle childhood is a time when, since the overriding influence of the family is beginning to lessen, the child's physical environment starts to loom large in his/her consciousness (Chawla 1992, Matthews 1992). Chawla (1992: 64) asserts that 'children are attached to a place when they show happiness at being in it and regret or distress at leaving it, and when they value it not only for the satisfaction of physical needs but for its intrinsic qualities' (quoted in Chatterjee 2005: 3). Although we saw plenty of evidence of children's strong attachments to place, we found little evidence of them recognising places' 'intrinsic qualities'. Our data suggest instead that their attachment is to people-in-place rather than to place itself. Indeed, our conception of place is that it is always necessarily *peopled*. That is, it is inevitably experienced by people through their social and interpersonal relations. There is a sizeable literature on sense of place that we cannot do justice to here. Nevertheless, it is clearly something that arises over time, and which depends to a considerable extent on the build-up of memories, feelings, values, images, and so forth that individuals accrue as they dwell in places (Proshansky et al. 1995). It is not controversial to point out that children will have developed fewer resources to draw upon of this kind, particularly in terms of long-established memories, than adults.

Yet this is not to say that locality is unimportant to children. Our data suggest that of the various dimensions of place we studied, the local realm (including the most local of all – the family home[s]) is clearly the most salient to them – psychologically, socially and culturally. Global influences in middle childhood, are also, however, significant in some senses. Children are increasingly important consumers, both in their own rights and by exerting influence with the family, and this consumption needs to be understood in terms of global influences because of the character of the market in children's goods. There is also an important dimension of 'imaginative travel' (Urry 2000) whereby children have, perhaps, more awareness of the wider world than in the past due to the increasingly global reach of the media. Some children in our sample have in fact had international holidays (although this is dependent on social class) and some have lived abroad. However, we would argue that the influence of the global dimension on children is also limited. In the general flow of talk about places, the children's sense of their immediate local environments is stronger than any global or national dimension. This is also the case for most adults because most of us spend most of our time in localities, but is especially true for children as their mobility is more limited than that of adults.

Urry (2000) has developed a sociology that moves beyond a focus on located societies and instead employs the concepts of flows, fluidities, networks and scapes. He provocatively argues that 'Thatcher was right when she said there was no such thing as society' (2000: 190). Whilst this bold reconfiguration of the sociological enterprise is highly relevant to the global economy in general, it does not so thoroughly take account of differences in age and generation. The extent to which our experience is more local or more global varies considerably according to age and the social organisation of age-bound opportunity. Urry (2000: 197) acknowledges that most people are not aware of the global dimension, but sees human activity as having a global impact:

> Most people most of the time act iteratively in terms of local information, knowing almost nothing about the global connections or implications of what they are doing. However, these local actions do not remain simply local since they are captured, represented, marketed, circulated and generalized elsewhere. They are carried along the scapes and flows of the emerging global world, transporting ideas, people, images, monies and technologies to potentially everywhere.

But children in middle childhood, though limited consumers, are not really producers in any adult sense. They certainly consume goods that are made on the other side of the world and marketed by global corporations. Some may occasionally participate in on-line interactions with children who live on the other side of the world, but their active contribution to global scapes and flows is limited. Instead, these flows are dominated by adults and their conceptions of what will appeal to children in marketing terms. Urry does not, of course, see globalisation as entailing homogenisation. In fact, he argues for the application of chaos theory and complexity theory to understanding global processes (Urry 2003). Others have observed that globalisation for some has meant localisation for others (see, for example, Bauman 1998). We would suggest that within the affluent West, those who are more localised include children in infancy and in early and middle childhood, because of their primary location being determined by adults.

Whilst it is true that children in middle childhood are likely to be more local in their outlook and approach than adults typically are because of limited mobility, we need to caution against seeing localism as necessarily narrow and backward, as we noted in Chapter 1. Being open to people from different social domains and open to alternatives to your own familiar local cultures does not necessarily require travel. It is, of course, possible to cover great distances and see many different places but remain resolutely local in outlook. As we noted earlier, a cosmopolitan disposition can be practised equally well at home or away (Hannerz 1990).

The children were open to the possibility of global mobility when we asked them about the projected future. We should not conclude too much from this one exercise. We cannot assume anything about actual mobility of course, but the children did show themselves to be familiar with certain other places, namely, high-status locations associated with leisure and conspicuous consumption. These places were most likely familiar because of routinised exposure to images of them in the media. This familiarity does not seem to be an engagement of self with other or some kind of reaching out to symbols of unfamiliar cultures, as the children seem to take for granted that other places are much like here and, in the children's own terms, the people in them are much the same. This finding reiterates the theme of place-as-people noted above. At base, places were equated in children's eyes with people, known and unknown, and their only real conceptions of people's differences turned on the divisions noted above (namely, the nice/nasty; friend/non-friend); further, these divisions were made manifest to the children by their own everyday concrete experiences. Taking all this into account, it follows that they had no reason to find much in the way of otherness when asked about countries they had never encountered. The categories of nice and nasty were not available to them in talking about these distant places; hence, people living in them were assumed to be just like the self. There was no suggestion, however, that the children were closed off to the possibility of 'otherness' or were defensive about their own national identities. This defensiveness is perhaps more likely to surface in places with a more recent history of conflict (see Connolly and Healy 2004, Spyrou 2002). There was, in fact, little sense of anywhere else at all, because the children saw other countries as much the same as home. That finding inevitably reverberates with our arguments that 'here' is not a fleshed-out, elaborated geo-cultural entity for the children either. We might observe the same phenomenon for many adults, although we would also remain open to the argument that a sense of place is likely to deepen as one develops into an adult and accrues the stock of memories and lived experiences that contribute to it.

In most parts of the world, children are expected to value the nation; this is even more the case in marginalised or recently devolved proto-nations such as Wales where there have been strenuous efforts on the part of the Government to promote the integrity of national identity. This is reflected in the stated identifications of many of the children in our sample who told us that being Welsh was important to them. As noted in Chapter 3, some psychological research in the developmental tradition suggests that at five and six years of age, children's gender, age and local identities tend to be more important to them than their national identity, but that national identity does typically increase in importance through middle childhood and may overtake age and local identity by eleven/twelve (Barrett et al. 2003). Whilst we do not wish to reject the insights of research on child development, findings from studies that overtly ask children about what the nation means to them (including aspects of our own qualitative research) may well be reflecting these powerful cultural expectations rather than delivering an accurate insight into the extent of children's actual commitments to nation. Such findings do not necessarily tell us about the ongoing and everyday importance of the nation to children's (and adults') identities.

We see the relative primacy of nation-level (as opposed to globe-level or local-level) representations in public, cultural discourse as important factors in explaining children's greater readiness to draw on national, as opposed to other place-based identity labels, when asked direct questions about what matters to them (for example in the card-sorting exercise). Their home localities in fact seemed to mean more to them than the nation, as we discuss further below, but they tended to make little use of a language of place-demarcation at the local level when collective identitifications were being discussed. Place-demarcation was, by contrast, made highly available for them in the case of the nation. This is particularly the case for Wales (where the underpinnings of Welsh identity represent a highly visible, and often contested, public cultural terrain), and also, we suggest, for children at this stage of childhood. Welshness is institutionally flagged on a daily basis in classrooms adorned with maps showing Wales in relation to the rest of Britain and Europe. National identity is particularly overt in Welsh-medium schools, where national linguistic identity is what marks the school as being distinctive within a predominantly anglophone environment (in two of the three Welsh-medium schools in our sample).

In middle childhood, children tend to become especially aware of the importance of sporting loyalty – it is expected of boys in particular. At this stage of the life course, sport is probably the most important resource for banal nationalism. In these contexts of schooling and sport, to mention just two aspects of the nationalising process, children know that they should feel loyalty to their nation. This is not uncontested, of course and, as we argued in Chapters 3 and 4, there is room for some (limited) agency in constructing a national identity. Some children will say that belonging to a nation or, more specifically, being one of the nationalities on offer to them, is not important to them. Children with choices to make because of diverse ethnic and national heritage, have to work out more actively how to express their relationship to Welshness or Britishness so that it becomes something they can reconcile with their familial identities and heritage. This indicates the extent of cultural pressure on children to express national loyalty – perhaps especially in school – something that has particularly difficult identity implications for those defined as marginal to mainstream culture. These children have to be far more careful what they say and circumspect in defining who they are, especially in front of their peers. Understanding the intertwining of these cultural norms with childen's own individual responses, family situations and biographies is a difficult project and one that our limited dataset could only begin to trace out.

Our study suggests that the children's conception of place is heavily mediated by notions of boundary. These boundaries are clear to the children when asked about the nation (they were sure, for example, who in their family was Welsh and who was not) and they were also clear to them when asked about locality (they had little trouble in specifying intra-locality zones and areas). This reflects arguments in geography about the importance of boundary to the whole idea of a sense of place (see Newman and Paasi 1998). However, the boundaries within the locality rather than the ones between nations were those that seemed to matter most to the children's conception of self-identity. There was more at stake psychologically and culturally for them in describing the zones that made up their immediate environments (for example, places where they should and shouldn't go, people whom they should or shouldn't associate with). We would argue that the national is, in fact, a less salient place identity in middle childhood than the local or the domestic. Although it does seem to represent a significant and certainly a well-rehearsed *boundary* for the children, we do not find much in their talk about the nation that defines it as a set of identifiable cultural attributes held to characterise a geographical territory (see also Carrington and Short [1995] on children's conceptions of Britishness). The nation emerges as a rather one-dimensional category, marked almost exclusively by reference to language and sport. There is little said about 'what people do' in, for example, Wales or 'how they look'. Perhaps this reflects the premises of the global network society as described by Castells (2003), a world in which, since overt markers of cultural difference are increasingly diluted or contested, it is language difference that becomes instead 'the refuge of identifiable meaning' (2003: 56). This heightened significance for language might be thought to apply to adults equally.

On the other hand, we have also noted that the media are replete with images of multiculturalism and cultural difference and that a general touristic discourse of geographically based differences pervades contemporary media representations of 'the world' (see Dicks 2003). It has also been widely noted that the specification of cultural difference in the context of the Muslim/non-Muslim divide is actually more starkly expressed now than ever before (Barber 1995). In this sense, it is more plausible to question why children reproduce so little of this language of sterotypes and differences in discussing places and nations. At least part of the explanation, we feel, must lie within age-related social factors. Children in middle childhood, by virtue of not being alive as long, have had less chance than adults to acquire a vocabulary of national identity which includes reference to visual images, literature, music, cultural stereotypes and so on. They are in fact surrounded by fairly elaborate, national imagery in school, in various aspects of the curriculum (most obviously history, geography, language and literature), as well as via classroom displays, songs and celebrations. However, when talking in the research context about national identities, they did not tend to make use of the categorisations provided by this material. Perhaps we can explain this in the context of the children's tendency to make sense of the world in relation to the self (what is like me/not like me). Whereas one can straightforwardly claim to speak a language or not, or to be born here or there, the relationship between more elaborated cultural content and the self is more abstract, more difficult to perceive. For the children we spoke to, at least, it seemed simply irrelevant to their sense of who they were.

The lack of culturally filled ideas of difference could also plausibly be connected to cognitive processes and to children's relatively underdeveloped abstract thinking at this age (however we understand that process of development). A more social and political understanding of development would emphasise the way the education system reflects the assumptions of cognitive developmental theory and is, therefore, geared towards the teaching and learning of more concrete thinking skills at this stage. The relative lack of reflexivity shown by the children we spoke to when compared with adults is perhaps not surprising since skills of critical thinking and questioning are generally reserved for education at the secondary level and above. Middle childhood is organised on the premise of defining children as concrete, relatively straightforward, and not to be troubled by existential thinking.

We have observed that at the level of locality, children also primarily conceive place through the construct of boundaries – in this case, boundaries between categories of people (especially class-based and moral ones). As in their descriptions of nation, there is little culturally elaborated language of place-identity. What there is, however, is an ability to describe quite a few salient features of their immediate landscapes, particularly in terms of the 'child's-eye view' of play spaces and hang-outs. These features could be anywhere in the sense that they do not serve to mark out the locality from elsewhere, but they are important in the sense that they attest to the children's strong attachments to the places they move in and their feelings for certain settings they can call their own. These vivid descriptions of locality from the children (generally more vivid than any talk of nation) are, again, not surprising. The local is more vivid for all of us at whatever age, because it is where we live out our daily lives, but this is especially so for children who are not as mobile as adults and are not economically active in any significant way. The places in which they move, both with adults and, to a lesser extent, independently, will be predominantly local ones.

There is diversity of local attachment amongst our sample of children according to their perception of quality of life. Children in the market town of Llwynirfon were markedly more positive about their locality than, for example, children on the deprived estate of Petersfield. This difference in quality of life is both imagined and real. On one level, children's categorisations of where 'bad' people live are simply reproducing the cultural stereotypes they have internalised, but this does not mean to say that there are no real differences between the two localities. Petersfield and Llwynirfon are indeed very different in socio-economic terms, and there are stark actual differences in recorded crime rates between these two districts. The children's constructions of quality of life in particular places do undoubtedly have some basis in actual socio-economic relations, not least in the fact that children living in poorer areas are more restricted in their mobility and, hence, perhaps more likely to perceive boundaries at the street rather than locality level (a hypothesis that has found some support in studies of child poverty – see Evans 2004). It is, rather, when they use morally loaded labels (such as 'nasty' or 'nice') to describe entire streets or estates that one can hear the language of cultural stereotyping and class-inflected discourse. (See Skeggs [2004] on the ways in which class discourse utilises a language of moral judgement; Southerton's study, too [2001] shows how people's expressions of class difference rely at least partly on evaluations of moral behaviour.)

We have noted several times already the fairly obvious point that the children's movement is restricted. Although few people move around with total freedom and independence, regardless of age, we have to acknowledge that mobility in middle childhood is limited in relation to adulthood. There are ambiguities here. Borland et al. (1998) note that at this stage of childhood parents typically allow more freedom of movement than they have for their children in early childhood. However, it is well known that in recent decades, independent movement for children at this age has decreased (see O'Brien et al. 2000). This has happened for a variety of reasons, including the increasing submergence of children's activities and identities within the family (Prout 2000), disproportionate concern about the possibility of sexual assault from strangers and much more rational concern about the increased volume and speed of traffic. Scott et al. (1998) have observed that a climate of risk anxiety has developed in relation to children in public spaces. It is not surprising then that much of the children's talk suggests the domestic arena to be the most significant spatial domain in their daily lives and also that family circumstances fundamentally affect place identity.

Prout (2000) argues, following Giddens, that there are tensions in high modernity between control and self-realisation. He sees children in contemporary Britain as subject to increasing regulation and their self-realisation as increasingly sequestered within the family, in an era of increased political preoccupation with parenting. In this context, we would expect children to identify with the family home as the place where they spend most time and which they are told is more important to them than anything else. The emphasis on the family reflects the particular position of children, though similar comments could be made about, for example, many parents of young children (and mothers in particular). The early and middle-childhood family is especially home-based, which inevitably affects place identity.

Conclusions

Chapters 4 and 5 have addressed the significance of various dimensions of place and space in middle childhood. The preceding discussion has highlighted some of the more important conclusions to be drawn. Despite the children tending to say when directly asked that national identity mattered to them and showing considerable facility in ascribing national labels to themselves and family members, we have to conclude that the overall picture is that locality is more vivid and meaningful to them. That said, there was little evidence of a culturally filled conception of place on either a global, national or local level. Attachments were more likely to be to known and significant others – people rather than places. Boundaries emerged as a key construct through which children could grasp the idea of place. Social class was an important factor that influenced the children's conception of locality, but there was little evidence, within the limits of our research design, of variation in social class affecting the children's sense of national identity.

Having presented a general overview of the significance of place to the children in our Welsh study, we now move on to some more specific aspects of place identity. The following two chapters deal first with inclusion and exclusion and then with language and accent. We begin in the next chapter by exploring the important issue of how the children categorised those who 'belonged' to the nation – who is in and who is out.

6   Insiders and outsiders

The preceding chapters have made it clear that when children talk about place they are engaged in the drawing of boundaries. This immediately brings up the question of belonging and who is an insider, who an outsider. As Newman and Paasi observe, 'boundaries, by definition, constitute lines of separation or contact [which] usually creates an "us" and an "Other" identity' (1998: 6). McCrone (1998: 116) identifies the same process in relation to the nation: '[n]ationalism has particularism built into it; hence every "us" has to have a "them" '. This 'othering' effect is deeply embedded in the construction of identities, since defining the self always involves specifying what the self is not. Accordingly, much of our preceding discussion in this book about children's boundary-drawing with regard to places and people is actually about the 'lines of separation or contact' that they draw between themselves and others. This chapter address national (and local) others, with particular reference to 'race' and the relation of minority-ethnic groups to national belonging. We are interested here in the aspects of children's accounts of Welshness that are either racialised or inclusive. In writing of racialisation, we refer to 'a dialectical process by which meaning is attributed to particular biological features of human beings' (Miles 1989: 76). In many ways, this whole book is concerned with ethnicity, if we define an ethnic group as one that shares ideas about common descent. In this chapter, however, we focus in particular on the aspects of the children's talk that highlight 'race' – that is, physical characteristics associated with ethnic groups – and explicitly refer to majority and minority racial and religious groups within Wales. Later in the chapter we also deal with how the children respond to constructs of Englishness.

Traditional approaches to children, 'race' and nation have emphasised development over time, either in terms of the cognitive and social development of children (from psychological perspectives see, for example, the review by Aboud and Amato [2001]) or socialisation (from social learning or sociological perspectives). More recently, some researchers have emphasised children's agency, their social aptitudes and sensibilities at an early age and the role of social interaction in the negotiation of 'race', in keeping with broader trends in the sociology of childhood (see, for example,

Connolly 1998 and Van Ausdale and Feagin 2002). This work has shown the interactions of even very young children to be highly racialised. The potential for identities in late modernity to be fluid, individualised and creative has been recognised in social-scientific writings for some time. Mac an Ghaill's research shows how minority-ethnic young people as well as adults can construct 'new syncretic versions of transculturally based identities' (Mac an Ghaill 1999: 148). As Song (2003) illustrates, there is an element of choice in contemporary ethnic identities, but this choice is also constrained and unequal in a racialised society. Williams (1999b) notes that there has been considerable research attention to metropolitan ethnicities, but that much less is known about the minority experience in largely white communities (although see subsequent papers by Connolly and Keenan [2002] and Scourfield et al. [2005]). Outside of its southern coastal cities, Wales is made up of very largely white communities. There is a very small minority-ethnic population across much of the country.

There has been some significant work done on various aspects of (adult) national identity in Wales (see, for example, the collection edited by Fevre and Thompson [1999]), but the position of ethnic minorities has not been to the fore in much of this work. There is simply not much available in the way of data on the minority-ethnic experience in Wales, although that is gradually improving (see the recent collection by Williams et al. [2003]). Although there has been considerable academic discussion of Welshness, Englishness and Britishness, there is a lack of data on people talking about Welshness that are analysed in terms of the racialisation of ethnic minorities (Day 2002). Our discussion is specifically about Wales and Welshness, although we also draw on the children's more general talk about 'race' where appropriate.

The chapter will discuss Welshness as racialised, children's views on being white and on being a minority and evidence of inclusivity amongst children. We then go on to consider the role of Englishness. We start with the various ways in which the children see the Welsh nation as racialised before moving on to consider the ways in which particular regions are seen as having a 'racial' character.

Racialised Welshness

As soon as the issue of nationality comes on the agenda there are questions to be asked about who can rightly claim it. In popular understandings of nationality, race is usually among the criteria for a rightful claim. It should also be acknowledged that there is nothing inevitable about the relationship between race and nation and that this is an area of political and academic debate, but the process of ascribing nationality can be seen as conceptually close to the process of ascribing race. As noted in Chapter 4, the children we spoke to tended to talk in terms of people having either full- or half-Welsh status. This is usually decided for them by place of birth or, more likely, by the nationality of their parents (with parents' nationality usually thought by the children to be about their place of birth), so for most of these children, having an English parent and a Welsh one means you are half Welsh and half English. In some conversations, such as the excerpt below, half-Welsh status is awarded on different grounds, but the commonest approach was recourse to parents' nationality. Some children with mixed heritage calculated this in a complex way and told us they were 'a quarter' of one nationality, for example. Ascribing this fractional- and full-Welsh status is conceptually close to racial categorisation, as we see here where Sian connects this concept with being 'half caste'.

Andrew: What does it mean then to be Welsh? You know, when somebody says what nationality, you say Welsh, what goes through your mind when you say that?
Aimee: You were born in Wales.
Andrew: Yeah, could somebody who wasn't born in Wales be Welsh?
Unidentified child: Yeah.
Aimee: Um . . . no.
Sian: They can be half Welsh.
Andrew: Yeah.
Sian: Yeah, they can be half. There is a girl in our class called Joanne she's half caste isn't she?

(Year 5 focus group, Petersfield School)

The legacy of Welshness being equated with Whiteness is vividly illustrated by eleven-year-old Dafydd, who would not want to be black since to him that would mean being English. Blackness is not only a challenge to whiteness here, but it is associated with a land beyond the border, so is doubly the other. England and Wales are both racialised.

Andrew: What about being white? Does that mean anything to you?
Dafydd: Means nothing that much. I'm glad I'm white because I don't want to be like a black person and 'cause I'd probably be an English person then.
Andrew: Yeah? Are there black Welsh people?
Dafydd: I don't know, I haven't seen any that much.

(Interview with Dafydd, Year 6, Ysgol Maes Garw)

We should not get too carried away with this one quotation. There are, in fact, competing notions of Welshness evident in our data, as will be seen as the chapter progresses. There is the question of how the interviewer frames the exchange in terms of 'whiteness'. This term conjures up its opposite to Dafydd, and in using the word 'black' he might well be thinking of African-Caribbean imagery, associated in media stereotypes quite strongly with English inner cities. Had the exchange deployed more precise ethnic labels such as 'Pakistani' or 'Bangladeshi' or 'Chinese' the topic might have been less polarised.

One quite clearly racialised aspect of children's experience in Wales is education. It is nothing unusual in the UK for schools to be segregated according to ethnicity (Tomlinson 1997). Even the ethnically diverse school we studied in Cardiff, around half of whose pupils come from minority-ethnic backgrounds, seems to be chosen by some parents (and not only white parents) in preference for the very largely Asian primary school nearby. One difference between Wales and the rest of the UK is the existence of Welsh-medium education. Welsh-medium schools are generally much whiter than English-medium schools in ethnically diverse areas of Wales (although we should also note that some English-medium schools in these areas are almost totally white). Given the historical population base of the Welsh language, this is to a degree unsurprising and unavoidable in respect of first-language Welsh-speakers. However, in eastern counties of Wales in particular, Welsh-medium schools are largely made up of children who speak only English at home, so in theory these schools could be well used by minority-ethnic families, though in practice they are not.

There is some evidence in our sample of minority-ethnic children feeling excluded from and hostile to the epithet 'Welsh'. Bahira (who describes herself as a British Muslim) says, in the excerpt below, that she would not want to go to a Welsh-medium school because of the lack of minority-ethnic children, meaning potential racism:

> Because they [children in Welsh school] might be racists or something, I don't know and I don't like Welsh. I hate Welsh [. . .] Yeah, because there is probably not one person who is Muslim there because not many Muslims are fluent in Welsh, like.
>
> (Interview with Bahira, Year 6, Highfields School)

Bahira has clearly identified the term 'Welsh' with a racist or anti-Muslim position. To put this in context, this same child was also concerned about people being 'more racist' in England and in London specifically than in Cardiff, with London being more racist because it is 'busier'. She observes that not many Muslims are fluent in Welsh, which is true enough. It is not surprising that Muslims who have moved to Wales within the past century are unlikely to speak fluent Welsh. Although some Muslim migration to Wales – particularly by Somalis and Yemenis – dates back to the early twentieth century, much has also been more recent. Cardiff, where most of these Muslims settled, has had a relatively low proportion of Welsh-speakers ever since its population rapidly expanded in the nineteenth century (Thomas 1998), although in recent decades it has acquired relatively large absolute numbers of Welsh-speakers, many of whom are members of the new Welsh-speaking 'bourgeoisie' (Aitchison and Carter 1999).

However, language use in minority-ethnic communities is always likely to be underscored by racialised discourses of the nation, and this is certainly the case with regard to Welshness and belonging (see Williams 1995, 1999a, 1999b). So, as Williams observes, the cultural nationalist ideology of the *gwerin*, meaning the (Welsh-speaking and rural) Welsh people (or folk) serves to exclude migrants who are not Welsh speakers from notions of 'true' Welshness: ' "gwerin" is essentially an appeal to a notion of cultural homogeneity and embodies a vision of culture and identity which is essentialist, static and based on ethnic absolutism' (Williams 1999a: 78).

And Wales is also racialised in situations where people are not aware of consciously racialised ideologies. Living in a very largely white community leads children to imagine their community as homogenous in terms of ethnicity. Although there has, in fact, been considerable migration in and out of Wales for centuries (Jenkins 1997), and even areas generally seen nowadays as having culturally homogenous populations such as the south Wales valleys have diverse ethnic histories (Scourfield et al. 2005), little of this inward migration, unlike England, has been from Britain's former colonies and large parts of Wales are indeed almost exclusively white. Hence, they have come to be discursively constructed as such, with this whiteness also having particular overtones of social class. Bonnett (2000) has described the process by which in late nineteenth-century Britain, whiteness became 'a popularist identity connoting superiority but also ordinariness, nation and community' (2000: 30).

The whiteness of Welsh-medium schools is reflected by Chloe in the following excerpt. Even though she lives in a part of Wales (the western valleys) that has a 98–9 per cent white population, so there would be very few minority-ethnic children in any schools, she is nonetheless aware that English-medium schools are 'blacker' than Welsh-medium schools.

Andrew:　Pa fath o blant sy'n mynd i ysgolion fel 'na?
Chloe:　Plant sydd ddim yn siarad Cymraeg.
Andrew:　Ie. Ydyn nhw'n wahanol i plant fan hyn neu ydyn nhw'r un peth?
Chloe:　Yr un peth.
Andrew:　Oes unrhyw beth yn wahanol amdanyn nhw?
Chloe:　Mae nhw'n gallu bod yn (.) plant du.
Andrew:　Oes 'na blant du sy'n dod i ysgolion Gymraeg?
Chloe:　Na.

[*Andrew*:　What type of children go to schools like that? [English medium schools]
Chloe:　Children who don't speak Welsh.
Andrew:　Yeah. Are they different from children here or are they the same?
Chloe:　The same.
Andrew:　Is there anything different about them?
Chloe:　They could be black children.

Andrew:　Are there black children that go to Welsh [-medium] schools?
Chloe:　　No.]

　　　　　　　　　　　　(Interview with Chloe, Year 5, Ysgol Maes Garw)

This extract indicates quite unambiguously the correlation in Chloe's mind between Welsh-medium schools and a uniformly white identity.

It was noted in Chapter 4 that there was very frequent collapsing of language ability and national identity across the whole sample of children: being Welsh and speaking Welsh, being English and speaking English. In terms of Billig's banal nationalism, the collapsing of language and nation occurs on an everyday level when children refer to Welsh-medium schools as 'Welsh schools' and English-medium schools as 'English schools'. This collapsing of language and identity does of course have 'racial' implications, when minority-ethnic Welsh people are less likely to be Welsh speakers. Hierarchies of Welshness according to language ability are highly problematic in relation to any attempts to develop an inclusive and multicultural Welsh citizenship.

An interesting example of a hierarchy of belonging was seen in a focus group in Highfields School, where Cerys, who described herself as 'mixed race' and also as 'African' rejected the 'Welsh' card in the first stage of the card-sorting exercise, to be corrected by Wasim, who said 'Yes you are', on the basis of her having a conspicuously 'Welsh-sounding' name. She was not swayed by Wasim, but in fact distanced herself from her name by saying 'My father gave it to me'. Here, a black child was seen by another in the class as able to claim a Welsh identity on the basis of a culturally authentic name (as opposed to an English-sounding or black-sounding name). In a similar vein, Melissa, a white child, who consistently struck an inclusive note in discussions on nationality (see 'inclusive Wales' below) justified black people's claim to Welshness at one point with reference to Welsh-speaking.

> I visit Ponty a lot on a shopping day or something on Saturday after dancing, so I go there then and there's not much of a mixture, like black people and white people. I mostly see white people so I don't think that that's fair. So I don't like it and I want black people to live there because some speak Welsh like and then like I like having a conversation in Welsh I do. I think it is really good like.
>
> 　　　　　　　　　　(Interview with Melissa, Year 6, Petersfield School)

This is an example of a child who is exercising some degree of agency in defining Welsh identity against the dominant grain.

Whilst we did not specifically ask questions about the children's view of Welsh history, there were a couple of incidental references to the Celts from children in Welsh-medium schools. These are, in effect, references to the racial history of Wales. In one case, this is used to differentiate Wales from England, and in another it is used to invoke common origins with France. In the first excerpt, the children refer to the Celts predating the Romans in the British Isles and thus Wales predating England as a 'nation'. This is an interesting projection of the notion of nationhood onto what we might call a 'pre-national' historical context. History is, of course, often used by nationalist movements in this way. These excerpts illustrate the caution that is needed in the teaching of such history as children can potentially take away ideas about essentialist racial origins. This is not, of course, the sole responsibility of teachers – such discourses are also found in simplistic media portrayals of Wales.

Leanne: Mae Cymru'n mwy o gwlad na fel Lloegr.
Andrew: Siwd 'ny, 'te?
Rachel: Dwi'n meddwl mae ganddo fo hanesion mwy achos mae ganddo
           nhw y Rhufeiniaid a mae ganddo ni y Celtiaid.

[*Leanne*:   Wales is more of a country than like England.
Andrew: How's that then?
Rachel: I think it's got more history because they've got the Romans and
           we've got the Celts.]

                            (Year 6 focus group, Ysgol y Waun)

Andrew: Beth mae pobl fel yn Ffrainc?
Llinos: Siarad Ffrangeg, siarad Saesneg ac—
Andrew: Beth byddan nhw'n meddwl am bobl o Gymru?
Llinos: Maen nhw'n debyg i ni achos maen nhw'n Celtiaid.
[*Andrew*:   What are people like in France?
Llinos: Speak French, speak English and—
Andrew: What would they think about people from Wales?
Llinos: They're similar because they're Celts.]
               (Interview with Llinos, Year 6, Ysgol y Porth)

These two excerpts were the only instances of children utilising history as a distinguishing cultural feature in Welsh identity. As the previous chapters observed, Welsh identity was mostly seen in the culturally 'thin' terms of sporting and language differences alone. This is backed up by Howard and Gill's (2001) research with indigenous and minority-ethnic Australian chidren who displayed little sense of being part of a national cultural entity.

Regional racial Wales

Skin colour is used as a marker of regional difference within Wales by some children. Interestingly, it is used as a marker of difference even where the children's knowledge of different areas is not good. So two children thought that when travelling towards the middle of Wales from where they lived (one in the north and one in the south), you would start to see black people. This is not particularly true, as the minority-ethnic population of mid-Wales is in fact very small and dispersed. What is interesting is that these two boys thought of skin colour when trying to imagine what could distinguish people in different parts of Wales. One of the boys quoted below, Joseph, said the same about travelling to London and to France. In a similar way, and much more frequently than reference to skin colour, children mentioned language and accent as markers of difference, even where their geographical know-ledge in this respect was vague or inaccurate.

Nathan: Some people would talk different and some people might be coloured or things like that.
Andrew: Where would that start to happen then, do you think?
Nathan: Somewhere round there.
Andrew: Somewhere round the middle [of Wales], yeah? OK.
                              (Interview with Nathan, Year 4, Ysgol y Waun)

Andrew: If you're going up this way then, OK there's Ammanford and Llandeilo and all the way up here into the middle of Wales. OK, where do you think people would start speaking different to you? Start moving this way.
Joseph: Might go, some people could be black.
                              (Interview with Joseph, Year 4, Ysgol Maes Garw)

Black identity seems to creep in here simply through an invitation to imagine otherness. Of the limited markers of otherness the children are familiar with (as our data show), skin colour is likely to be one of the few that comes readily to mind, through the general prevalence of racialised discourse (per-haps made more potent by the fact that the speakers both live in areas that are almost exclusively white).

Some children also racialised their own areas – this part of Wales is white. When asked what he thought about the 'white' card, Llyr, from Bryntawel in north-west Wales replied 'Wel, dyna be 'di lliw ni rownd fan'ma' (Well, that's what our colour is round here). Haf, from the same school, thought she was happy to be white, 'oherwydd lliw yna 'dwi, a mae 'na lot o bobl o Bryntawel yn gwyn' (because that's the colour I am, and there's a lot of people from Bryntawel are white). Maes Garw in the western valleys was also seen by the children as very white, to the extent that Rowland felt he needed to point out in a focus group when various minority identities were mentioned that 'Chinese people live down here in the Chinese shop'. These people were worthy of mention precisely because they were thought to be so unusual. That Chinese people are only to be found in the 'Chinese shop' would strike many living in more multi-ethnic parts of the UK as extraordinary. Llanhywel in the eastern valleys was also seen as a white place. People in *EastEnders* are different from people in Llanhywel because they have a 'different colour skin', we were told in a focus group. Cardiff, on the other hand, the nearest city, was seen as multicultural by children in Llanhywel. Melissa embraces this, and Jason sounds more wary, not thinking the Muslims in Cardiff are really part of *his* country.

> I do like living in Llanhywel. Llanhywel is a bit [*recording unclear*] but um, they are a bit the same. I have walked round Cardiff and seen people speaking Welsh. There is black people there and white people as well. There is a mixture. That is what I like about it.
>
> (Interview with Melissa, Year 6, Petersfield School)

Andrew: Are people different in Cardiff than here do you think?
Jason: Maybe Muslims live in Cardiff. There would be loads of things, it would be all right.
Andrew: Yeah, are there Muslims in Llanhywel at all?
Jason: No. No way.
Andrew: No? What do you think people from Cardiff would think about people from Llanhywel, do you think that they would like them?
Jason: Yes if they have ever been down here.
Andrew: Do you think the Muslims in Cardiff would like to visit Llanhywel?
Jason: No. Don't know. They would go to their country.

(Interview with Jason, Year 4, Petersfield School)

Being white

At this point, it is worth saying something about what whiteness meant to the children. As previously mentioned, we included the label 'white' in our card-sorting exercise. Most children said it meant 'nothing much' to them to be white. Whiteness is taken for granted by these children, so they have not had to stop and think about what it might mean. Of those who were positive about being white, they had no reason to give beyond this being the dominant skin colour in their local area. Unsurprisingly, it was more difficult to own up to liking being white. As Rowland put it 'I didn't want to pick white because then that would be a racist comment'. In the following excerpt, several children initially say it is important to be white but this is challenged. Lindsay thinks it is important enough to challenge it that she switches to English (her first language). The children are all 'white', although Gianni describes himself more than once as 'brown' (he says his Italian father is 'very brown').

Andrew: O reit, OK. Beth am fod yn wyn 'te? Ydy hwnna'n bwysig i unrhyw un? [Oh right, OK. What about being white then? Is that important to anyone?]
Voices: Ydy. [Yes it is.]
Andrew: Ydy? [It is?.]

Lindsay:	Wel, dwi ddim, ddim lliw fi, wel. [Well I'm not, not my colour, well]
Gianni:	Dim bwys. [No importance.]
Caryl:	Dwi'n licio bod yn gwyn 'de ond ddim ond lliw yw gwyn. [I like being white but it's only colour, white.]
Lindsay:	Achos . . . [Because . . .] Can I say in—?
Andrew:	Yeah, go on – say it in English.
Lindsay:	The colour doesn't matter – it's just what's inside that counts.
Gianni:	I'm a bit brown as well in me because my (.) I could have been a brown child.
Andrew:	So this . . . this isn't really – is it important or isn't it?
Gianni:	Not really.

(Year 4 focus group, Ysgol y Porth)

There are also instances of children saying they are glad they are white because black children have a difficult time due to racism. Jane told us it was important (but not very important) to be white because black people get treated badly.

Being a minority

The perspectives of the minority-ethnic children on identity were very interesting and have important implications for attempts in political and cultural life to construct an inclusive notion of Welshness. The number of minority-ethnic children was small (eleven) and all except one came from one school, Highfields in Cardiff, so caution is of course needed in drawing conclusions, but it was nonetheless revealing that not one of these children used the term 'Welsh' as an umbrella identity. One child, Wasim, mentioned the term 'Welsh' for himself but alongside other alternative identities, such as Muslim and Italian. The avoidance of Welsh as an umbrella term might reflect ideas about alternative nationalities – that you cannot be simultaneously Pakistani and Welsh for example. It cannot, it seems to us, be understood properly outside of the overwhelmingly 'white' identity associated with Welshness, as illustrated in the above sections. Interestingly, some were content to describe themselves as British (for example, 'British Muslim') and refer to 'their country' as Britain.

Table 6.1 opposite shows the identities that children in Highfields School chose in the card-sorting exercise. We have grouped the children in their focus groups to show any interactional dimension to their choices, how they may have influenced each other. We have identified the white children to facilitate comparison with the other children, who are from a variety of minority-ethnic backgrounds. We do not mean to suggest that the white children are a homogenous group. They were not, as there were children born and brought up in England as well as Wales and also a child with an Australian parent. It is worth repeating at this point the exercise that the

Table 6.1 Identity choices in Highfields School, Cardiff

	Edward (white)	Muhammad	Sion (white)	Nim	Bahira	Shamsa
Focus group 1						
first round of cards	Australian	Muslim	Welsh	Girl	British Muslim	Somali Muslim
second round of cards	Cardiff City FC	Muslim	Hockey Club	Religion	Religion	My country (Britain) and my family

	Stephen (white)	Satnaam	Nicola (white)	Julia (white)	Ashid	
Focus group 2						
first round of cards	From Blackmill (area of Cardiff)	Asian	From Birmingham	British	Black	
second round of cards	England football	Pet fish	Family, Mam and Dad	Clothes, hair and stuff	Muslim	

	Wasim	Zubaida	Sabirah	Danny (white)	Joe (white)	Cerys
Focus group 3						
first round of cards	from Cardiff	Muslim	Muslim	Welsh	Welsh	African
second round of cards	Playing wrestling with my sister	Pakistani	My family and grandparents	David Beckham	Welsh	My Dad

children were asked to complete. They were asked to keep only the one most important card from a batch that included various nationalities, sex, local identity, colour (white/black), religion and a choice card. Following this initial choice, they were then given back all cards and asked to add in something else (a free choice) that was important to them, such as a person, pet or hobby, and to choose between the entire set of cards which was the most important of all. As can be seen from Table 6.1, some children maintained their original choice in the second round but most changed between rounds. Some rethought their original choice and selected for the second vote something that was already available to them first time around.

We do not present this table in order to make grand claims from any comparison, bearing in mind the small numbers, purposive sample and the contingent nature of such identities. Nonetheless, it is interesting that only three children, all of whom were white, chose the 'Welsh' card. This card was the most popular first-round choice in the other five schools. In keeping with the tendency for contemporary ethnic identities to be hybrid and complex (Mac an Ghaill 1999), we can see relatively little commonality across the children's choices. Only minority-ethnic children chose religion as important. There is interesting material in the table concerning gender, with the boys tending to choose something sport-related in Round 2 and the girls more focused on the importance of family.

Despite the minority children's reluctance to claim Welshness, there were examples in every school of white children telling us that of course black people are included in Welshness (see the section 'Inclusive Wales' below); the scope of their stated conception of Welshness was inclusive. There is an interesting exchange in one of the Highfields focus groups where Nim (Cardiff-born, Chinese parents) and Edward (Cardiff-born to Scottish mother and Australian father) are in the process of considering inclusive Welshness and negotiating the criteria:

Andrew: No, right great. What about being Welsh, is that important to anyone?
Nim: Yes it is.
Child (identity unclear):   No.
Edward: I am not particularly Welsh.
Siôn: It is important. [*To Edward*] Where were you born?
Edward: Cardiff (.) I don't have any Welsh blood.
Siôn: Yeah you are 'cause you were born here.
Nim: Some people say I'm Welsh, some people I'm from Cardiff.
Andrew: What do you say you are?
Nim: I say I'm from Cardiff but at the same time I like to think I'm Welsh.

(Year 6 focus group, in Highfields School)

Nim seems to be aware of both inclusive and exclusive notions of Welshness. She shows that she can in theory be considered Welsh and is interested in applying this label to herself. Her tentative 'Some people say' and 'I like to think' make it clear she knows that this inclusive version of Welshness would also be contested by some.

Another interesting aspect of minority identities from our research was the contesting of whiteness by some children. It was noted above that Gianni, a child with an Italian father and white British mother, described himself more than once as 'brown' in the context of the labels 'white' and 'black' being available. Gemma, a girl with a slightly darker skin than the others, whose heritage we were not aware of but who was not thought of by school staff as a minority-ethnic child, also describes herself as brown with confidence. There are multiple discourses of 'race' evident here – a racialised comment from Gemma about black people, the assumption of whiteness as normal (I'm not any colour) and a universalist comment: it doesn't matter what colour you are.

Andrew:	What about being white and being black then?
Emma:	It doesn't matter.
Paula:	It doesn't matter what colour you are.
Gemma:	If you are black you have got more rhythm. But I'm not both, I'm just brown.
Paula:	And me.
Emma:	I'm not any colour.
Jack:	No you're not, you're white.
Gemma:	No I'm not, I'm brown.
Jack:	I'm white.
Gemma:	I'm brown, I'm definitely brown.

(Year 4 focus group, Petersfield School)

In this exchange, race is framed by the interviewer at the outset in terms of a polarity: black and white. Perhaps it is this that sets the tone for the girls to try and avoid identifying with either term. Only Jack makes a claim on whiteness but can't persuade the others to do likewise. Gemma declares an alternative identity – 'brown' – and sticks to it. This does indicate that when race is offered to these children in terms of a stark opposition, they are uncomfortable locating themselves within its terms. To an extent, one can hear a rejection here of simple racialised labels, perhaps because the children at this age are becoming conscious that the acceptability of such labelling is at issue.

Inclusive Wales

Despite the racialised discourses of Welsh identity that were outlined earlier in the chapter, there was also evidence in every school of children contesting these narrow definitions of the nation. This contestation does not take away from the exclusion felt by many black and minority-ethnic people in Wales, but it does suggest that there is hope for a more inclusive Welsh citizenship. This is not particularly a naïve universalism that the children are proclaiming either, as many of these comments are made in the context of observations about racism. There are examples of children spotting racism and rejecting it.

> My gran would say she's British. She's glad to be white. She's racist. I hate it when she says things like that.
> (Interview with Phillip, Year 6, Ysgol Maes Garw)

Joanna: Because some white people go out with black people or they are best friends and it's unfair to make fun of them, because you wouldn't like it if you was black and then say someone made fun of a black person they wouldn't like it if they were black and a white person made fun of them.

Melissa: Um, long ago, right, um, English and black people used to not go near each other because they used to fight each other. There is no point, because they are same whether they are black or white, they are the same inside.

Andrew: Yeah.

David: Like the Taliban they probably done that for a reason because they are black and they are proud of it and they don't like the white people.

Unidentified child: Yeah.

Sean: Black and white people still got the same blood.

Joanna: They still feel the same.

> (Year 6 focus group, Petersfield School)

Melissa's statement ('the same inside', that physical differences are irrelevant) is an attempt by her to reject racialised labels, though her distinction 'English'/'black' remains intact. David's comment is intriguing. His understanding is that the Taliban 'don't like white people' and, in the context of both Joanna and Melissa's saying that it is wrong to make judgements based on race, he has found a way of making sense of this dislike (they are 'proud' of being black) that allows him, too, to reject the 'anti-black' sentiment condemned by the girls. Children in Petersfield come across as especially aware of racism, with several comments about trying to understand the position of the Taliban. As noted earlier in the book, these focus groups took place during the Afghanistan war in late 2001, not long after 9/11, and it is likely that teachers had discussed this with children in the school. In no other school were sympathetic comments made about the Taliban. It may be that a special effort had been made in Petersfield as there had been organised racist activity in the area recently. It is a school in a virtually all-white area, as were all those we studied with the exception of the Cardiff school.

There were frequent comments of a generally universalising nature made by the children, even though comments suggest a case needs to be argued and blackness is (at least potentially) stigmatised.

Andrew: Beth am gwyn te, ydi o'n bwysig i fod yn wyn neu?
Several: Na.
Nerys: Does dim ots pa lliw wyt ti.

[*Andrew*:   What about white then, is it important to be white or?
Several: No.
Nerys: It doesn't matter what colour you are.]

(Year 4 focus group, in Ysgol Maes Garw)

No. They just the same person. They can be as nice as white people as well.

(Interview with Julia, Year 4, Highfields School)

Andrew: Okay, what about being black or white then, is that important or—?
General response: No, not really.
Sian: It depends on what's on the inside.

(Year 5 focus group, Petersfield School)

Again, Sian's comment makes use of a humanist 'what's inside counts' discourse to reject the terms 'black' and 'white'; in general, these responses – like the others above – suggest the children are consciously ducking away from the polarised racial labels presented to them.

There were also inclusive comments made by the children we spoke to about Wales specifically. Other studies have found similar inclusiveness in studies of children's views of the nation. Howard and Gill's (2001) qualitative research in Australia found that the children of minority-ethnic and indigenous backgrounds all celebrated the idea of Australia as being a multicultural mix (even though they displayed little in the way of cultural or historical knowledge abut the nation). Carrington and Short (1995), in surveying children about Britishness, reported the fairly optimistic finding that few children made racialised distinctions about belonging to the British nation. It was noted above that attempts were made by white children to include minority-ethnic children within their notion of Welshness even where the minority children themselves were reluctant to go along with this. A few comments were made about an inclusive Wales when we showed a video clip of the Welsh national anthem at a Wales versus France rugby international (to prompt discussion), as there were black players in the team that was lined up during the anthem.

Andrew: What did you think of that when you were watching it?
Melissa: I think we should be proud of where we live, and who we live with and your family, if we are black or not.

Joanna: They play for Wales and some of them are black.

(Year 6 focus group, Petersfield School)

It seems to be the case that many of the white children were aware of the potential for black and minority-ethnic people to be excluded or feel excluded from mainstream notions of Welshness. There was a feeling that at least in the virtually all-white schools we visited (such as Petersfield above) the children needed to argue the case for black people being 'Welsh too', rather than taking it as a given. Not unsurprisingly, it is difficult for them to see Wales as multicultural in environments that are so uniformly monocultural; nevertheless, they make efforts to do so. This was seen in the earlier excerpts where black people were co-opted into Welshness on the basis of having a 'Welsh-sounding' name or speaking the Welsh language. In Highfields School, where ethnic diversity was an everyday reality for the children, there was less evidence of them having to work hard to justify the notion of an inclusive Wales. The fact that the children seem aware that Wales is traditionally a white construct is perhaps evidence of the resilience of this version of the nation. The children are not naïve in proclaiming universality but are consciously contesting a version of Wales they know is at odds with the vision of inclusion promoted to them. In this sense, even an inclusive version of Wales is necessarily racialised in so far as the children are conscious of race and racism and are trying to reconcile their knowledge of what ought to be said with their knowledge of what often is said, perhaps by adults they know.

Englishness

Constructions of England and Englishness have to be of central importance to identifying and understanding what is meant by 'Welshness'. Englishness is arguably the most significant 'other' for Welsh identity, and Welshness could be seen as defined in relation to it. McIntosh et al. (2004: 53) suggest from research in Scotland that 'perhaps the English continue to be the central "Other" [. . .] which defines what it means to be Scottish' and we could speculate that a similar – though of course not identical – phenomenon might be identified within dominant constructions of Welsh identity. Not surprisingly, this relational definition of national identity has been noted outside the UK as well. To give just a couple of examples from research on children, Spyrou (2002: 259) notes with regard to his study of Greek Cypriot children that 'There are Greeks because there are Turks'. Jukarainen's (2003) research on the Finnish–Russian and Finnish–Swedish borders found that, 'In each of the borderlands cases studied, spatial identities – whether municipal, regional or of a smaller village – were almost systematically created *in relation to the different national Other*, neighbouring nation or bordering state' (Jukarainen, 2003: 220, italics in the original).

The boundary label of Britain/Britishness was not mentioned by many of the children, but the English–Wales boundary was frequently highlighted. It was clear that the children were very aware of the border with England and generally had a clearer sense of England than of Britain. There is an interesting contrast to be drawn here between Welsh and English children. Barrett (1996) found English children much more likely to describe their homeland as 'England' than 'Britain', which on the surface is a similar finding to ours. However, this English phenomenon is likely to be a collapsing of national categories, whereby Britain becomes England in routine referencing of nationality, rather than the children making a conscious decision to exclude Wales and Scotland. However, the children in our study were generally very aware of England being a different country rather than the term referring to an overarching Britishness, as illustrated in the following excerpts:

Andrew: Why did you choose that one ['Welsh' card] above the rest?
Jenny: Well I just like being Welsh. I don't want to be English or anything [*laughs*].
                              (Interview with Jenny, Year 6, Llwynirfon School)

I don't like being British because when I go over to Ireland to see my relatives they say 'oh, how's England this time of year?' and I say 'I don't live in England, I live in Wales'
                              (Year 6 focus group, Ysgol Maes Garw)

In general, the children tended to have little to say about any distinction between people within the UK. In so far as they did see differences, these were mainly those of accent and the ability to speak the Welsh language. So if any Welsh/English distinction was identified (references to Scotland and Ireland were rare) this was not usually expressed through what we would regard as culturally 'filled' categories, such as 'what they do' or 'who they are', but rather with reference to 'how they speak'. The boundary here is defined in communicational terms rather than in what we might call anthropological terms. This relates to our analysis in the previous chapter in which we observed that although the children were conscious of the nation in terms of boundaries, these boundaries did not demarcate cultural entities so much as linguistic and sporting differences. The latter, in particular, suggests that the differences were taking shape in the children's minds in terms of competition and rivalries. To some extent, the same could be said of the language issue, for electing to use the Welsh language can often also be about making a choice of allegiance (as we saw in Chapter 4, the Welsh-speaking children sometimes seemed to feel guilty about using English). However, the extent to which this awareness of boundaries and allegiances constitutes part of their 'identities' is open to question. Indeed, what we see is a thinner and more one-dimensional definition of national difference than the term 'identity' would, perhaps, merit. Indeed, when we asked if there was any difference between those attending Welsh-medium and English-medium schools, children from all schools tended to assert that children in both types of schooling were 'just the same'.

In national contexts where there is more at stake in negotiating national identity, perhaps because of recent conflict, research has found children to be hostile to any reference to the culture of the national other (see, for example, Spyrou [2002] on Cyprus). The children in the Welsh study were positive about Englishness, however, when it was not overtly marked as such. So, for example, they identified with television programmes that are clearly English in setting but perhaps project a less specific 'middle Britain' image, such as *Hollyoaks*, whose characters children in Petersfield thought they resembled. English popular culture has a great deal of power in these children's lives, because England is the much more populous nation and Englishness tends to dominate the London-based UK media. However, there were also more negative messages about England from the children when it explicitly cropped up in discussion. Although in general the children tended not to comment explicitly on social class – which is not to say that class was not central to their understandings of place identity (see Chapter 5) – the excerpts below show that for the children part of a discourse of distinction between Wales and England is to construct England and English people (from London in the second excerpt) as both better off, arrogant and privileged ('more posh') in comparison with Wales. Within the exception of the 'we have more history' comment from Rachel earlier in this chapter, this was the only culturally filled conception of national difference within the UK that our data revealed. It echoes McIntosh et al.'s (2004: 50–1) observation from a Scottish context that 'an English national identity is one which is very often understood as being quintessentially "middle class" '.

Siôn: I just hate England. They just think that they're posh heads or something. They just think, they think they're the best, they're the biggest country in the world.
Andrew: Did you say that your dad was from England?
Siôn: Yeah.
Andrew: How do you think he would feel about that?
Siôn: He wouldn't mind too much actually. I don't think he would. He has come to be more Welsh than he is English.
                          (Interview with Siôn, Year 6, Highfields School)

Mae o'n dipyn bach yn wahanol oherwydd . . . mae Llundain yn dipyn bach mwy posh. [It's a little bit different because . . . London's a little bit more posh.]
                          (Interview with Eleri, Year 4, Ysgol y Waun)

I'm not against Britain or anything but it's just like, in Wales, it's like we said on Tuesday, it's just England have got all the things like.
                          (Interview with Phillip, Year 6, Ysgol Maes Garw)

For Siôn this is personal, more personal, perhaps, than much of the children's talk about identities. He is distancing himself from the nationality of his parents. He is clearly backed up in this by his father and in fact may be taking a lead from his father. His language is strong; he hates England. The others offer less emotional responses.

There were no examples of Englishness being associated with criminality and deviance, although that clearly does feature in some constructions of English incomers in rural Welsh-speaking areas – the reverse of English people being seen as 'posh'. Jones (2002) noted young people in their early teens clearly associating deviant behaviour with 'rough' English youth in the rural Welsh towns she studied. This construction did not surface in our study. There were other examples of negativity. In our focus groups there were a couple of instances of children expressing disapproval or even shock about the possibility that others in the group might have chosen the 'English' identity card. In one of these groups a child with some English roots felt the need to make use of our offered secrecy in saying 'I chose between, something and something'. Here we maybe see an echo of the reluctance reported by Condor (2000) of English respondents to talk about the 'delicate topic' of Englishness in categorical terms. McIntosh et al. (2004: 45) note that in Scotland, English people face 'constant reminders of their *difference*'. We would suggest that this is also the case in many parts of Wales, though not all. Unlike Scotland, where only 8 per cent of the population is English-born, 20 per cent of Wales's population is made up of people born in England (statistics from the 2001 UK Census). Williams (2005) reminds us that there are more people in Wales who are English-born than there are Welsh-speakers. In some parts of Wales, such as middle-class districts of Cardiff, for example, it is routine to encounter people who identify themselves (and would be seen by others) as English, and this is not problematic – or even particularly noteworthy – for them in routine interaction. There was some negativity about England and Englishness to be found in our dataset, however. A few children said 'I hate the English' when discussing the 'English' identity card in interviews and focus groups. In the face of this, we noted in Chapter 3 that an example of children's going against the grain in 'doing' national identity is maintaining an English identity where they are aware this is not approved of. It is worth returning to this issue here. Joshua worried that someone might 'start a fight or something like that because of what I put in' during the focus-group exercise. When asked about this in a subsequent interview, he modified his concern:

Andrew: Do you think it is difficult being half English and half Welsh in Wales?

Joshua: Nothing exactly happens because I am half English and half Welsh.

Andrew: Yeah.

Joshua: But like if something did I would be quite sad about that.

Andrew: Yeah sure.
Joshua: Because it doesn't I can walk about and stuff.
(Interview with Joshua, Year, 5, Llwynirfon School)

So there is potential difficulty that Joshua anticipates, but in fact he gets away with his dual heritage and dual identity. Maintaining the duality seems important for him, and it is perhaps a source of pride. We could speculate that some ambivalence might surround the children's reactions to English identities. There is clearly an idea around that to be English is antithetical to being Welsh and, perhaps, that an English identity implies that you think you are better than others. However, Englishness is also culturally affirmed for the children, particularly in the media they consume. Their favourite television programmes have English settings and they support English football teams. Joshua is perhaps aware of some ambivalence. He worries that he might get into trouble for being half English but in fact finds that 'nothing exactly happens' and he can in fact 'walk about and stuff'.

Discussion

Although we have noted racialised and exclusive discourses of Welsh identity, we can also report evidence of children resisting racialised conceptions of national belonging and constructing broader, more inclusive alternatives. This is particularly noticeable where they are invited to respond to the polarised terms of 'black' and 'white', which they tend to sidestep or actively resist. Amongst the existing published research on children and ethnicity we can similarly find both pessimistic findings, such as explicit racism in very young children (Connolly 1998, Van Ausdale and Feagin 2002) and also more optimistic material on inclusivity (Carrington and Short 1995, Howard and Gill 2001). There are multiple and somewhat contradictory findings here, as Connolly (1997) notes in relation to research on racialisation.

What do the aspects of our research findings we have presented in this chapter tell us about how children negotiate ethnicity and national identity? As a corrective to what were perceived as passive models of socialisation and deficit models of childhood from traditional sociological approaches and from developmental psychology, there has been increasing emphasis in recent sociological studies on children's agency and sophistication and on the importance of their interaction with peers in helping to shape their identity choices and positions. Van Ausdale and Feagin, for example, emphasise these perspectives in their research on racism in children: 'In our analysis, young children are no less able than adults to interact and learn from interaction. Within the contexts of interaction they deliberate and decide on actions, often of a very sophisticated kind' (Van Ausdale and Feagin 2002: 19).

We were able to observe some interaction in the relatively artificial environment of focus groups, and we discussed the role of gendered interaction in the negotiation of national identities in Chapter 3, but we cannot claim to have much depth of insight into how children 'do' race in everyday interaction because of the relative brevity of our time with these children and the presence of a sanctioning adult (Van Ausdale and Feagin 2002). We can, however, make some further comment on the role of agency in the everyday construction of the nation, from the data we have presented in this chapter.

What we see in many of the data excerpts is the children again reproducing a limited range of received ideas about Wales and England. This is not necessarily because they are children, with less developed cognition or social awareness, but because all that most of us, of whatever age, have available to us is a limited repertoire, derived from the dominant discourses of the nation. Nevertheless, we have also made it clear in previous chapters that the children's classroom environments are replete with far more in the way of culturally defining material – particularly on nationality – than the children made use of in their interviews or focus groups. For them, the categories of nation (and, indeed, place, as the previous two chapters showed) were defined in terms of boundaries and allegiances, but not in terms of manifest cultural content. Nevertheless, the children are conscious of stereotypes and images and the pressures to conform to them. Some will go against the grain and demonstrate independent agency – for example where they maintain identities, such as Englishness, which are in some respects marginalised. They also demonstrate agency when they consciously dismiss racialised notions of nationality and proclaim instead a humanist discourse of 'everyone's the same inside'. This discourse is not outside of the mainstream, however, since it chimes with inclusive and multi-ethnic visions of Wales that are promoted on some classroom walls, in official discourse and in the media (to some degree). Yet the children are clearly conscious of negotiating perceived obstacles to this inclusive vision (perhaps in the form of racialised discourse heard in everyday contexts) when they make these proclamations. What is revealing is that when the children apply inclusiveness to Wales specifically (as opposed to more general comments about people being all the same inside), it tends to be framed within a traditional and exclusive discourse. So, for example, black people are Welsh too because some speak Welsh or play rugby for Wales, or a black child deserves the label 'Welsh' because she has a Welsh-sounding name. What they do not do is define Welshness itself *as* multicultural.

How active can children or adults be in relation to something that is out of their reach? The influence that ordinary people have over the public-discursive construction of the nation is very limited. Certainly, the ongoing reproduction of the nation works through human interaction, but all that most of us have to go on is available public discourse and representations. This may be slightly more open to critique for adult academic and cultural elites who are actively engaged in debating nationhood, but even for these people, dominant discourses of the nation have to be contended with – accepted, rejected or somehow negotiated. They cannot be bypassed. We would suggest that it is as legitimate to emphasise here the limitations on children's agency (and that of adults) in doing national identity as it is to emphasise their active role. What is more evident from our data is not how active these children are in negotiating Welshness, but how untouched they are by the (albeit limited) range of ideas about national belonging in circulation.

The question needs to be asked as to whether Welshness could be said to be *more* racialised than other nationalities within the UK. Of course, no grand claims can be made either way on the basis of this project with no comparative data. It is, nonetheless, an interesting question to ask. Are the terms 'British Muslim' or 'Black British' easier to use than the Welsh equivalents, for example? If so, the same could perhaps be said about the use of 'English' in this context. Ifekwunigwe (1999) has noted the association of Englishness with whiteness, and in an excerpt earlier in this chapter, Melissa set up a binary of English/black. Although it has been criticised for many things, including its associations with England, the concept of Britishness is perhaps vague enough to encompass ethnic hybridity such as the term 'British Muslim'. However, Saeed et al. (1999) found in their research with Glasgow Pakistani teenagers that hybrid terms such as 'Scottish Pakistani' and 'Scottish Muslim' were more popular choices for describing ethnic identity than were hybrid terms including the label 'British'. It would be interesting to use Saeed et al.'s method in Wales with children of similar ages for purposes of comparison. The racialisation of the nation is, of course, highly regionally specific. To consider our dataset as a whole, and not just the data on minority-ethnic children, we were working in a virtually all-white context. Had we conducted research in parts of England or Scotland with a similar ethnic profile, we may well have encountered some similarly racialised discourse of the nation.

It is certainly true that there is work that needs to be done if we are to build an inclusive Wales. As May (2001) observes, there is a tendency for people to believe that in Wales there are only English people, Welsh people and long-standing assimilated ethnic minorities. May goes on to say that 'the new conception of Welshness apparent in Wales has yet to be extended to the formal recognition of the cultural and linguistic histories of its various ethnic minorities' (2001: 269). Day (2002: 242) is optimistic in writing that 'it is reasonable to suppose that, as Wales has become a more diverse and fragmented place, so the number of possible varieties of Welshness have increased'. Our data suggest that amongst the children we spoke to, the traditional 'white' version of Welshness is being contested, but this contesting tends to be framed within a traditional version of belonging – having an 'authentic' name or speaking Welsh. Although we can see children insisting on an inclusive Welshness with respect to 'race', it is perhaps more difficult to imagine any conception of Welshness that is not set up in opposition to Englishness, given that these two national identities are, perhaps, inextricably bound up with one another. Indeed, it may also be difficult to imagine the fading of popular constructions of Englishness as privileged and 'posh', given the continuing relative economic disadvantage of Wales (Day 2002).

Conclusion

We have presented some insights into children's 'race' talk in Welsh schools, based on our qualitative research on national and local identities. We have also reflected on the role of Englishness in relation to Welshness. We have highlighted aspects of the data where children spoke about Wales as racialised, either to support such an image of Wales or to contest it. There are examples of children uncritically seeing their Wales as white and also examples of white children wanting to contest a white Wales and instead construct an inclusive nation. In these latter instances, there is a sense that the children are aware that a case for inclusivity needs to be argued against a traditional white model, sometimes using traditional ideas of cultural authenticity to argue their case. The limited data we have on the views of black and minority-ethnic children indicate a reluctance to claim Welshness and, in particular, a reluctance to use 'Welsh' as an umbrella identity within which other ethnic identities can be expressed. There is material here to argue a pessimistic case about Welsh identity as narrow, exclusive and still tending to whiteness. There is also evidence from the research that could support the potential for an inclusive citizenship in Wales to be developed. We have also highlighted the construction of Englishness as the central 'Other' of Welshness and the tendency for England and English people to be seen as privileged and arrogant. There is ambivalence about Englishness and potential for children with English identities to maintain these even under pressure, though of course this process is contingent on a number of very local factors.

This chapter has dealt with some particular aspects of national identities, namely the negotiation of boundaries of nationhood – ideas about racial belonging and relations with the neighbouring nation. The 'others' of the nation have to be considered an integral part of the picture of national identities, for children as for adults. In many ways, we can see continuity between the identities that these children have to negotiate and those of adults. It is fundamental predicaments of national and ethnic identity, regardless of age, that strike us in reading our research data, rather than any sense of primary-school children inhabiting different worlds of identification, either because of developmental trajectories or because of particular cultures of childhood. In the final empirical chapter we move on to consider a specific aspect of identification with the nation, namely the significance of language in a bilingual nation.

7 Ways of speaking

Nations are often thought of as communities united – or divided – by language. People living in them are supposed to speak the same language – both linguistically and culturally; where they do not, the assumed unifying powers of language are missing and the nation as imagined community becomes 'at issue' (as the examples of Belgium, Italy, Canada and, indeed, Wales, suggest). So language is a crucial aspect of successful and confident nation-building, and in bilingual and multilingual nations there is always a language 'problem' to be navigated. But is this a problem for public pronouncements and programmes alone, or does it trouble people's own sense of who they are? And where do children figure in this? Language emerges, of course, in childhood – but to what extent and how do children use it as a resource in their constructions of nation and, indeed, place-belonging? This chapter, then, addresses children's use of and attitudes to language – particularly in terms of the minority/majority language relations existent in bilingual nations.

It is important, in our view, to examine how questions of language contribute to children's relationships with nation and place, since it is an issue frequently pointed to by politicians, governments, the media and other institutional stakeholders as a significant barometer of collective identity and belonging. For these reasons, it is a frequently politicised and contentious issue in public discourse – particularly in devolved, proto-nations such as Wales. This could be thought of as the 'public' status of a national language – how important it is felt to be in identifying the nation and drawing boundaries around and within it. It is also important to consider, however, the more personal dimensions of language, the extent to which children see the language they speak as essential to their own conceptions of self-identity and who they are. These two aspects of language and identity – one public, one more personal – overlap, of course, and to some extent are mutually constitutive; nevertheless, they can be distinguished, especially perhaps in bilingual nations where one language is far less dominant than another. What we find in our own research is that the children know that the Welsh language is of public importance, but most have a very taken-for-granted sense that English is their language of 'self'. They may (as other chapters have shown) frequently identify themselves as 'being Welsh', but they do not see the language they speak – whether English or Welsh – as impinging on this to any significant extent.

It was noted in Chapters 4 and 5 that language and accent are key boundary markers for the children we spoke to in relation to both national and local difference and are important resources for national identity, in Wales at least. This chapter will explore the significance of ways of speaking in more depth. It deals with language first and then accent. As noted in Chapter 4, language is cited by the children as a boundary marker of both national and supranational divisions. Yet language, as we explore in this first section, also has important implications for how children relate to the constructs of place and nation at a more local level. There will be attention given to language conflict, language as a marker of difference, the use of Welsh in Welsh-medium schools, the attitude towards Welsh in English-medium schools and language as identity or commodity. There is more attention to the Welsh language because its minority status makes it more of a talking point than English, whose presence is largely taken for granted.

Language

Joseph argues that 'the entire phenomenon of identity can be understood as a linguistic one' (2004: 12) and that 'language and identity are ultimately inseparable' (2004: 13). Joseph has a particular take on what is important about language and identity. He sees the primary linguistic function as interpretation, rather than communication or representation as in traditional linguistics. Interpretation involves placing people in categories with others, a process of identity ascription (Joseph 2004: 40). This chapter deals both with how children go about ascribing identities to others and how they accept or reject identities ascribed to them.

There is, of course, a considerable body of research relevant to children, language and identity from several different academic disciplines. The field of linguistics includes fine-grained work on the detail of language and theoretical perspectives on the meaning and place of language from a range of social-science perspectives: sociological, psychological and political. To consider only the study of children in a bilingual context, relevant studies include work on bilingual education (Baker 2002, Morris Jones and Singh Ghuman 1995), the social psychology of language attitudes in children (Baker 1992) and the development of children's dual language use (Bialystok 1991). This chapter is not as specialist as any of these literatures, but rather aims to give a general sociological overview of what the children say about the significance of language in their lives, with some comment on this with reference to the social context of language use in Wales.

Any chapter that deals with the issue of language in a bilingual nation enters, willingly or unwillingly, into heavily disputed territory characterised by ongoing, contemporary debate, as well as drawing on a contested history.

As Patten and Kymlicka (2003: 12) observe, 'debates over regional languages are never just debates over languages'. For all children in school in Wales, these debates form a backdrop to their own experience of being educated in a country where more than one language is in daily use. For some, language considerations will be far more than a backdrop. The decision made by their parents between a Welsh-medium or English-medium education will have foregrounded a set of considerations which are summed up in language choice, but which go far beyond that single consideration. In some instances, also, the matter of language will not be simply an active consideration for families, but will be an issue of community engagement and part of a wider social and political discourse. In either case, language in Wales forms part of the raw material from which identity is negotiated at a series of different levels – personal, local and national, spatial and social.

This chapter aims to explore the way in which children themselves report and discuss their understanding of language issues as it impacts on that question of identity formation. May (2001: 132) illustrates from first principles both the long-standing and deep-rooted nature of the debates to which they are inheritors when reminding us that, 'The Welsh word "iaith" originally meant both language and community; the word for a compatriot, "cyfiaith" means "of the same language" '. This community-based sense of language stood in sharp contradistinction to the predominant theories of the nineteenth-century nation-state when, as O'Reilly (2001: 8) puts it:

> certain languages came to be seen as the vehicles of rational thought while others were deemed 'emotional' or simply inadequate. Those that were believed to have the capacity to promote reason came to be linked to the rational idea of the modern state, while the others remained 'stateless' and linked to the realm of the traditional. Because the 'stateless' languages tended to be linked to the old order, they were often perceived as a threat to the state and became the subject of neglect or outright hostility.

The practical impact of such views were most famously evident in Welsh history (see Morgan 1991) in the 1847 report popularly remembered by the phrase *Brad y Llyfrau Gleision* (The Treachery of the Blue Books), in which education inspectors from London reached the conclusion that the inability of the Welsh-speaking children interviewed to answer simple questions was the product of ignorance and the habit of speaking Welsh, which was variously blamed for dirtiness, laziness, ignorance, superstition, promiscuity and immorality. The report concluded that, 'The Welsh language is a vast drawback to Wales and a manifold barrier to the moral progress and commercial prosperity of the people. It is not easy to over-estimate its evil effects' (Reports of the Commissioners of Enquiry 1847: 66).

Nor were such attitudes confined to Wales. The experience of Breton speakers in France (Timm 2001) and of minority-language users in liberal

Sweden (Peura 2000) reflect the same set of underlying attitudes that persisted, albeit in a diluting way, right up to the 1970s. A number of factors then combined to challenge, and to some extent, reverse these earlier practices. These included a new concern at the fact that, as Boran (2001) puts it, 'the world's languages are dying', as well as the impact of the European Union, where bilingualism was the norm (O'Riagain 2001) and cultural diversity specifically underlined in the Maastricht Treaty (O'Reilly 2001: 11). There is also, moreover, the wider context of cultural renewal in the 1970s, a decade that saw the beginnings of the subsequent boom in conservation, heritage, 'roots', identity politics and a concern with the 'authenticity' of place (Dicks 2003, Samuel 1994).

If the general climate for minority and regional languages had altered for the better, it is important to note that this does not imply any simple or linear process. Hussain (2000), for example, writing in the Danish context, suggests that globalisation and the fragmentation of identities have produced new pressures upon majority cultures to attempt to shore up the coherence of their own distinctiveness. These attempts produce, he argues, an impact upon wider patterns of social cohesion and stability because of 'an intensified ethnification of the minorities, which the politics of identity requires for the maintenance of a unique Danish identity' (Hussain 2000: 145). In other words, promoting a greater sense of majority cohesion relies upon a greater emphasis on the 'otherness' of non-majority groups in the population, setting up new tensions over language issues in the process.

More generally, Patten and Kymlicka (2003) argue that most European states have responded by conceding pragmatic accommodations to multi-lingualism, rather than by establishing new political rights. In Wales, improvements in the protections and promotions offered to the Welsh language have often been accompanied by majority-language interests arguing that attempts to promote Welsh are 'exclusive' or even 'racist' in their effects on non-Welsh speakers. May (2001) observes that those who make such arguments very rarely apply their 'anti-nationalist' scrutiny to their own nationalism. He further argues that it is these majority-language interests, rather than policies to bolster minority languages, that are illiberal. This set of attitudes and ambivalences form the context to the question of why should the Welsh language be singled out for particular treatment in Wales? It is by no means the only minority language spoken within its boundaries, particularly following the growth of populations from the Indian subcontinent. In the current state of policy-making in devolved Wales, it is possible to see the distinction proposed by Patten and Kymlicka (2003) in which it is only national minorities who can demand as *of right* formal inclusion of their languages and cultures in the civic realm. Welsh speakers are thus afforded with a set of promotion rights, while other linguistic minorities have recourse to tolerance-orientated rights (see Kloss 1977 for a first exposition of this distinction).

This chapter is particularly concerned with language in the context of education – an area which Skutnabb-Kangas (2000) identifies as one of particular language controversy around the world. For as Patten and Kymlicka (2003) suggest, the aims of language policies go far beyond the delivery of effective education, being concerned as they are with shaping the language use of future generations. In this way, schools become 'important sites of social and cultural reproduction' and the sites of political struggles over the language of instruction (Heller 1999: 18). In the highly politicised atmosphere of Canada's linguistic policies, Heller emphasises that the way in which schools construct and implement rules about language use can only be properly understood as part of a more general discourse of power and identity. Those wider issues flow in both directions between a school and the homes and neighbourhoods in which students live. In this way, language-policy issues emerge in very concrete ways in the lives of individual children – as their own views in this chapter illustrate.

Before moving directly to that material, however, it is important to understand that, in Wales, also, the recent history of Welsh-medium education has been one of struggle to ensure the availability, at primary- and secondary-school levels, of a sufficient supply of places to meet latent demand. It was not until the 1988 Education Reform Act that a Welsh education system in its own right with a specific Welsh curriculum was established and the Welsh language became a subject that all pupils within Wales would study (as well as being the language of instruction in Welsh-medium schools). The Welsh language is now seen by the Government as being a key means (perhaps *the* key one) of affirming Welsh identity in the public eye, as well as being important for individual citizens' self-identities. In that, the Welsh children find themselves in the mainstream of bilingual experience elsewhere (see Churchill [2003] on Canada).

In this chapter, our aim is to emphasise the way in which language acts as a lightning rod for a far wider series of identity questions. Thus, while language in Wales lies at the heart of ongoing debates about a national – or at least civic – identity that is capable of encompassing all Welsh citizens, it inevitably attracts the sort of attention which Churchill (2003: 25) describes as unavoidable when language policies are 'used as a symbol or proxy for larger interest clashes which language alone cannot resolve. Official language policies will continue to be blamed as a scapegoat for the failure to resolve other non-linguistic social and political difficulties'.

These social and political questions have a spatial as well as civic dimension, as far as identity formation is concerned. Historically, minority languages have been subject to 'diglossia', in which speakers of a marginalised language progressively confine its use to contexts of intimacy – with family, friends and close associates – while switching to a different, higher-status language in public domains. The growth of Welsh-medium education places children in middle childhood at the nexus of these intersecting factors, by emphasising the use of the language in new and 'official' settings. The impact of this change has to be analysed in context: the negotiation that will be needed by a child from a Welsh-speaking family in a Welsh-speaking area will differ from that experienced by a child in a Welsh-medium school from an English-speaking home and in a predominantly Anglicised part of Wales. Yet further compounds of agency and socialisation will occur in relation to language and identity in English-medium schools in Wales. The general context of language use in the six schools researched in this study is set out in detail in Chapter 2. Chapter 4 has also discussed the symbolically significant relationship between language and national identity in Wales. It concluded that collapsing linguistic and national categories (speaking Welsh and being Welsh and so on) was pervasive amongst the children we spoke to but that, almost invariably, children also told us they thought non-Welsh-speakers were just as Welsh as Welsh-speakers. In this chapter, we aim to explore these issues in more detail as well as considering a number of other ways in which children negotiate language as raw material in identity formation.

Language conflict

The Welsh language is a site of conflict in Wales, as explained above. Our research explored this issue at three different levels: community, family and individual. In recent years, much of the public controversy that has lasted so long has crystallised most overtly around an organisation called Cymuned, literally translated as 'Community', which campaigns specifically in order to preserve the linguistic integrity of what it regards as primarily Welsh-speaking areas. Considering the high profile of this issue in the Welsh media and in areas such as 'Bryn Tawel' in north-west Wales (the location of one of our Welsh-medium schools, Ysgol y Porth) in particular, where Cymuned slogans were fly posted around the town, the children spoke surprisingly little of language conflict in interviews and focus groups. Even in a part of Wales where identity and language use featured prominently in public discourse, attitudes to language use amongst children were generally practical rather than ideological. The children in our study were generally very matter of fact about people's language use, accepting that some children prefer to speak English and that some of their classmates' parents do not speak Welsh. Children from Ysgol y Porth were more aware than those in the other localities we studied of speaking a different language from the rest of Britain, and they did also express a stronger sense of Welsh national identity, as Chapter 4 outlined. Jane, for example, worried that if she were to move to Australia she would 'colli'r iaith' (lose the language). Children from this school seemed to regard a willingness by incomers to learn Welsh as a 'test', but they saw this 'test' as one of practicality – because Welsh is the preferred language for many people in the area – rather than of cultural commitment. Glad to speak Welsh themselves, because it allows them to speak directly with other Welsh-speakers, their expectation that newcomers to their area should learn Welsh was framed by children as sensible rather than dogmatic.

Nevertheless, it does underline children's sense here that there is a potential linguistic disjuncture between incomers and themselves – something that was not so evident in the other localities, in which Welsh was less widely spoken.

At a family level, only a small number of children reported language conflict as a feature of their own experience. The views of Mandy at Ysgol Maes Garw noted in the previous chapter on p. 95 ('My Dad . . . says . . . sheep speak Welsh') illustrate some of the different ways in which cultural and ethnic identities can play out according to how they connect to personal histories. This conflation of Welsh-speaking with rural backwardness is an enduring theme in Welsh identity formation. Here, language is just one way in which family conflict emerges between urban and valley perspectives. Mandy's father draws on a collective piece of myth-making and makes that grist to the mill of family discord. Culture, language and ethnicity are thus contingent on individual circumstances, just as individual identifications with collectivities cannot be understood without reference to the social and political context of those collectivities (Jenkins 1996).

We attempted to explore the issue of language and conflict for individuals. We asked all our respondents about their views on English- and Welsh-medium education and whether they would like to go to a school with a different language medium from their own. Language itself featured far less in their consideration than the character of children in these other schools, which chimes with our more general observation that the children seemed to prioritise people over place and place-cultures. Children worry at the prospect of moving school, but it is other children, other teachers and other rules that concern them, not the use of another language.

The conclusion we might draw from these examples is that although language is understood as a marker of difference, of and by themselves language questions are not regarded as being of overriding importance to identity. They are part of a wider canvas in which language can be a matter of practical importance, of interfamily conflict or a relatively minor factor in negotiating a personal pathway through potential difficulty. Language matters, but even in conflictual situations, it is only a part of any picture.

Language as a marker of difference

Despite its fairly weak association with conflict, language emerged in the children's talk as the most immediate marker of difference between groups of people. As we noted in earlier chapters, it often signifies nationality and also regional difference, and it is very often the only distinguishing factor between national groups (and language groups in Wales) that the children report. Even when children have an indifferent grasp of the specifics of where languages are spoken in Wales, they are clear that speaking a different language will be a signifier of difference. This understanding is situational as well as geographical. For children able to speak both Welsh and English, especially, the way in which others choose to use language – at school, in the playground, with family and friends – marks the world out as shared or strange, and as a key component in identity formation.

Other than speaking different languages, the children we spoke to thought that children in different language-medium schools would be 'just the same' or 'yr un fath' (the same type/kind) and would share a common children's culture. As David puts it in the excerpt below, this expresses a universalism of diversity. Children in Welsh-medium schools are the same in so far as everyone is different.

Andrew: What do you think of the sort of children that go to those kinds of schools? Are they the same as children here?
David: Not the same because everyone is different but . . . like some naughty, some bad. I mean some's naughty, some's good.
(Interview with David, Year 6, Petersfield School)

Use of Welsh: children in Welsh-medium schools

In order to get below the surface of this general tendency towards universalism, we now turn to the issue of language use in different school contexts. As far as children's use of Welsh in the school setting is concerned, the linguistic life of a school can only really be understood in the context of the language circumstances outside the school door (Heller 1999). By middle childhood, the children we spoke to have a clear understanding of the situations where Welsh does and does not get used. In Bryntawel and Maes Garw – the two traditionally Welsh-speaking areas – we were told similar tales of old people speaking Welsh and young people not so much. The 2001 Census results in fact report significant growth in Welsh-speaking amongst children in Wales, but this is likely to be a feature of the growth of Welsh-medium education. The children's testimony in the study might perhaps be a more accurate reflection of the generational character of actual language use – what you actually speak rather than your knowledge of a language.

Andrew: O't ti'n gweud, Jane, bod lot o hen bobl yn siarad Cymraeg. Beth am y bobl ifanc? ydyn nhw'n siarad Cymraeg neu—?
Jane: Weithiau.
Llinos: Ychydig.
Andrew: Ydyn nhw'n gallu siarad Cymraeg?
Lleisiau: Yndy.
Andrew: Ond jyst—
Anthony: —ddim yn siarad Cymraeg.

[*Andrew*:   You were saying, Jane, that lots of old people speak Welsh. What about young people? Do they speak Welsh or—?
Jane: Sometimes.

Llinos: A bit.
Andrew: Are they able to speak Welsh?
Lleisiau: Yes.
Andrew: But just—
Anthony: —don't speak Welsh.]

(Year 6 focus group, Ysgol y Porth)

Use of Welsh also distinguishes within, as well as between, generations. At Ysgol Maes Garw, younger children reported that older pupils were less likely to speak Welsh, although that was not something that was particularly observable from spending time around the school, in so far as few children of any age could be seen using Welsh outside the classroom. Mandy told us that while she spoke Welsh inside and outside the classroom, older children 'in Years 5 and 6 they're always doing it [speaking English outside the classroom] but they swear like that. . . . They just think they're better than everybody 'cause they're in Year 5 and Year 6'. There is a hint here of English being used by older children – or younger ones perceiving them as using it – as a kind of subcultural expression of resistance to the school standard.

More generally, some children in all three Welsh-medium schools told us they use more English outside class because it's easier – even at the risk of official disapproval. At Ysgol y Waun, for example, in the area of Wales within our sample that had the weakest Welsh-language social base in the surrounding area, there was a strong ethos that children ought to speak Welsh wherever they can, including in non-lesson school times, doubtlessly in recognition that there will be little support for the language outside school. Of the Welsh-medium schools researched in this study, its approach to language use comes closest to that reported by Heller (1999), in which minority-language schools enforce use of that language most strictly in those areas where the language is least used in surrounding communities.

Several children in this school spoke of 'those children' (always others) who don't speak Welsh around the school, implying that they themselves do. Olwen from Ysgol y Waun adopts a censorious tone about those who 'pan mae nhw'n adre' efo ffrindiau nhw'n siarad Saesneg a chwarae yn Saesneg a popeth' (when they are at home within their friends, they speak English and play in English and everything), while Eleri prefers a more practical explanation of the same behaviour: 'maen nhw eisiau siarad Saesneg oherw- ydd maen nhw'n gwybod y enwau (.) ond maen nhw jyst yn lazy' (they speak English because they know the words . . . but they are just being lazy).

Stephen was unusual in saying frankly that 'we' speak English because it's a bit 'boring' to speak Welsh for the whole of playtime. These data suggest that use of Welsh was a resource used by children in drawing divisions amongst themselves, especially along the lines of what they felt they 'ought' and 'ought not' to be doing.

By contrast, children in Ysgol y Porth in Brynyawel, the community we visited where Welsh-speaking was by far the strongest (at around 80 per cent of the population), were quite matter of fact about language and were particularly relaxed about bilingualism, both inside the school and out of it. They simply told us that people speak Welsh in the area so children have to learn Welsh if they move there – it is simply the normal thing to do. Children understand that newcomers will speak a good deal of English at first but will quickly learn Welsh because it is around them all the time. Allowances are made for the fact that some children speak Welsh at home while others do not. As Gianni suggests, you generally choose your language according to this: 'I speak Welsh to some of the kids, but my other friend Ashley, he's from Sheffield, so I just speak English a bit to him'.

At Ysgol Maes Garw, in the western valleys of south Wales, a traditionally Welsh-speaking area where the Welsh language has been in decline, the position was more mixed. None of the children we interviewed spoke Welsh at home and most of the Year 6 children who were in their last year of primary school were moving on to a bilingual school with English as the dominant language, rather than a Welsh-medium school. Rowland, the most politically nationalist child of all those to whom we spoke is in this position. Asked about his experience of attending a Welsh-medium school, he echoed an older discourse of the Welsh language 'holding you back': 'It's alright. But I don't want to get too stuck with Welsh. It would be good to have the skill of Welsh but it wouldn't help me if I spoke Welsh to everybody'.

While language may not be a crucial site of conflict for children in middle childhood, the views of children in Welsh-medium education illustrate very clearly the many ways in which language demarcates a series of important borders in their lives. These demarcations lie at the frontiers of identity. Language is a marker of difference between age cohorts within school and between the generations; it has to be negotiated between native speakers and incomers; it marks out territory between conformity and rebellion and it has to be weighed up in relation to a series of different components of identity, cultural and instrumental.

Attitudes towards the Welsh language in English-medium schools

Children in English-medium schools showed a real mixture of positive and negative attitudes towards the Welsh language, but with more positive attitudes than might perhaps have been expected. It was noted above that the Welsh language was referred to quite often as a marker of Welshness, even by children from English-medium schools. There was at least some sense from these children of positive attitudes towards the value of the language, with some children echoing the notion that Welsh is a useful acquisition in the general context of extra languages being globally useful. Melissa from Petersfield, for example, explains her friend's attendance at 'a Welsh school' because she wants to be an air hostess, 'and she has got to learn different languages'. We return to this view below where we discuss language as commodity.

We asked children in all schools about the prospect of moving to a school with a different language medium. For the English-medium children, aside from the obvious anxiety that they would not understand what was being said, most regarded any change of school as unwelcome but, as with children from Welsh-medium schools, for social reasons, rather than language per se. William from Llwynirfon School was typical in telling us that he probably wouldn't want to go to any new school, whatever the language of instruction.

As well as similarities, however, some important differences emerged in the ways in which children in English-medium schools regarded language issues, in comparison with their Welsh-language contemporaries. For some, there was an understanding that Welsh is simply the first language for a lot of people. Melissa from Petersfield School was markedly positive about the Welsh language, largely because of having a Welsh-speaking grandmother. She also described the Welsh language as important to a Welsh national identity Asked why she thought people spoke Welsh, Sian from the same school replied simply that it was because 'it's their natural language'. But this kind of differentiation is fairly unusual. More typical were comments about children in Welsh-medium schools being 'just the same'. As Billig's (1995: 17) notion of 'banal nationalism' would suggest, there is a sense that in an English-speaking world it is normal to speak English. 'Just the same' here, perhaps, means that language is not seen as important: English-speaking is so taken for granted that, even when education takes place in a different language, it does not disrupt a sense of an essentially English-speaking world.

In this way, children in English-medium schools differ in their views and their linguistic experience from those who attend Welsh-medium schools. Even Welsh-speaking children in north-west Wales, where Welsh is widely spoken in public, were very well aware of the presence, and in some cases of the pressure, of English all around them. No sense of pressure or threat was spoken of by the children in English-medium schools. Emma from Petersfield, an area where it would be unusual to hear any language other than English being spoken, told us that 'I reckon English is normal', a sentiment echoed almost exactly by Cerys from multi-ethnic Highfields School who, in a very multilingual setting (though not including much in the way of Welsh-language use) was still able to sum up her own understanding quite simply as 'I just think that it is normal to speak in English'.

The taken-for-granted way in which speakers of majority languages assume their own position to be the 'norm' was noted at the start of this chapter as a phenomenon that goes far wider than Wales. It also goes far wider than language. Children will very likely regard being 'white' as such a default position as not to think of white as a colour at all. So these positions – speaking English and being white – were completely taken for granted by the white anglophone children in our study. In Chapter 6, we showed how they were nevertheless compounded by a fairly strong and widespread association in all the children's minds between *being Welsh* and whiteness.

This did not mean that *speaking* English, however, was equated with a more multi-ethnic identity. On the contrary, speaking English was simply how the children communicated, which did not by any means rule out their thinking of themselves as Welsh – and being open to the idea of speaking Welsh. In our research, Welsh children in English-medium education display a range of responses to the Welsh language, most of which are positive and some of which contain an identity component. Usually, however, English-speaking Welsh children do not appear to include language as significant raw material in the negotiation of their own identity. They speak English and, as far as that is concerned, there is nothing else to be said.

Identity or commodity?

At this point, we discuss in a little more depth the issue mentioned earlier about language as commodity. Monica Heller's (1999) book on linguistic minorities in Quebec describes a shift to the language being seen as a commodity rather than as a source of identity (see also Heller 2003). She suggests (1999: 270–1) that for most students, 'French is not about identity, or even about a politics of identity; French is about the accumulation of the symbolic capital that will allow them to enjoy the fruits of what the French-Canadian politics of identity has won'. This echoes what we found in the schools in Wales. The children were more likely to make connections between language and linguistic capital than to speak of a personal attachment to language or language being fundamental to who they were. We would, perhaps, not expect the English language to be spoken of in terms of depth of attachment, because its dominance is so taken for granted. We might, however, have expected to hear more about personal attachment to the Welsh language, precisely because of its minority status. A word of caution is needed here because, despite the fact that half of all the 105 children we spoke to attended Welsh-medium schools, only six of them spoke Welsh at home. This equates to less than 6 per cent of our whole sample and 22 per cent of the children we spoke to in Welsh-medium schools. Data gathered by schools in Wales in 2001–2 on the languages that children of primary-school age speak at home show the proportion using Welsh with their families to be similar to the proportion in our sample, at 6 per cent (Welsh Assembly Government 2004: 5). The low numbers of children speaking Welsh at home might, of course, explain some of the lack of talk in our dataset about the Welsh language as personal attachment or part of who the children think they are.

Phillip referred to advantages within Wales in being bilingual: 'It's good because I can speak Welsh and now you get a better job if you speak Welsh'. Other children said that learning one language in addition to your 'mother tongue' can then help you learn a further language. Nathan put it this way, 'Well, at least then you can speak more than one language. And then when you go to high school, you can learn other languages as well, like French and

Spanish and things'. Lisa declared that 'mae Mam eisiau iddyn ni cael manteision fel siarad fel dau iaith' (Mum wants us to have the advantages like speaking two languages). These views reflect a prevalent contemporary educational discourse about extra languages being good for learning – being bilingual will make it easier for you to learn further language. This discourse has to be understood in the context of increasing globalisation and mobility, especially in the employment market, although it is only in Wales of course (and then largely in specific public-sector jobs) that speaking Welsh would in itself be seen as giving an advantage in the job market.

Language choice for these children, it seems, is about 'what I can do' rather than 'who I am'. In previous chapters we have questioned the extent to which 'place' and 'nation' – though salient boundaries for children – are actually meaningful for them in terms of their own self-identities. It seems to us, from our small study at least, that children's use of these boundaries certainly helps them define 'who I am' and 'where I come from', but cannot be said to be central *in their own terms* to their sense of self. Such is the case, it seems to us, with their relationship to language. Welsh is recognised by them as the national language and, therefore, as important in a public sense (however vaguely that may be defined) but not considered particularly crucial to their sense of who they are as individuals. It is important, of course, not to imply a judgement that a 'commodity' rationale for speaking Welsh is somehow less acceptable than one which emphasises identity. With the historical context in mind, it could be argued that for the Welsh language to become seen as a useful commodity in the job market is an achievement for its supporters when, as with many other minority languages, the previous perception of it as a barrier to progress led to a large drop in the numbers of people speaking Welsh, as we observed earlier in the chapter. Of course, one could argue that realistically if Welsh-speaking does not have a deeper personal meaning to the children, they will not be motivated to use the language skills they have in a Wales that is bilingual in theory but in practice is in most areas dominated by the everyday use of English.

We might observe that the actual currency of Welsh-speaking as commodity might not in fact match the expectations of some children and that we should not, therefore, emphasise too strongly commodification as a rationale for parents and children to use Welsh-medium education. For one thing, a Welsh-medium education does not necessarily confer full fluency. Children from homes where only English is spoken and schools in highly Anglicised areas can often struggle to achieve full fluency in the Welsh language. In this situation, the experience of a school such as Ysgol y Waun in north-east Wales is very close to that found elsewhere in bilingual nations. Churchill's review of the Canadian experience (2003: 23) is very positive about bilingualism, but nonetheless he concludes that native English-speaking students, receiving their education through the medium of French, generally achieve 'functional bilingualism, though not necessarily to the high levels of literacy required for many types of employment in French'.

An identity dimension of language does at times rise to the surface. Examples exist in the dataset of children from non-Welsh-speaking families associating the Welsh language with birthplace and heritage (see also Davies et al. 2006). There is some talk of the minority status of the Welsh language adding to its cultural importance and to the value of being able to speak it. As noted in a previous section, Rowland from Maes Garw is the most territorially nationalist of all our respondents. While his is often an instrumental view of the language – some is alright, but not too much – he is still able to articulate the distinctiveness that the language provides and the value to be derived from this in identity terms. 'Welsh is our language', he says, 'and if it dies out we may as well be called England'. His use of the word 'we' here points to Rowland's keen sense of the importance of the language to Wales' *collective* and public identity, but it does not necessarily mean that he sees it as important to him.

Heller (2003) argues that it is important to locate the commodification of linguistic and cultural identity within the economic bases of social and cultural reproduction. To consider that context in Wales, as Aitchison and Carter (1999) note, increased Welsh-speaking in Anglicised areas, the decline in traditional industries and an increase in service industries (including the large Welsh public sector) has led to the emergence of a new bourgeoisie with a large Welsh-speaking element. More generally, there could be seen to be a genuine economic advantage in speaking Welsh within Wales itself, as already noted. Drinkwater and O'Leary (1997) found a significant association between Welsh-speaking and lower levels of unemployment in their analysis of the 1991 UK census. They further found that differences in characteristics between Welsh and non-Welsh speakers did not account for the entire employment differential according to language abilities, especially in west Wales. It could be argued, then, that there is an objective advantage in being bilingual.

Accent

McIntosh et al. (2004) observe that somewhat surprisingly there has been relatively little attention to accent in sociological research on national identities. This is, perhaps, because of traditional disciplinary boundaries, in so far as research attention to accent tends to be confined to the field of linguistics. Accent as well as language marks Wales out as different from other places for the children in our study. Along with language, it is also the principal national and regional difference they spoke of. At one level, as we have seen, the children in our study share a dominant idea of cultural and national difference which is that people are the same – at least in the West. Language is one way in which boundaries *within* that sameness are marked out. Accent is another way in which people speak differently according to where they live. Kathryn, for example, straightforwardly states that accent (in English) and the presence of the Welsh language (she goes to a

Welsh-medium school but speaks English at home) mark out Wales as being different to London.

Accent makes children aware of their difference from others, both within Wales and when mixing with other British children. Many of the children were aware both of being categorised by others and of categorising themselves as being different on the basis of accent. Sometimes, this categorisation irks them, as when Emma found herself marked out as Welsh on a holiday where she mixed with English children who made fun of her accent. But in much of their talk about accent, it is spoken of as a mundane (and obvious) difference amongst people who are otherwise the same. David from south-east Wales agrees that people in Cardiff are 'different', but puts this firmly in perspective: – 'They have just got different accents that's all'. In identity terms, it is a difference without an important distinction. Yet, once below the surface, again, accent emerges as a rich source of raw material for the drawing of boundaries, particularly between self and other, a process that we have suggested is bound up with identity formation. As noted in earlier chapters, the repertoire and range of identity-making resources on which children can draw is limited. Accent emerges as one of the most readily available means by which we are all able to position ourselves in relation to others. Here are a series of ways in which children in middle childhood actively draw on accent in identity work.

To begin with, there are *degrees of Welshness*. For some children, accent is even more local than Wales itself. Bahira, from Highfields School in inner-city Cardiff and whose chosen identity card was 'British Muslim', doesn't think of her own accent as Welsh at all. Asked by Andrew if 'we in Wales have got a funny accent', she replied, 'I don't. I don't really notice, because I think I have got a Cardiff accent'. Yet, for those outside Cardiff, this accent too is grist to the mill of 'Welshness'. Asked by Andrew if she had ever been to Cardiff, Jenny from Llwynifron immediately identified the fact that 'they have got different accents', as proof of the difference between her own town and the capital city. For her, the significance of that different accent was that Cardiff people sounded 'really Welsh. We're not like that'. For Phillipa, in Petersfield (literally a 20-minute drive from Cardiff), the difference was even more pronounced. Asked by Andrew if she knew about the Welsh Assembly, she replied 'You'd have to say it in Cardiff accent. Cardiff hasn't got the same language as us'.

More generally within Wales there is the distinction, which children in more than one place share, of sounding more 'Welshy'. The term covers an amalgamation of different identity components. It is possible both to sound Welshy without being more Welsh and to be *more* Welsh by being more 'Welshy', which is a different thing from accent. When Phillip, in this next excerpt, uses the term 'Welshy', he means something about the quality of Welsh language. It is 'stronger', by which he might mean Welsh is spoken more often or perhaps that they speak a purer Welsh that is less tainted with

English constructions. Andrew, the researcher, is asking Phillip about an area which is not very far from his own home:

Andrew: What would people be like there do you think?
Phillip: They talk more Welshy up there.
Andrew: Talk more Welsh or Welshy?
Phillip: More Welsh and more Welshy.
Andrew: Ok, what's more Welshy?
Phillip: The language.
Andrew: Yeah? So they speak more Welsh the language, yeah? What about more Welshy? What does that mean?
Phillip: They, like, speak it stronger.

Interview with Phillip, Year 6 Ysgol Maes Garw

In adult Wales there are deep-rooted identity issues for some which revolve around the perceived differences between north and south and, separately, around a belief that another Welsh speaker's command of the language will, somehow, be 'purer' or more authentic than your own. Our interviews suggest that, by middle childhood, these nostrums are already embedded in the way children develop identity. In north-east Wales, several children were sure that more Welsh is spoken in the south. Stephen (Ysgol y Waun) thinks people in the south speak 'Hen Cymraeg' (Old Welsh) with 'a deep voice'. Rowland, from the western valleys of south Wales, expresses the reverse: 'People in the north talk really strange and in Welsh they talk strange. They got their own words in Welsh'.

Second, and using the same sort of fine differentiation, accent is a marker of *internal geography*. Here, Andrew is asking the same sort of question as above about a nearby area to children in mid-Wales, all of whom are monolingual English speakers. The same sense of agency can be seen at work, as accent is used to mark out territory between the very local and the none too distant:

Andrew: Are people different in Nant y Bwlch or are they same as people here?
Jasmin: They are all the same but they talk a bit different.
Andrew: How do they talk different?
Jasmin: Well, they don't talk Welsh but sort of when they talk they talk fast and you can't understand them.

(Interview with Jasmin, Year 4, Llwynirfon school)

Third, as well as local differentiation, accent is one of the main ways in which our respondents were able to set themselves apart from *far away places*. There is a distinction that children draw between 'borders', as seen below, and those who live well beyond Wales. Bahira, despite her ambivalence about her own accent, is quite clear that, once you get as far away as Bradford or Scotland, people will have 'funny accents'. Sian, from Petersfield, echoes the same phrase. The further away from Wales, the 'more English' things become, with 'funny accents' setting in by Newcastle. David, also from Petersfield, describes a complex set of identities, which he nevertheless works through on the basis of language and accent combined: 'My Nan, she's English, but she don't talk proper English, like, she talks Welsh, she don't like talk how the English talk. She talks a bit like them, but she was born in England and everything'.

The influence of television can be seen in the way children understand, and use, accent as a way of sorting out identity issues. The popularity of Australian soap opera and wildlife programmes enabled Emma, at Petersfield, to illustrate the way in which they 'talk differently': 'Because they go like [*in Australian accent*] "Oh that's a beauty" and like that. He sees a snake and goes [*in Australian accent*] "I'm going to sneak up on him now and grab him by his neck" and all that, they speak different'.

Fourth, accent is used by our children as a way of *being 'normal'*. For those who have never lived away from their place of birth, accent becomes one of those taken-for-granted elements of what it means to be 'normal', along with language and 'race'. Emma knows that Australians are different and understands something of the relativism that this implies. She also knows, however, that when a judgement has to be made, it is the local that sets the standard, as the following exchange illustrates:

Emma: They [people in Australia] would think that they speak right and we don't, that we have a different accent. We think that we speak right and they don't get it.
Andrew: So how do we speak then?
Emma: Normal.

(Interview with Emma, Year 4, Petersfield School)

This sense of local accent being within a 'normal' British mainstream emerged further at Petersfield in a focus-group discussion that considered accent in the context of *Hollyoaks*, a popular youth soap opera set in Chester, in which the characters tend to speak with an English accent that is not strongly regionally marked. 'Is your accent Welshy?' Aimee was asked. 'No', she replied. 'It's like on the *Hollyoaks*'. To someone from neither locality, the difference between a Chester and a Petersfield accent is readily apparent. A number of different explanations may lie behind the reply quoted above: it may be that the significance of accent is being downgraded in favour of a more general identification with a popular television programme; the contrast cited may rest on a closer claimed alignment between accents along the Welsh–English border than the 'Welshy' accents of north and west Wales. She may be revealing the higher status of Received Pronunciation – perhaps an accent that is not seen as either particularly 'posh' or 'rough' (in the children's terms) but as apparently classless. Whatever the explanation, however, the conclusion reached is the product of agency. Children use accent as a means of positioning themselves in a series of social and spatial contexts, in which identity has to be created, rather than simply received.

This process can be seen clearly in our fifth example, accent as a means of *fitting in*. If accent is an important marker of 'normality', then it is also important and more problematic raw material for boundary-drawing amongst those children who are not natives of the area in which they now go to school. As far as accent is concerned, the strength of the assumption that local is normal provides a challenge for these individuals in which agency is clearly required if it is to be negotiated successfully. Joshua had moved from Yorkshire to Llwynirfon School. His contributions tread a fine line between emphasising how much he likes his new surroundings – it is a 'nice school' – and pointing out that being an outsider means that people can make fun of you: 'like put on funny accents and stuff'. There is a suggestion here that he is policing his own speech in order to minimise embarrassment or difficulty and to make 'fitting in' easier to accomplish.

The extent to which accent plays an active part in children's sense of identity is well illustrated in the following excerpt. For the most part, the children in our research were alert to the protocols that govern school life. They responded to Andrew as someone from 'adult' life and respect the boundary of what can, and what can not, be included in discussion with him. Here, however, on the matter of accent – and to general laughter from others – Lianne, from Ysgol y Waun in north-east Wales trespasses knowingly along that border when she tells him that, coming as he does from south-west Wales, 'Dw i ddim yn bod yn gas ond 'dach chi'n siarad yn ffyni' (I'm not being nasty, but you speak funny).

For adults, the most obvious way in which accent is used as a guide to 'fitting in' revolves around *social class*. In our research, this is the sixth way in which children also actively deploy accent as a means of refining identity. As an explicit theme in the interviews and focus groups overall, social class emerges relatively rarely. This is unsurprising as in order to recognise class as a factor or presence in the world, facility in a language of class differences and class relations is required – something that has arguably diminished in adult discourse and that could hardly be expected to figure much in children's. As previous chapters have shown in discussing the nice/nasty divisions that for them characterise children's local landscapes, class demarcation is already another taken-for-granted part of the social world of middle childhood, unremarked upon because it is so unremarkable. Some support to this contention is provided by the way in which, when the connections between language, accent and class do rise to the surface, children seem able, readily enough, to make sense of them. Thus, while to be English is to be 'posh', and to speak in a 'posh language' (Mandy), Gwenllian, a first-language Welsh-speaker from north-west Wales, still understands that accent in *EastEnders* is used for the purposes of class demarcation. She tells Andrew that, 'D'yn nhw ddim yn gorffen eu geiriau' (They don't finish their words), giving as an illustration that, 'Maen nhw'n dweud "yeah" yn lle "yes" ' (They say 'yeah' instead of 'yes').

Inside Wales, too, accent is understood, and used, by our respondents, as a way of marking class difference. Ysgol Maes Garw is situated in the valleys near Swansea: Phillip, Year 6, told Andrew in interview that, 'if they're from Townhill [a very poor district of Swansea] they speak different'. Asked about the difference, in less than ten words, he brings together language, accent and action as markers of identity and social class difference, referring to a familiar criminalisation of a poor community:

Andrew: How do they talk then?
Phillip: Like 'mush' and they always nick things up there.

In all of the above discussions, accent emerges as a way of drawing boundaries between people, and the children are fully fluent in these kinds of social categorisation. This brings us to our seventh and final way in which accent is deployed as an active ingredient in the way children understand and shape identity: marking the borders between England and Wales. In many ways, this is the point that emerges most strongly from our data. As Chapter 4 made clear, the England–Wales boundary is the most salient one to the children, not surprisingly considering the powerful cultural narratives and histories that have been constructed through this particular national division. Melissa, at Petersfield, seems generally anxious about being seen as English. She points out that it is her cousin who is really from England: 'She comes down at Christmas. She has got an accent like'. The physical border with England shifts with different respondents. For Sian, it starts 'around the Bristol area'. For David, at Petersfield, it was either 'Gloucester' or 'past Ebbw Vale, they're English'. It is left to Rowland, the child in our sample with the most overtly nationalistic views, to use accent as a strict way of marking difference along the Wales–England border. Tracing the line on a map with Andrew, he suggested that 'they'd have a bit of a Welsh accent there because they're exactly on the border', with the boundary between Welsh and English ways of speaking marked specifically by the Severn Bridge.

Conclusion

This chapter has considered the ways in which language and accent are regarded and employed by the children we studied as part of the process of identity formation. Despite the highly contested and controversial nature of language debates in Wales, most of our respondents reported an understanding in which language and accent were obvious markers of difference, but where such differences were the cause of little concern, difficulty or indeed overt self-identification. Part of that reaction, particularly amongst first-language English-speakers, rests on a taken-for-granted sense of English being the norm against which any difference has to be measured. Below this secure surface, however, a good deal of more active negotiation is clearly taking place, as the analysis of identity and accent demonstrated.

We can see the influence of globalisation in more than one respect in relation to language. There is, of course, the increasing global dominance of the English language that can help to explain the attitudes of the children to both English and Welsh. There is also the notion of language as a commodity and the idea that bilingualism is 'good for you', both in terms of the Welsh job market and because it enhances your ability to learn further languages. In a sense, this reveals a globalised discourse of social mobility that connects with the children's imagined global mobility we noted in Chapter 4: living abroad as adults. Walkerdine (2003) writes of the 'neo-liberal subject' in a labour market dominated by employment that is increasingly 'flexible' (or precarious, to give a more pessimistic tone). What she is referring to is the self-invention that is spoken of in the context of an apparently limitless employment market: 'the apparently limitless possibilities are all possibilities of being SOMEBODY' (2003: 244). The children are aware of this discourse in speaking of the 'advantages' of being bilingual in a competitive employment context. References to language as a source of identity, in the thicker sense of a culturally filled category, were notably lacking. Language was generally a thinner boundary-drawing marker of national or regional difference, as we noted in Chapter 4.

8 Conclusion

In this book, we have tried to convey some of the complex issues involved in researching and thinking through children's relationships to place. We have found it necessary to consider place in children's lives at a number of levels: domestic, local, national and supranational. All of these are intertwined in children's sense of the relations of space that surround and, to some degree, define them, and are frequently conveyed through symbolic oppositions: here/there, known/unknown, home/away, self/other, nice/nasty. In writing the preceding chapters, we have been struck by the extent to which children's talk about place turns on their consciousness of being enmeshed in a world of social and cultural, as well as geographical *boundaries* – operating on a number of different levels. We have discussed these through general observations drawing on the extant literature, but we have also been carefully sketching out and interpreting the findings derived from our own small-scale study of children in Wales. Although we cannot make bold generalisations from this study, nor was it intended to produce standardisable results, it has allowed us to contribute to developing knowledge about how children relate to these different scales of space. At the same time, it has allowed us to engage with theorisations of childhood and nation and to shed a little more light, we hope, on some of those ongoing debates. In these concluding few pages, we return to these debates in the process of mapping out and reiterating some of our arguments – first, through outlining our thoughts about children, place and nation and, second, by drawing out their significance for thinking in particular about children in Wales.

Making sense of place identity in middle childhood

In the first chapter, we wondered how far a sense of place-belonging is inculcated through top-down cultural representations in general circulation and how much it is a product rather of the enmeshment of the self in local social networks. To what extent does children's sense of national (and general collective) belonging come about through their exposure to pre-existing discourses and representations that propagate the existence of national and place identity; conversely, to what extent is it the nature of their social networks and relationships (with family, neighbours and peers in particular) that is the most important field wherein their collective identities are formed? To some extent, such a question echoes the differences of approach outlined in Chapter 1 in relation to Smith and Gellner's debate over the origins of national identity, in that the social network approach fits quite well with Smith's emphasis on the durability and importance of ethnic ties and 'spontaneous cultures', whilst the representational approach sees national symbols and narratives as top-down cultural constructs propagated through the education system (see Gellner 1998, Smith 1999). The evidence from our own qualitative and local study cannot resolve this difference of emphasis, but it does show both kinds of influence in action. When called upon to talk about the nation in front of and for each other – as focus-group methodology entails – children certainly 'perform' particular scripts of the nation and belonging differently than when they narrate them in single interviews – as in the boys in Chapter 3 who were all trying to outdo each others' claim on 'cool' sporting iconography. Gender, here, was a major aspect influencing what they were prepared to say – as was ethnicity for participants from minority groups. Nevertheless, of course, in making different kinds of claims to it, the children are not inventing this national iconography; it is composed from well-rehearsed cultural scripts and discourses that provide the resources with which they 'do' national belonging as gendered, classed, racialised (and aged) social beings. Hence, we can conclude that children do exercise agency in constructing identities from limited resources (they do not simply soak up and regurgitate them), yet always within pretty strict limits. National identity could be seen to limit possibilities more than expand them, particularly where, as always, it is inflected and enacted through the constraining threads of social relations such as age, gender, ethnicity and class. We noted that the same observation would have to be made about adults, although greater exposure over time to resources for national identity might give adults more options.

So we would conclude that national and local identitites are always gendered, classed and racialised to varying degrees. Specifically, in Chapter 3 we noted how micro-level negotiation of collective identities can be gendered. Gender cropped up again at various points of the book, but not as a major theme. Our study did not show children from different social class backgrounds dealing with the nation in markedly different ways. There were, however, notable differences to be seen in how they regarded their localities. In particular, it was through the lens of class distinctions that interlocality boundaries were drawn between the 'nice' areas and the 'nasty' areas. Discourses of the nation were found to be racialised, with a strong elision made between Welshness and whiteness, though there were tensions around inclusive and exclusive versions of Wales. Similarly, there was ambiguity surrounding Englishness and its relation to Welshness, even though this was one of the boundaries that children most clearly perceived. Indeed, it was this nation boundary as well as boundaries *within* the locality (where to go and where not to go; whose company to embrace and whose to avoid) that were the most salient ones for children. Each has both representational and interactional aspects. Representations are clearly resources for them to draw on (since the England–Wales boundary is the most intensively flagged in the media, sport and other fora of 'banal nationalism'; likewise, it is the generalised system of class distinction that informs their calibrations of groups of local people). In parallel, such affiliations are also clearly reproduced through children's daily experiences and interactions, since their consciousness of both national and local divisions arises also through the micro-level ties and meanings that characterise the local milieux in which they move.

In many senses, these two approaches – interactional and representational – are two sides of the same coin. What we need to understand better is how cultural representations come to gain purchase in different ways for different children within the varying contexts of their lives. Likewise, we need to know how to reconcile the ever-shifting and multifarious nature of individual children's autobiographical experiences with the influence of these more public and durable constructs. This reflects the wider question touched on in Chapter 2 in our discussion of the debates that characterise the various social and psychological approaches to childhood. How does culture 'get into' children's lives and minds, and what do they do with it when it is there? What is really needed for a sophisticated social science of children's place identities is an approach that gives attention to the psychological, cultural, social, economic and political influences on children. We do not claim to have done that in this book. Our focus has been primarily social and cultural and, even then, we will not please all readers who think we have neglected particular aspects of the social and cultural context. We have asserted the need for a psycho-social and political understanding of place identity, although we ourselves do not claim to have provided such a breadth of analysis from our own data. Certainly, child development has to be part of the picture, but a social and political understanding of the social construction of immaturity in children also has to be brought to bear, as does an appreciation of the constraints and limitations imposed on children through the expectations and preoccupations of adults. We cannot answer the question of whether children's difference – such that it is – is explained by their developmental stages as opposed to their culturally and socially constrained environments. We can, however, pose it anew and call for new directions in research that seek to make the link between the developmental and socio-cultural agendas.

Although we acknowledge that identities are contingent on social interaction, we have made some attempt at assessing the apparent strength of children's attachments to various different domains of place identity. Despite the children asserting the importance of national identities when explicitly asked about their attachments, our analysis of more general talk led us to be rather more sceptical about this. There seemed to be little talk about explicit attachments to places at all, although, as we show in

Chapter 5, children had their own 'child's-eye view' view of their home turf and knew its affordances (in terms of their own social agendas) intimately. Although we must, of course, appreciate the importance of their location in global markets and global cultures, the local was in fact most vivid to the children, as one would expect, given the day-to-day parameters of their lives. For the children, the world seemed to be seen in relation to the self. Other people and other places were defined in relation to the self. They were conscious of inhabiting worlds divided by boundaries, but here was little sense of a culturally filled conception of place or nation. The resources they could draw on for the doing of national identity were very limited and were mainly expressed through language and sport – both of which we have noted tend to pose the issue of national identity in terms of competing allegiances. Locality is grasped mainly through boundaries between categories of people, as already noted, and through a handful of culturally salient features that define children's daily leisure and schooltime trajectories.

It seems to be people rather than places that mean most to the children – family members and friends. The family home is, perhaps above all, the place they identify with. That might be expected in the context of the social location of middle childhood and the centrality of an ideology of hearth and home and of community more generally. What does it tell us about the importance of relations of space, place, boundary and locality in determining children's sense of who they are? To what extent in our analysis of children's feelings for place are we actually talking about their identities, something that is 'at stake' for the terms of self – or are we referring to something thinner and less psychologically salient? In general, our findings lead us tentatively to suggest that boundary construction appears to be a significant, and perhaps foundational, feature of children's efforts at representing (to us at least) their sense of who they are. Their use of distinctions between here/there and self/other in talking about, for example, where they lived and what mattered to them was readily apparent to us. More culturally filled notions of place and space, however, were noticeably absent. Indeed, children seemed to take for granted the nature of the environments and cultural content of both the marked-off spatial entities (whether localities, 'the world' or nations) and the markers themselves (such as language).

Given the assumptions that are often made within social science about how national projects are achieved, children ought to be a central topic for study. Our book has hopefully raised some issues for further discussion and further research. In new times where place identities are being challenged by detraditionalisation and globalisation and are also (in reaction?) being hardened into exclusive and aggressive political movements in some parts of the world, attachments to nation and locality have to be a crucial topic for consideration and debate. We hope that the perspectives of children will become increasingly important in these debates.

Wales and Welshness

Two crucial issues for Welshness are distinctiveness and inclusivity. In an era where cultural authenticity is widely felt to be at risk in the context of global capitalism (whether through increasing homogeneity or, conversely, fragmentation), Wales claims distinctive national status (if not the status of a separate state) within Britain. Clearly not all people in Wales see themselves as part of a distinctive culture, but in a sense the raison d'être of Wales as a nation is to be distinctive in some way from England, Scotland and Northern Ireland. At the same time, there is a concern about inclusive citizenship and about Wales being a place to which diverse peoples can belong.

To take the issue of inclusivity first, many of the children displayed an inclusive notion of what it is to be Welsh. This was often done by connecting non-traditional Welsh citizens (such as black people) with an aspect of 'traditional' Welshness, such as a 'Welsh-sounding' name or the ability to speak Welsh. There was minimal hostility spoken of between children who attend English-medium and Welsh-medium schools. There was some tension surrounding children with 'English' identities, however. Although many children displayed an ethnically inclusive notion of Welshness, we note that within our small sample of minority-ethnic children, none chose the label 'Welsh' as a primary national identity and there was no expectation that it could be used as an umbrella identity (for example, Welsh Muslim).

In many national contexts we might conclude that resources for national identity are limited, especially in childhood, given the lower exposure children have had to cultural resources. However, we might conclude that the association of national identity in Wales with birthplace, sport and language, above all, is problematic for the development of an inclusive Welshness. Any idea that to belong you have to be born in the country (although we should note that not all children voiced this) runs against the idea that citizenship should include all people resident in the country. Also, the connection of Welshness with the Welsh language – even if this is only a symbolic connection – does of course at least cause some identity tension for the four out of five people in Wales who do not speak Welsh. The fact that the talk of inclusivity we heard from the children relied on co-option of minority-ethnic Welsh people within very traditional discourses of Welshness such as Welsh-speaking or having a Welsh-sounding name might suggest that the dominant ideas of Welshness are restrictive.

These resources for Welshness suggest we are some way from the 'post-national' Wales sketched out by Williams (2005). Williams sees a post-national Wales in terms of an autonomy that would have:

> a liberating effect for all citizens, and not just for those who subscribe to conventional views of what the characteristics and direction of that nation-state should be. It would be a society that has discarded the

notion of a homogenous nation-state with singular forms of belonging, in favour of inclusivity and cultural diversity.

(Williams 2005: 16)

Whilst we would not wish to impose a compulsory Welsh identity on all children who move to Wales from elsewhere, or whose parents are not Welsh, we believe that it is important that this identification remains an *option* for all living in Wales. Promoting an inclusive notion that incorporates many ways of being Welsh is not only important for visibly minority-ethnic children, but also for children whose families have migrated from other parts of the UK (for example, those who are English-born) and for monoglot English-speaking children in Wales. In practical terms, a more vigorous promotion of diverse Welsh identities in the media and educational materials might be one step forward. As well as combating the idea that an ability to speak the Welsh language is necessarily core to Welsh identity, another very different strategy would be to open up that language by making it more accessible to a diverse population. Welsh-medium schools and Mudiad Ysgolion Meithrin (an early years organisation) might, for example, ensure that their facilities are actively promoted amongst minority-ethnic communities.

We turn now to the issue of distinctiveness. It was noted in Chapter 4 that in some respects the children in the largely Welsh-speaking area of Bryntawel were more aware of their difference within Britain than were the children in the other schools. This is, of course, not a comment about rights to any particular identity and not a comment on citizenship, but is simply noting a sense of difference. We live in a world that is increasingly diverse in some respects with more global mobility resulting in greater cultural diversity. But in other respects we see increasing homogenisation. Certainly, the English language is becoming more dominant all the time, particularly via the expansion of global media, trade and travel. This poses a challenge to a country like Wales whose most obvious claim to distinctiveness is its unique language.

Although the children made frequent connections between *being* Welsh and *speaking* Welsh in routine talk about the nation, our research findings do not necessarily bode well for the future of the Welsh language. The use of Welsh in Ysgol Maes Garw, a school in an area where the language has traditionally been very strong, could clearly give cause for concern if it is at all indicative of what is going on elsewhere. Although the children there were fluent in Welsh, they did not see the language as having practical use as a community language. It was something that old people spoke and that these children had to speak in school. The view of the Welsh language as a commodity could lead to the optimistic conclusion that the language now has status in public life to the extent that it is seen as useful in the job market – a great improvement on the scenario fifty years before when it was seen as holding people back. Any market incentive to learn Welsh must be an important motivating factor. However, the lack of personal attachment to the language in middle childhood – with the proviso that relatively few of the children in our sample spoke Welsh at home – could be interpreted as potentially undermining policies designed to extend the use of Welsh. The risk is that we get a Wales with more people able to understand the language if not speak it but who do not actually use it at all in their everyday lives because they do not need to and because it does not really matter to them.

We could, therefore, conclude with a rather pessimistic picture both for an inclusive Welsh citizenship and for Welsh distinctiveness with regard to language. However, there are contrary findings. Some children were actively and creatively engaged in finding new ways to construct an inclusive Wales. The linguistic territory was pretty free of tensions and trouble for the children and those who were bilingual tended to be very relaxed in their dual language use.

To bring together the twin issues of distinctiveness and inclusivity, we could turn to Appiah (1997), who writes optimistically about 'rooted cosmopolitans', people who are attached to a specific place and its own particular culture whilst 'taking pleasure from the presence of other, different places that are home to other, different people' (2005: 617). We suggest that it is rooted cosmopolitans that Wales needs. We do not wish to suggest that children should be simply expected passively to incorporate an adult-driven expanded vision of Welshness. Instead, we suggest that we encourage children's agency in constructing their own creative visions of Wales and what it means to be Welsh citizens.

References

Aboud, F. E. and Amato, M. (2001) 'Developmental and socialization influences on intergroup bias', in R. Brown and A. Gaertner (eds) *Blackwell Handbook of Social Psychology: Intergroup Processes*, Oxford: Blackwell, pp. 65–85.

Agnew, J. (1989) 'The devaluation of place in social science', in J. Agnew and J. Duncan (eds) *The Power of Place*, Boston, MA: Unwin Hyman, pp. 9–29.

Agnew, J. A. and Duncan, J. S. (1989) 'Introduction', in J. Agnew and J. Duncan (eds) *The Power of Place*, Boston, MA: Unwin Hyman, pp. 1–8.

Aitchison, J. and Carter, H. (1999) 'The Welsh language today', in D. Dunkerley and A. Thompson (eds) *Wales Today*, Cardiff: University of Wales Press.

Albrow, M. (1997) 'Travelling beyond local cultures', in J. Eade (ed.) *Living the Global City: globalization as a local process*, London: Routledge.

Alldred, P. and Burman, E. (2005) 'Hearing and interpreting children's voices: discourse analytic contributions', in S. Greene and D. Hogan (eds) *Researching Children's Experience: approaches and methods*, London: Sage.

Anderson, B. (1991) *Imagined Communities*, 2nd edn, London and New York: Verso.

—— (1996) 'Introduction', in G. Balakrishnan (ed.) *Mapping the Nation*, London: Verso, in association with *New Left Review*.

Anthias, F. (2002) 'Where do I belong? Narrating collective identity and translocational positionality', *Ethnicities*, 2 (4): 491–514.

Appadurai, A. (1990) 'Disjuncture and difference in the global cultural economy', in M. Featherstone (ed.) *Global Culture: nationalism, globalisation and modernity*, London: Sage.

Appiah, K. A. (1997) 'Cosmopolitan patriots', *Critical Inquiry*, 23 (3): 617–39.

Archer J. and Lloyd, B. B. (2002) *Sex and Gender*, 2nd edn, Cambridge: Cambridge University Press.

Aries, P. (1962) *Centuries of Childhood*, New York: Vintage.

Backett, K. and Alexander, H. (1991) 'Talking to young children about health: methods and findings', *Health Education Journal*, 50 (1): 106–16.

Bagguley, P., Mark-Lawson, J., Shapiro, D., Urry, J., Walby, S. and Warde, A. (1990) *Restructuring: place, class and gender*. London and Newbury Park, CA: Sage.

Baker, C. (1992) *Attitudes and Language*, Clevedon: Multilingual Matters.

—— (2002) 'Bilingual education', in R. Kaplan (ed.) *The Oxford Handbook of Applied Linguistics*, New York: Oxford University Press.

Balsom, D. (1985) 'The three Wales model', in J. Osmond (ed.) *The National Question Again? Welsh Political Identity in the 1980s*, Llandysul: Gomer.

Barber, B. R. (1995) *Jihad vs. McWorld*, New York: Random House.

Barrett, M. (1996) 'English children's acquisition of a national identity', in G. Breakwell and E. Lyons (eds) *Changing European Identities: social psychological analyses of social change*, Oxford: Butterworth-Heinemann, pp. 349–69.

—— (2002) 'Children's views of Britain and Britishness in 2001', Keynote Address at the annual conference of the Developmental Psychology section of the British Psychological Society, Sussex, September.

—— (2005) 'Children's understanding of, and feelings about, countries and national groups', in M. Barrett and E. Buchanan-Barrow (eds) *Children's Understanding of Society*, Hove: Psychology Press.

Barrett, M. and Short, J. (1992) 'Images of European people in a group of 5–10-year-old English school children', *British Journal of Developmental Psychology*, 10 (4): 339–63.

Barrett, M. and Whennell, S. (1998) 'The relationship between national identity and geographical knowledge in English children', poster presented at XVth Biennial Meeting of the International Society for the Study of Behavioural Development, Berne, Switzerland.

Barrett, M., Wilson, H. and Lyons, E. (2003) 'The development of national in-group bias: English children's attributions of characteristics to English, American and German people', *British Journal of Developmental Psychology*, 21 (2): 193–220.

Barth, F. (ed.) (1998) *Ethnic Groups and Boundaries: the social organisation of cultural difference*, first published 1969, Prospect Heights, Ill.: Waveland Press.

Bauer, O. (1996) 'The nation', in G. Balakrishnan (ed.) *Mapping the Nation*, London: Verso, in association with *New Left Review*.

Bauman, Z. (1996) 'From pilgrim to tourist – or a short history of identity', in S. Hall and P. Du Gay (eds) *Questions of Cultural Identity*. London: Sage.

—— (1998) *Globalization: the human consequences*, Cambridge: Polity.

—— (2000) *Liquid Modernity*, Cambridge: Polity.

Bechhofer, F., McCrone, D., Kiely, R. and Stewart, R. (1999) 'Constructing national identity: arts and landed elites in Scotland', *Sociology*, 33 (3): 515–34.

Bhabha, H. (1990) 'DissemiNation: time, narrative and the margins of the modern nation', in H. Bhabha (ed.) *Nation and Narration*, New York: Routledge.

Bialystok, E. (1991) *Language Processing in Bilingual Children*, New York: Cambridge University Press.

Billig, M. (1995) *Banal Nationalism*, London: Sage.

Bonnett, A. (2000) *White Identities: historical and international perspectives*, Harlow: Pearson Education.

Boran, I. (2001) 'Global linguistic diversity, public goods, and the principle of fairness', in C. C. O'Reilly (ed.) *Language, Ethnicity and the State, Vol I: Minority Languages in the European Union*, Palgrave: London.

Borland, M., Laybourn, A., Hill, M. and Brown, J. (1998) *Middle Childhood: the perspectives of children and parents*, London: Jessica Kingsley.

Bott, E. (1957) *Family and Social Network*, London: Tavistock.

Bourchier, A., Barrett, M. and Lyons, E. (2002) 'The predictors of children's geographical knowledge of other countries', *Journal of Environmental Psychology*, 22 (1–2): 78–94.

Bourdieu, P. (1986) *Distinction*, London: Routledge.

Bowie, F. (1993) 'Wales from within: conflicting interpretations of Welsh identity', in

S. Macdonald (ed.) *Inside European Identities: ethnography in western Europe*, Oxford: Berg.

Boyden, J. (2003) 'Children under fire: challenging assumptions about children's resilience', *Children, Youth and Environments*, 13 (1). Retrieved (August 2005) from <http://colorado.edu/journals/cye>.

Boyden, J. and de Berry, J. (eds) (2004) *Children and Youth on the Front Line: ethnography, armed conflict and displacement*, Oxford: Berghahn.

Brannen, J., Heptinstall, E. and Bhopal, K. (2000) *Connecting Children: care and family life in later childhood*, London: Routledge Falmer.

Brown, J. S., Collins, A. and Duguid, P. (1989) 'Situated cognition and the culture of learning', *Educational Researcher*, 18 (1): 32–42.

Bryman, A. (1988) *Quantity and Quality in Social Research*, London: Routledge.

Buckingham, D. (2004) 'New media, new childhoods? Children's changing cultural environment in the age of digital technology', in M. J. Kehily (ed.) *An Introduction to Childhood Studies*. Maidenhead: Open University Press.

Burman, E. (1994) *Deconstructing Developmental Psychology*, London: Routledge.

Calhoun, C. (1997) *Nationalism*, Buckingham: Open University Press.

Carrington, B. and Short, G. (1995) 'What makes a person British? Children's conceptions of their national culture and identity', *Educational Studies*, 21 (2): 217–38.

—— (1996) 'Who counts; who cares? Scottish children's notions of national identity', *Educational Studies*, 22 (2): 203–24.

Casey E. S. (1993) *Getting Back into Place: toward a renewed understanding of the place-world*. Bloomington, IN: Indiana University Press.

Castells, M. (2003) *The Power of Identity*, 2nd edn, Oxford: Blackwell.

Chatterjee, Sudeshna (2005) 'Children's friendship with place: a conceptual inquiry', *Children, Youth and Environments*, 15 (1): 1–26. Retrieved (August 2005) from <http://www.colorado.edu/journals/cye/>.

Chawla, L. (1992) 'Childhood place attachments', in A. Altman and S. M. Low (eds) *Place Attachment*, New York: Plenum.

—— (ed.) (2002) *Growing Up in an Urbanising World*, Paris: UNESCO.

Childress, H. (2004) 'Teenagers, territory and the appropriation of space', *Childhood*, 11 (2): 195–206.

Christensen, P. and Prout, A. (2005) 'Researching children and childhood', in S. Greene and D. Hogan (eds) *Researching Children's Experience: approaches and methods*. London: Sage.

Churchill, S. (2003) *Language Education, Canadian Civic Identity and the Identities of Canadians*, Strasbourg: Council of Europe

Cohen, A. (1982) *Belonging: identity and social organisation in British rural communities*, Manchester: Manchester University Press.

Cohen, A. P. (1985) *The Symbolic Construction of Community*, London: Tavistock.

Cohen, L. and Manion, L. (1994) *Research Methods in Education*, London: Routledge.

Cohn, I. and Goodwin-Gill, G. S. (1994) *Child Soldiers: the role of children in armed conflict*, Oxford: Clarendon.

Cole, M. (1999) 'Culture in development', in M. H. Bornstein and M. E. Lamb (eds) *Developmental Psychology: an advanced textbook*, Mahwah, NJ: Lawrence Erlbaum.

Condor, S. (2000) 'Pride and prejudice: identity management in English people's talk about "this country" ', *Discourse and Society*, 11 (2): 175–205.

Connolly, P. (1997) 'In search of authenticity: researching young children's perspectives', in A. Pollard, D. Thiessen and A. Filer (eds) *Children and Their Curriculum*, London: Falmer Press.

—— (1998) *Racism, Gender Identities and Young Children*, London: Routledge.

Connolly, P. and Healy, J. (2004) *Children and the Conflict in Northern Ireland: the experiences and perspectives of 3–11 year olds*, Belfast: Office of the First Minister and Deputy First Minister Research Branch.

Connolly, P. and Keenan, M. (2002) 'Racist harassment in the white hinterlands: the experiences of minority ethnic children and parents in schools in Northern Ireland', *British Journal of Sociology of Education*, 23 (3): 341–56.

Cook, D. (2004) *The Commodification of Childhood: the children's clothing industry and the rise of the child consumer*, Durham, NC: Duke University Press.

Corsaro, W. A. (1997) *The Sociology of Childhood*. Thousand Oaks, Calif.: Pine Forge Press.

Crain, W. (2005) *Theories of Development Concepts and Applications*, 7th edn, Upper Saddle River, NJ: Pearson/Prentice Hall.

David, M., Edwards, R. and Alldred, P. (2001) 'Children and school-based research: "informed consent" or "educated consent"?' *British Educational Research Journal*, 27 (3): 347–65.

Davies, C., Charles, N. and Harris, C. (2006) 'Welsh identity and language in Swansea 1960–2002', *Contemporary Wales*, 18: 28–53.

Day, G. (2002) *Making Sense of Wales: a sociological perspective*, Cardiff: University of Wales Press.

De Cillia, R., Reisigl, M. and Wodak, R. (1999) 'The discursive construction of national identities', *Discourse and Society*, 10 (2): 149–73.

Dicks, B. (2003) *Culture on Display*, Buckingham: Open University Press.

Drinkwater, S. J. and O'Leary, N. C. (1997) 'Unemployment in Wales: does language matter?' *Regional Studies*, 31 (6): 583–91.

Dunn, J. (1993) *Young Children's Close Relationships: beyond attachment*. Newbury Park, Calif.: Sage.

—— (2005) 'Naturalistic observation of children in their families', in S. Greene and D. Hogan (eds) *Researching Children's Experience: approaches and methods*, London: Sage, pp. 87–101.

Ennew, J. and Swart-Kruger, J. (2003) 'Homes, places and spaces in the construction of street children and street youth', *Children, Youth and Environments*, 13 (1). Retrieved (August 2005) from <http://colorado.edu/journals/cye>.

Epstein, D. (1993) *Changing Classroom Cultures: anti-racism, politics and schools*, Stoke-on-Trent: Trentham Books.

Evans, G. (2004) 'The environment of childhood poverty', *American Psychologist*, 59 (2): 77–92.

Evans, J. (1999) 'Introduction: nation and representation', in D. Boswell and J. Evans (eds) *Representing the Nation: a reader*. Routledge, pp. 1–8.

Exell, N. (2006) 'Observance of St. David's Day in secondary schools in Wales: a national survey, 2002', *Contemporary Wales*, 18: 72–90.

Factor, J. (2004) 'Tree stumps, manhole covers and rubbish bins: the invisible play-lines of a primary school playground', *Childhood*, 11 (2): 142–54.

Featherstone, M. (1995) *Undoing Culture*, London: Sage.

Fevre, R. and Thompson, A. (eds) (1999) *Nation, Identity and Social Theory: perspectives from Wales*, Cardiff: University of Wales Press.

Fishman, J. (ed.) (2000) *Can Threatened Languages Be Saved? Reversing language shift revised: a 21st century perspective*, Clevedon: Multilingual Matters.

Flavell, J. (1992) 'Cognitive development: past, present and future', *Developmental Psychology*, 28 (6): 998–1005.

Frosh, S., Phoenix, A. and Pattman, S. (2001) *Young Masculinities*, London: Palgrave Macmillan.

Fryer, P. (1984) *Staying Power: the history of black people in Britain*, London: Pluto Press.

Gellner, E. (1983) *Nations and Nationalism*. Oxford: Blackwell.

—— (1998) *Nationalism*, London: Phoenix.

Giddens, A. (1991) *Modernity and Self-Identity: self and society in the late modern age*, Cambridge: Polity Press.

—— (2002) 'Agency, structure', in C. Calhoun, J. Gerteis, J. Moody, S. Pfaff and I. Virk (eds) *Contemporary Sociological Theory*, Oxford: Blackwell.

Giggs, J. and Pattie, C. (1992) 'Wales as a plural society', *Contemporary Wales*, 5: 25–63.

Gilligan, C. (1982) *In a Different Voice: psychological theory and women's development*. Cambridge, MA: Harvard University Press.

—— (1987) 'Women's place in men's life cycle', in S. Harding (ed.) *Feminism and Methodology*, Milton Keynes: Open University Press.

Gittins, D. (1998) *The Child in Question*. Basingstoke: Macmillan.

Glendinning, A., Nutall, M., Hendry, L., Kloep, M. and Wood, S. (2003) 'Rural communities and well-being: a good place to grow up?' *The Sociological Review*, 51 (1): 129–56.

Goffman, E. (1990) *The Presentation of Self in Everyday Life*, first published 1959, Penguin: London.

Graue, M. E. and Walsh, D. J. (1998) *Studying Children in Context: theories, methods, and ethics*. Thousand Oaks, CA: Sage.

Greene, S. and Hill, M. (2005) 'Researching children's experience: methods and methodological issues', in S. Greene and D. Hogan (eds) *Researching Children's Experience: approaches and methods*. London: Sage, pp. 1–21.

Greenfield, P. M. and Cocking, R. R. (eds) (1994) *Cross-Cultural Roots of Minority Child Development*, Hillsdale, NJ: Lawrence Erlbaum.

Gruffudd, P. (1995) 'Remaking Wales: nation-building and the geographical imagination, 1925–50', *Political Geography*, 14 (3): 219–40.

Gupta, A. and Ferguson, J. (1992) 'Beyond culture: space, identity and the politics of difference', *Cultural Anthropology*, 7 (1): 6–23.

Hall, S. (1993) 'Culture, community, nation', *Cultural Studies* 1 (3): 249–363.

—— (1996) 'Introduction: who needs identity?' in S. Hall and P. Du Gay (eds) *Questions of Cultural Identity*, London: Sage, pp. 1–17.

Hall, T., Coffey, A. and Williamson, H. (1999) 'Self, space and place: youth identities and citizenship', *British Journal of Sociology of Education*, 20 (4): 501–13.

Hamilton, H. (2003) *The Speckled People*, London: Fourth Estate.

Hannerz, U. (1990) 'Cosmopolitans and locals in world culture', in M. Featherstone (ed.) *Global Culture: nationalism, globalization and modernity*. London: Sage, pp. 237–51.

Harden, J., Scott, S., Backett-Milburn, K. and Jackson, S. (2000) 'Can't talk, won't talk? Methodological issues in researching children', *Sociological Research Online*, 5 (2). Available on-line at <http://www.socresonline.org.uk/5/2/harden.html>.

Harvey, D. (1989) *The Condition of Postmodernity: an enquiry into the qrigins of cultural change*, Oxford: Basil Blackwell.

—— (1993) 'From space to place and back again: reflections on the condition of postmodernity', in J. Bird, B. Curtis, T. Putnam, G. Robertson and L. Tickner (eds) *Mapping the Futures: Local Cultures, Global Change*, London and New York: Routledge, pp. 3–29.

Hart, J. (2002) 'Children and nationalism in a Palestinian refugee camp in Jordan', *Childhood*, 9 (1): 35–47.

Hart, R. (1979) *Children's Experience of Place*, New York: Irvington.

Heath, A. (2003) 'Who is British? Presentation to CREST conference, Devolution Five Years On', Cardiff, 7 February.

Hechter, M. (1975) *Internal Colonialism: the Celtic fringe in British national development 1536–1966*, London: Routledge & Kegan Paul.

Heller, M. (1999) *Linguistic Minorities and Modernity: a sociolinguistic ethnography*, Longman: Harlow.

—— (2003) 'Globalization, the new economy, and the commodification of language and identity', *Journal of Sociolinguistics*, 7 (4): 473–92.

Hengst, H. (1997) 'Negotiating "us" and "them": children's constructions of collective identity', *Childhood*, 4 (1): 43–62.

Henriques, J., Hollway, W., Urwin, C., Venn, C. and Walkerdine, V. (1984) *Changing the Subject: psychology, social regulation, and subjectivity*, London: Methuen.

Hester, S. and Housley W. (eds) (2002) *Language, Interaction and National Identity*, Aldershot: Ashgate.

Hobbs, S. (2002) 'New sociology and old psychology', in B. Goldson, M. Lavalette and J. McKechnie (eds) *Children, Welfare and the State*, London: Sage, pp. 29–41.

Hobsbawm, E. and Ranger, T. (1983) (eds) *The Invention of Tradition*, Oxford: Blackwell.

Hogan, D. (2005) 'Researching "the child" in developmental psychology', in S. Greene and D. Hogan (eds) *Researching Children's Experience: approaches and methods*. London: Sage, pp. 22–41.

Holloway, S. and Valentine, G. (2000a) 'Spatiality and the new social studies of childhood', *Sociology*, 34 (4): 763–83.

—— (2000b) 'Corked hats and Coronation Street: British and New Zealand children's imaginative geographies of the other', *Childhood*, 7 (3): 335–57.

—— (eds) (2000c) *Children's Geographies: playing, living, learning*, London: Routledge.

Housley, W. and Fitzgerald, R. (2001) 'Categorisation, narrative and devolution in Wales', *Sociological Research Online*, 6 (2). Available on-line at <http://www.socresonline.org.uk/6/2/housley.html>.

Howard, S. and Gill, J. (2001) ' "It's like we're a normal way and everyone else is different": Australian children's constructions of citizenship and national identity', *Educational Studies*, 27 (1): 87–103.

Hussain, M. (2000) 'Exclusion as discursive practice and the politics of identity', in R. Phillipson (ed.) *Rights to Language: equity, power and education*, London: Lawrence Erlbaum, pp. 144–48.

Ifekwunigwe, J. O. (1999) *Scattered Belongings: cultural paradoxes of race, nation and gender*, London: Routledge.

Jahoda, G. (1964) 'Children's concepts of nationality: a critical study of Piaget's stages', *Child Development*, 35: 1081–92.

James, A. and Prout, A. (eds) (1990) *Constructing and Reconstructing Childhood: contemporary issues in the sociological study of childhood*, London: Falmer Press.

James, A., Jenks, C. and Prout, A. (1998) *Theorising Childhood*, Cambridge: Polity.

Jenkins, G. H. and Williams, M. A. (2000) 'The fortunes of the Welsh language 1900–2000', in G. H. Jenkins and M. A. Williams (eds) *Let's Do Our Best for the Ancient Tongue: the Welsh language in the twentieth century*, Cardiff: University of Wales Press, pp. 1–28.

Jenkins, R. (1996) *Social Identity*, London: Routledge.

—— (1997) *Rethinking Ethnicity*, London: Sage.

—— (2005) 'Taking childhood seriously: identity, networks and integration', paper delivered at Childhoods 2005 conference, University of Oslo.

Jenks, C. (ed.) (1992) *Sociology of Childhood: essential readings*, London: Batsford.

—— (2005) *Childhood*, 2nd edn, London: Routledge.

Jones, J. (2002) 'The cultural symbolism of disorder and deviant behaviour: young people's experiences in a Welsh rural market town', *Journal of Rural Studies*, 18 (2): 213–17.

Joseph, J. E. (2004) *Language and Identity: national, ethnic and religious*, London: Palgrave Macmillan.

Jukaramen, P. (2003) 'Definitely not yet the end of nations: northern borderlands youth in defence of national identities', *Young. Nordic Journal of Youth Research*, 11 (3): 217–34.

Kahn, J. S. (1995) *Culture, Multiculture, Postculture*. London: Sage.

Kellett, M., Forrest, R., Dent, N. and Ward, S. (2004) ' "Just teach us the skills please, we'll so the rest": empowering ten-year-olds as active researchers', *Children and Society*, 18 (5): 329–43.

Kiely, R., Bechhofer, F., Stewart, R. and McCrone, D. (2001) 'The markers and rules of Scottish national identity', *Sociological* Review, 49 (1): 33–55.

King, R. (1978) *All Things Bright and Beautiful? A sociological study of infants' classrooms*, Chichester: Wiley.

Kloss, H. (1977) *The American Bilingual Tradition*, Rowley, MA: Newbury House.

Kohlberg, L. (1969) 'Stage and sequence: the cognitive-developmental approach to socialization', in D. A. Goslin (ed.) *Handbook of Socialisation Theory and Research*, Chicago, IL: Rand McNally.

Korpela, K., Kytta, M. and Hartig, T. (2002) 'Children's favorite places: restorative experience, self-regulation and children's place preferences', *Journal of Environmental Psychology* 22 (4): 387–98.

Lave, J. (1990) 'The culture of acquisition and the practice of understanding', in J. W. Sigler, R. A. Shweder, and G. Herdt (eds) *Cultural Psychology: essays on comparative human development*, Cambridge: Cambridge University Press, pp. 309–27.

—— (1991) 'Socially shared cognition', in L. Resnick, J. Levine, and S. Teasley (eds) *Perspectives on Socially Shared Cognition*, Washington, DC: American Psychological Association.

Lave, J. and Wenger, E. (1991) *Situated Learning: legitimate peripheral participation*, New York: Cambridge University Press.

Lee, N. (1998) 'Towards an immature sociology', *Sociological Review*, 6 (3): 458–82.

Lefebvre, H. (1991) *The Production of Space*, Blackwell: Oxford.

Lopez, A. M. (2003) 'Collecting and tabulating race/ethnicity data with diverse and mixed heritage populations: a case-study with US high school students', *Ethnic and Racial Studies*, 26 (5): 931–61.

Mac an Ghaill, M. (1999) *Contemporary Racisms and Ethnicities*, Buckingham: Open University Press.

McCrone, D. (1998) *The Sociology of Nationalism*, London: Routledge.

—— (2002) 'Who do you say you are? Making sense of national identities in modern Britain', *Ethnicities*, 2 (3): 301–20.

McHale, S., Crouter, A. C. and Tucker, C. J. (1999) 'Family context and gender role socialisation in middle childhood: comparing girls to boys and sisters to brothers', *Child Development*, 70 (4): 990–1004.

McIntosh, I., Sim, D. and Robertson, D. (2004) ' "We hate the English, but not you because you're our pal": identification of the "English" in Scotland', *Sociology*, 38 (1): 43–59.

Massey, D. (1994) *Space, Place and Gender*, Cambridge: Polity.

—— (1995) 'The conceptualisation of place', in D. Massey and P. Jess (eds) *A Place in the World? Places, cultures and globalisation*, Oxford: Oxford University Press, pp. 45–86.

Massey, D. and Jess, P. (1995) (eds) *A Place in the World? Places, cultures and globalisation*, Oxford: Oxford University Press.

Matthews, M. H. (1992) *Making Sense of Place: children's understanding of large-scale environments*, Hemel Hempstead: Harvester Wheatsheaf.

Matthews, H., Taylor, M., Sherwood, K., Tucker, F. and Limb, M. (2000) 'Growing up in the countryside: children and the rural idyll', *Journal of Rural Studies*, 16 (2): 141–53.

May, S. (2001) *Language and Minority Rights: ethnicity, nationalism and the politics of language*, London: Longman.

Meek, M. (ed.) (2001) *Children's Literature and National Identity*, London: Trentham Books.

Merton, R. (1957) *Social Theory and Social Structure*, Glencoe: IL: Free Press.

Meyrowitz, J. (1985) *No Sense of Place: the impact of electronic media on social behaviour*. Oxford: Oxford University Press.

Miles, R. (1989) *Racism*, London: Routledge.

Morgan, P. (1983) 'From a death to a view: the hunt for the Welsh past in the romantic period', in E. Hobsbawm and T. Ranger (eds) *The Invention of Tradition*, Cambridge: Cambridge University Press pp. 43–100.

—— (ed.) (1991) *Brad Y Llyfrau Gleision : Ysgrifau ar hanes Cymru*, Llandysul: Gomer.

Morley, D. and Robins, K. (1995) *Spaces of Identity: global media, electronic landscapes and cultural boundaries*, London: Routledge.

Morris Jones, B. and Singh Ghuman, P. (1995) *Bilingualism, Education and Identity*, Cardiff: University of Wales Press.

Morrow, V. (2001) *Networks and Neighbourhoods: children's and young people's perspectives*, London: Health Development Agency.

Morrow, V. and Richards, M. (1996) 'The ethics of social research with children: an overview', *Children and Society*, 10 (2): 90–105.

National Assembly for Wales (2001) *Welsh in Schools*, Cardiff: National Assembly.

Newman, D. and Paasi, A. (1998) 'Fences and neighbours in the postmodern world: boundary narratives in political geography', *Progress in Human Geography* 22 (2): 186–207.

Newson, J. and Newson, E. (1976) *Seven Years Old in the Home Environment*, London: Allen & Unwin.

O'Brien, M., Jones, D., Sloan, D. and Rustin, M. (2000) 'Children's independent spatial mobility in the urban public realm', *Childhood*, 7 (3): 257–77.

O'Reilly, C. C. (2001) 'Introduction: minority languages, ethnicity and the state', in C. C. O'Reilly (ed.) *Language, Ethnicity and the State, Vol I: Minority Languages in the European Union*, London: Palgrave, pp. 1–19.

O'Riagain, D. (2001) 'Many tongues but one voice: a personal overview of the role of the European bureau for lesser used languages in promoting Europe's regional and minority languages', in C. C. O'Reilly (ed.) *Language, Ethnicity and the State, Vol I: Minority Languages in the European Union*, London: Palgrave, pp. 20–39.

Oakes, P., Haslam, S. A., Turner, J. (1994) *Stereotyping and Social Reality*, Oxford: Blackwell.

ODPM (Office of the Deputy Prime Minister) (2001) *Housing in England 1999/2000 Summary Trends in Moving Households*, London: Stationery Office.

Parsons, T. (2002) 'An Outline of the Social System', in C. Calhoun, J. Gerteis, J. Moody, S. Pfaff, K. Schmidt and I. Virk (eds) *Classical Sociological Theory*, Oxford: Blackwell.

Patten, A. and Kymlicka, W. (2003) 'Introduction: language rights and political theory – context, issues and approaches', in W. Kymlicka and A. Patten (eds) *Language Rights and Political Theory*, Oxford: Oxford University Press, pp. 1–51.

Peura, M. (2000) 'Creating a successful minority school', in R. Phillipson (ed.) *Rights to Language: equity, power and education*, London: Lawrence Erlbaum, pp. 219–26.

Phillips, R. (1998) *History Teaching, Nationhood and the State: a study in educational politics*, London: Cassell.

Phillips, T. (2002) 'Imagined communities and self-identity: an exploratory quantitative analysis', *Sociology*, 36 (3): 597–617.

Piaget, J. (1965) *The Moral Judgement of the Child*, New York: Free Press.

—— (2001) 'The stages of the intellectual development of the child', first published 1962, in M. Gauvain and M. Cole (eds) *Readings on the Development of Children*, 3rd edn, New York: Worth, pp. 17–21.

Piaget, J. and Weil, A. M. (1951) 'The development in children of the idea of the homeland and of relations to other countries', *International Social Science Journal*, 3: 561–78.

Pollard, A. (1987) 'Studying children's perspectives: a collaborative approach', in G. Walford (ed.) *Doing Sociology of Education*, London: Falmer.

Postman, N. (1983) *The Disappearance of Childhood*, London: W. H. Allen.

Poveda, D. and Marcos, T. (2004) 'The social organization of a "stone fight": Gitano children's interpretive reproduction of ethnic conflict', *Childhood*, 12 (3): 327–49.

Pred, A. (1983) 'Structuration and place: on the becoming of sense of place and structure of feeling', *Journal for the Theory of Social Behavior*, 13 (1): 45–68.

Proshansky, H. M., Fabian, A. K. and Kaminoff, R. (1995) 'Place-identity physical world socialization of the self', in L. N. Groat (ed.) *Giving Places Meaning*, London: Academic Press.

Prout, A. (2000) 'Children's participation: control and self-realisation in British late modernity', *Children and Society*, 14 (4): 304–15.

—— (2001) 'Representing children: reflections on the children 5–16 programme', *Children and Society*, 15 (3): 193–201.

Pryke, S. (2001) 'Comment on Frank Bechhofer, David McCrone, Richard Kiely and Richard Stewart, "Constructing national identity: arts and landed elites in Scotland" ', *Sociology* 35 (1): 195–9.

Qvortrup, J., Bardy, G., Sgritta, G. and Wintensberger, H. (1994) *Childhood Matters: social theory, practice and politics*, Aldershot: Abebury.

Rasmussen, K. (2004) 'Places for children – children's places', *Childhood*, 11 (2): 155–73.

Reay, D. (2000) 'Children's urban landscapes: configurations of class and place', in S. R. Munt (ed.) *Cultural Studies and the Working Class*, London: Cassell, pp. 151–64.

Relph, E. (1976) *Place and Placelessness*, London: Pion.

Renold, E. (2002) 'Close encounters of the "third kind": researching children's sexual cultures in the primary school', in G. Walford (ed.) *Doing a Doctorate in Educational Ethnography: studies in educational ethnography*, Boston, Mass.: JAI Imprint.

—— (2005) *Girls, Boys and Junior Sexualities: exploring childrens' gender and sexual relations in the primary school*, London: RoutledgeFalmer.

Reports of the Commissioners of Enquiry into the State of Education in Wales (1847) London: Her Majesty's Government.

Richards, M. and Light, P. (1986) (eds) *Children of Social Worlds*, Cambridge: Polity.

Roberts, B. (1995) 'Welsh identity in a former mining valley: social images and imagined communities', *Contemporary Wales*, 7: 77–95.

Robertson, R. (1995) 'Glocalization: time-space and homogeneity-heterogeneity', in M. Featherstone, S. Lash and R. Robertson (eds) *Global Modernities*, London: Sage.

Rogoff, B. (1990) *Apprenticeship in Thinking: cognitive development in social contexts*, New York: Oxford University Press.

Rutland, A. (1998) 'English children's geo-political knowledge of Europe', *British Journal of Developmental Psychology*, 16: 439–45.

—— (1999) 'The development of national prejudice, in-group favouritism and self-stereotypes in British children', *British Journal of Social Psychology*, 38 (1): 55–70.

Saeed, A., Blain, N. and Forbes, D. (1999) 'New ethnic and national questions in Scotland: post-British identities among Glasgow Pakistani teenagers', *Ethnic and Racial Studies*, 22 (5): 821–44.

Said, E. (1994) *Orientalism: western conceptions of the Orient*, Harmondsworth: Penguin.

Samuel, R. (1994) *Theatres of Memory*, London: Verso.

Scott, S., Jackson, S. and Backett-Milburn, K. (1998) 'Swings and roundabouts: risk anxiety and the everyday world of children', *Sociology*, 32 (4): 689–705.

Scourfield, J. and Coffey, A. (2006) 'Access, ethics and the (re)construction of gender: the case of researcher as suspected "paedophile" ', *International Journal of Social Research Methodology*, 9 (1): 1–12.

Scourfield, J., Evans, J., Shah, W. and Beynon, H. (2005) 'The negotiation of minority ethnic identities in virtually all-white communities: research with children and their families in the South Wales valleys', *Children and Society*, 19 (3): 211–24.

Segrott, J. (2006) 'Lessons in nationality: constructing identities at Ysgol Gymraeg Llundain', *Contemporary Wales*, 18: 122–39.

Sennett, R., and Cobb, J. (1972) *The Hidden Injuries of Class*. New York: Random House.

Shields, R. (1991) *Places on the Margin: alternative geographies of modernity*, London: Routledge.

Skeggs, B. (1997) *Formations of Class and Gender: becoming respectable*, London: Sage.

—— (2004) *Class, Self, Culture*, London and New York: Routledge.

Skutnabb-Kangas, T. (2000) *Linguistic Genocide in Education – or Worldwide Diversity and Human Rights?* Mahwah, NJ: Lawrence Erlbaum.

Smart, C., Neale, B. and Wade, A. (2001) *The Changing Experience of Childhood: families and divorce*, Cambridge: Polity.

Smith, A. D. (1979) *Nationalism in the Twentieth Century*, Oxford: Martin Robertson.

—— (1996) 'Nationalism and the historians', in G. Balakrishnan (ed.) *Mapping the Nation*, London: Verso, in association with *New Left Review*.

—— (1999) 'History and modernity: reflections on the theory of nationalism', in D. Boswell and J. Evans (eds) *Representing the Nation: A Reader*, London: Routledge.

Song, M. (2003) *Choosing Ethnic Identity*, Cambridge: Polity.

Southerton, D. (2001) 'Boundaries of "us" and "them": class, mobility and identification in a new town', *Sociology*, 36 (1): 171–93.

Spyrou, S. (2002) 'Images of "the other": "the Turk" in Greek Cypriot children's imaginations', *Race, Ethnicity and Education*, 5 (3): 255–72.

Stainton Rogers, R. and Stainton Rogers, W. (1992) *Stories of Childhood: shifting agendas of child concern*, Hemel Hempstead: Harvester Wheatsheaf.

Stainton Rogers, W. (2003) 'What is a child?' in M. Woodhead and H. Montgomery (eds) *Understanding Childhood: a interdisciplinary approach*, Chichester: John Wiley & Sons, in association with the Open University.

Stargardt, N. (2005) *Witnesses of War: children's lives under the Nazis*, London: Jonathan Cape.

Stephens, S. (1997a) 'Editorial introduction: children and nationalism', *Childhood*, 4 (1): 5–17.

—— (ed.) (1997b) 'Special edition: children and nationalism', *Childhood* 4, 1.

Strange, V., Forest, S., Oakley, A. and the RIPPLE study team (2003) 'Using research questionnaires with young people in schools: the influence of the social context', *International Journal of Social Research Methodology*, 6 (4): 337–46.

Thomas, O. J. (1998) 'The Welsh language in Cardiff c.1800–1914', in G. H. Jenkins (ed.) *Language and Community in the Nineteenth Century*, Cardiff: University of Wales Press.

Thompson, A. (2001) 'Nations, national identities and human agency: putting people back in to nations', *The Sociological Review*, 49 (1): 18–32.

Thompson, J. B. (1995) *The Media and Modernity*, Cambridge: Polity.

Thomson, R. and Holland, J. (2004) *Youth Values and Transitions to Adulthood: an empirical investigation*, London: London South Bank University.

Thorne, N. (1993) *Gender Play: girls and boys in school*, New Brunswick, NJ: Rutgers University Press.

Tilly, C. (1973) 'Do communities act?' *Sociological Inquiry*, 43 (December): 209–40.

Timm, L. (2001) 'Ethnic identity and minority language survival in Brittany', C. C.

O'Reilly (ed.) in *Language, Ethnicity and the State, Vol 1: Minority Languages in the European Union*, London: Palgrave, pp. 104–27.

Tomlinson, S. (1997) 'Diversity, choice and ethnicity: the effects of educational markets on ethnic minorities', *Oxford Review of Education*, 23 (1): 63–76.

Tomlinson, J. (1999) *Globalisation and Culture*, Cambridge: Polity Press.

Urry, J. (2000) 'Mobile sociology', *British Journal of Sociology*, 51 (1): 185–203.

—— (2003) *Global Complexity*, Cambridge: Polity.

Urwin, C. (1984) 'Power relations and the emergence of language', in J. Henriques, W. Hollway, C. Urwin, C. Venn and V. Walkerdine (1984) *Changing the Subject: psychology, social regulation, and subjectivity*, London: Methuen.

—— (1986) 'Developmental psychology and psychoanalysis: splitting the difference', in M. Richards and P. Light (eds) *Children of Social Worlds*, Cambridge: Polity.

Valentine, G. (1997) 'A safe place to grow up? Parenting, perceptions of children's safety and the rural idyll', *Journal of Rural Studies*, 13 (2): 137–48.

Van Ausdale, D. and Feagin, J. R. (2002) *The First R: how children learn race and racism*, Lanham, MD: Rowman & Littlefield.

Van Leeuwen, T. (2000) 'It was just like magic: a multimodal analysis of children's writing', *Linguistics and Education*, 10 (3): 273–305.

Vanderbeck, R. M. and Dunkley, C. M. (2003) 'Young people's narratives of rural–urban difference', *Children's Geographies*, 1 (2): 241–59.

Vygotsky, L. (1978) *Mind in Society*, Cambridge, Mass.: Harvard University Press.

Walkerdine, V. (1984) 'Developmental psychology and the child-centred pedagogy: the insertion of Piaget's theory into primary school practice', in J. Henriques, W. Hollway, C. Urwin, C. Venn and V. Walkerdine (eds) (1984) *Changing the Subject: psychology, social regulation, and subjectivity*, London: Methuen.

—— (1986) 'Post-structuralist theory and everyday social practices: the family and the school', in S. Wilkinson (ed.) *Feminist Social Psychology: developing theory and practice*, Buckingham: Open University Press.

—— (2003) 'Reclassifying upward mobility: femininity and the neo-liberal subject', *Gender and Education*, 15 (3): 237–48.

—— (2004) 'Developmental psychology and the study of childhood', in M. J. Kehily (ed.) *An Introduction to Childhood Studies*, Maidenhead: Open University Press.

Waterman, A., Blades, M. and Spencer, C. (2001) 'Is a jumper angrier than a tree?' *The Psychologist*, 14: 474–9.

Wells, G. (1987) *The Meaning Makers: children learning language and using language to learn*. London: Hodder & Stoughton Educational.

Welsh Assembly Government (2004) *Welsh in Schools 2003*, Statistical Bulletin 16/ 2004 (R), Cardiff: Welsh Assembly Government.

Wertsch, J. (1981) 'The concept of activity in Soviet psychology: an introduction', in J. Wertsch (ed.) *The Concept of Activity in Soviet Psychology*, Armonk, NY: Sharpe.

West, C. and Zimmerman, D. (1987) 'Doing gender', *Gender and Society*, 1 (2): 125–51.

Williams, Charlotte (1995) 'Race and racism: some reflections on the Welsh context', *Contemporary Wales*, 8: 113–31.

—— (1999a) 'Passports to Wales? Race, nation and identity', in R. Fevre and A. Thompson (eds) *Nation, Identity and Social Theory: perspectives from Wales*, Cardiff: University of Wales Press.

—— (1999b) ' "Race" and racism: what's special about Wales', in D. Dunkerley and A. Thompson (eds) *Wales Today*, Cardiff: University of Wales Press.

—— (2003) 'Strange encounters', *Planet*, 158: 19–24.

Williams, Charlotte, Evans, N. and O'Leary, P. (eds) (2003) *A Tolerant Nation? Exploring ethnic diversity in Wales*, Cardiff: University of Wales Press.

Williams, Chris (2005) 'Problematizing Wales: an exploration in historiography and postcoloniality', in J. Aaron and C. Williams (eds) *Postcolonial Wales*, Cardiff: University of Wales Press.

Williams, R. (1961) *The Long Revolution*, Harmondsworth: Penguin.

Wyn Jones, R. (2004) *Methiant Prifysgolion Cymru/The Failure of the Welsh Universities*, Cardiff: Institute of Welsh Affairs.

Yuval-Davis, N. (1997) *Gender and Nation*, London: Sage.

Index

Note: page numbers in *italics* refer to figures or tables